RHETORICAL ACCESSABILITY

At the Intersection of Technical Communication and Disability Studies

Edited by

Lisa Meloncon
University of Cincinnati

Baywood's Technical Communications Series
Series Editor: Charles H. Sides

Baywood Publishing Company, Inc.
AMITYVILLE, NEW YORK

Baywood Publishing Company, Inc.
26 Austin Avenue
P.O. Box 337
Amityville, NY 11701
(800) 638-7819
E-mail: baywood@baywood.com
Web site: baywood.com

Library of Congress Catalog Number: 2012022189
ISBN: 978-0-89503-788-6 (cloth : alk. paper)
ISBN: 978-0-89503-789-3 (paper)
ISBN: 978-0-89503-790-9 (epub)
ISBN: 978-0-89503-791-6 (epdf)
http://dx.doi.org/10.2190/RAA

Library of Congress Cataloging-in-Publication Data

Rhetorical accessability : at the intersection of technical communication and disability studies / edited by Lisa Meloncon.
    p. ; cm. -- (Baywood's technical communications series)
  Includes bibliographical references and index.
    ISBN 978-0-89503-788-6 (cloth : alk. paper) -- ISBN 978-0-89503-789-3 (pbk. : alk. paper) -- ISBN 978-0-89503-790-9 (epub) -- ISBN 978-0-89503-791-6 (epdf)
    I. Meloncon, Lisa K. II. Series : Baywood's technical communications series (Unnumbered)
  [DNLM: 1. Biomedical Enhancement. 2. Biomedical Technology--instrumentation. 3. Communication. 4. Disabled Persons. 5. Internet--standards. 6. Self-Help Devices--standards. W 82]

  610.28'4--dc23
                                                                2012022189

Dedication

To Mark, Melissa, Coby, Jacob, and Daniel

Table of Contents

Acknowledgments

This volume would not have been possible without the support and guidance of Sean Zdenek, the belief of Charles Sides, and the friendship and keen eye of Heather Hall. To each of them, I am thankful and grateful. I also owe a special and huge thank you to the contributors for their great ideas, multiple edits, and good humor. A final thank you goes out to my Professional Writing colleagues at the University of Cincinnati and the students in the capstone course that inspired this project, Lisa G., Megan V., Megan C., Rebecca, Lauren, Kristina, Lisa M., and Brittany. Finally, this book is dedicated to my sister, brother-in-law, and three of my beautiful nephews for their patience, strength, and grace.

Introduction

Lisa Meloncon

I'd like to start with a short story, one that provides the background to how this volume was conceived, because the story makes an important point. Like many universities that offer a Master's degree in Technical and Professional Communication (TPC), the University of Cincinnati requires a capstone course as the students' cumulative experience in the program. In the capstone, students typically work with a community partner to help them solve various communication problems within their organization.

As anyone who has done service-learning coursework knows, finding a community partner is no easy task since the project or projects must result in deliverables directly tied to course and program outcomes while also providing adequate challenges for the students. In preparation for the spring 2009 capstone course, I had narrowed the list of potential community partners down to three and then discussed the list with my colleagues. While all the potential partners would have offered the students a rich capstone experience, the primary rationale for choosing the Inclusion Network[1] was that it would require students to be exposed to issues of disability studies and accessibility, which, at the time, were an underdeveloped area within the curriculum.

While I was excited about the possibilities the overall project posed, I was also a bit panicked because I knew little about disability studies and had little understanding of how to weave in accessibility issues into an already jammed

[1] The mission of the Inclusion Network was to educate, assist, and support organizations in their efforts to include people with disabilities by creating welcoming environments. The economic downturn forced the Inclusion Network to cease operations in June 2009. One of the authors of chapter 4, Margaret Gutsell, helped direct that organization.

10-week term. Since "narrative is complex perspective affecting the way research and pedagogical issues in professional communication are viewed" (Perkins & Blyler, 1999, p. xiv), readers should know that this story has affected the shape of this project. As I found out, TPC practitioners and academics have few resources to understand issues related to disability studies and accessibility, and many disability scholars have little to no understanding about TPC and how it can be beneficial to the work they do. We—the authors and I—wanted to address this situation. We wanted to produce a volume that could be used in both TPC and disability studies classrooms. We wanted a volume that introduced a breadth of issues valuable to both TPC and disability studies. We wanted to start a scholarly conversation.

Worldwide, the United Nations (UN) estimates there are at least 650 million people with disabilities (2006). Presently, 41.3 million people in the United States, or about 15% of the population, have "some level of disability" (U.S. Census, 2008). Eurostat (2009), the clearinghouse of data and statistics for the European Union, estimates that in the 25 European Union nations 16.2% of the working age population (those aged 16 to 64) has either a long-standing health problem or a disability. Other worldwide statistics include the following:

- India: approximately 20 million people are disabled (Qureshi, 2010)
- Russia: 10 million are disabled people, and approximately 700,000 of those are children and young adults up to the age of 18 (Roza, 2005)
- China: 83 million people are disabled (People's Daily Online, 2006)
- Canada: 4.4 million people, or 14.3% of the population, are disabled (Human Resources, 2006)
- Australia: 1 in 5 people report a disability (Physical Disability Australia, 2003)

If these statistics are not enough, consider alongside them an aging population. Today, 1 of every 10 persons is 60 years old or over, totaling 629 million people worldwide. The United Nations projects that by 2050 one of every five persons will be 60 or older and that by 2150 this ratio will be one of every three persons (UN Information Service, 2002). Additionally, 21.4% of the U.S. population is over the age of 55, with that percentage expected to rise to 31.1 by 2050 (Trace Research, n.d.), and these older Americans face increased burdens of disabilities (Seeman, Merkin, Crimmins, & Karlamanga, 2010).

However, people with disabilities and an aging population hold enormous power and influence. With $220 billion in discretionary income, people with disabilities wield significant consumer power (Cheng, 2002). In the United States, people over 50 account for half of the country's discretionary spending (Dee, 2002), and the senior market (55 to 65+) accounts for $7 billion of online sales annually (Suddenly Senior, 2002). It becomes a moot point whether or not marketers and businesses recognize the power of these numbers because they are a market reality.

Although the United Nations cautions against comparison across countries because of the "differences in concepts and methods used to identify persons with disabilities" (n.d., para. 1), the fact remains that disability is a global concern. Further, in 2006, the United Nation's Convention on the Rights of Persons with Disabilities was supported by 82 member countries, indicating the international focus—and need—for sustained attention by technical communicators on issues of disability and, more specifically, the field of disability studies. Offering a more thorough account of the potential connections between technical communication and disability studies, this collection of new essays will explore, promote, and make a case for disability studies as a key location of technical communication scholarship and practice. Along the way, it considers and develops the relationship between disability studies and accessibility and between technical communication and accessibility.

LOCATING THE INTERSECTIONS BETWEEN TPC AND DISABILITY STUDIES

Words and their origins make for fascinating explorations. Take for instance one of the key concepts that underscore this project: innovation. Innovation can be dated to the mid-sixteenth century, a time that embodies the definition of the word. It is Latin in origin: *in* from "into" and *novare*, "to make into something new." Embedded within this making of something new is the presupposition that the new comes from something already out there. In this case, this volume's innovation resides in bringing together the already out there, yet seemingly divergent, fields of disability studies and technical communication. Our title, *Rhetorical AccessAbility*, pertains to and plays on the important ways the fields intersect—rhetoric and accessibility. Disability studies and technical communication share common theoretical grounds. Both see a need to bring rhetorical analysis to bear on understanding the construction of disability through a study of "the social meanings, symbols, and stigmas attached to disability identity" (Siebers, 2008, p. 3). Work by disability studies scholars (e.g., Davis, 1995; Linton, 1998; Tichkosky, 2007) will seem somewhat familiar to technical communicator scholars. These disability studies scholars do sophisticated work with language and discourse to highlight the power of words and their overarching impact on binaries that are of interest to technical communicators such as theory/practice, self/other, author/reader, and dependence/interdependence.

Regardless of the profession, discipline, or organization, rhetoric plays a major role in how knowledge is created, codified, shared, revised, contested, and enacted. Rhetorical criticism and rhetorical analysis are concerned with more than persuasive language. Rhetoricians want to know what language does and how it moves people to action. As self-identified rhetoricians, we chose rhetoric because rhetorical analysis can help identify and expose embedded ideologies in a variety of discourses and situations, and even though rhetoric can be seen as a theoretical grounding, it is more importantly practical and situated. Rhetoric can be an instrumental tool to position and craft effective communication strategies, and rhetorical analysis exposes how knowledge and values are composed and communicated. These inherent ideologies bind together communities and highlight relations and relationships within those communities. In the case of this project, chapter authors are examining the relationships between production, dissemination and circulation of discourse, ideas, and ideologies. One of the primary arenas for promoting social change and for moving toward universal access is through changing the discourse and through changing material conditions (such as access to Internet sites).

Technical communication and disability studies also employ a social constructionist view of science and technology that demands detailed and theoretically grounded analyses of the ethical, social, cultural, and political effects of discourse (Palmeri, 2006). Technical communication practitioners created the accessibility special interest group of the Society for Technical Communication, but practitioners have performed only a handful of research studies (e.g., Roberts & Pappas, 2009; Smith, 2010). On the other hand, technical communication academics have done only moderately better with studies focusing on specific areas. For example, several studies have examined disability studies and teaching technical communication (Palmeri, 2006; Walters, 2010; Wilson 2000) and legal guidelines (Carter & Markel, 2001), and one study has looked at the rhetorical aspects of web accessibility (Spinuzzi, 2007). More specific studies focus on distinct types of users, such as those with visual disabilities (Leuthold, Bargas-Avila, & Opwis, 2008; Theofanos & Redish, 2005), older users (Lippincott, 2004; O'Hara, 2004), users with intellectual disabilities (Karreman, van der Geest, & Buursink, 2007), and deaf users (Zdenek, 2009, 2011). The only area to receive any sort of sustained research is universal design and usability (e.g., Dolmage, 2009; Mbipom, 2009; Meiselwitz, Wentz, & Lazar, 2009). Although the two fields share a common ground, current scholarship in technical communication has not adequately explored these intersections, nor has scholarship in disability studies.

Disability studies fully emerged as a field in the early 1990s as a way "to advance the cause of the disabled and promote social change by analyzing the present social formations that contribute to maintain the walls of exclusion" (Wilson & Lewiecki-Wilson, 2001, p. 9). Whereas the medical model defines a disability as a personal defect or lack in need of medical or therapeutic intervention, disability studies scholars define *disability* more broadly to include environmental and technological barriers that may prevent people from having equal access to goods, services, interfaces, and information. The medical definition, according to Linton, views disability as "a personal matter and 'treat[s]' the condition and the person with the condition rather than 'treating' the social processes and policies that constrict disabled people's lives" (2010, p. 225). For disability studies scholars, disability is a "complex phenomenon, reflecting an interaction between features of a person's body and features of the society in which he or she lives" (World Health Organization, n.d., para. 2).

Throughout this book, various definitions of *disability*, *disabled*, and *people with disabilities* are used. As scholars in disability studies have shown, there is no singular, commonly accepted definition. (See Wendell, 2006, for an overview of the definitions of *disabled*.) Even though some have argued for a specific definition of *disability* (Iezzoni & Freedman, 2008), we hesitate to offer one. Moreover, legal definitions, like the one found in the Americans with Disabilities Act or the one offered by the World Health Organization, leave much room for interpretation and conversation. With the disabled community so diverse and multifaceted, it seems to make sense that no single, homogeneous definition could adequately describe the whole of the disability community/communities.

Beyond a theoretical common ground, the two fields also share a pragmatic foundation in their concern with accessibility (i.e., the material practice of making social and technical environments and texts as readily available, easy to use, and understandable to as many people as possible, including those with disabilities).[2] Through its concern with the pragmatic but theoretically grounded work of helping users interface effectively and seamlessly with technologies, the field of technical communication is perfectly poised to put the theoretical work of disability studies to practice. In other words, technical communication could ideally be seen as a bridge between disability theories and web accessibility practices.

Accessibility is a central concern of technical communication instructors, practitioners, and scholars. When we filter our understanding of accessibility through the diverse and growing body of literature in disability studies, our attention is drawn to the ways in which technologies enable and include or disable and exclude both users and practices. Even though disabilities studies have grown into a robust and theoretically rich field, current scholarship has yet to engage fully the complex intersections of technology and disability. Goggin and Newel (2003) offer a view of the social construction of disability in new media, which they view broadly as the Internet, television, and telecommunication networks. They provide a "critical gaze upon the very technologies that are supposed to provide the solution to disability—and show how new media technologies actually build in disability" (p. xv). But since their book-length work, disability studies has confined itself to a more narrow analysis of social networks (Huang & Guo, 2005; Pescosolido, 2001) and a potpourri of intriguing investigations found, mostly, in two special issues of *Disability Studies Quarterly* in 2005 (Goggin & Newell). These two special issues were themed around

---

[2] This definition in its clarity and usefulness owes much to Sean Zdenek.

"access, equity and citizenship" and "ethics, utility and possibility." Since 2005, technology has all but disappeared from disability studies scholarship.

Accessibility, then, becomes the practical incantation of making a product, document, service, or environment. When we design for the web, for example, we may unconsciously activate a set of normative beliefs about how well or how poorly people move, see, hear, think, learn, know, act, and use specific technologies (Zdenek, 2009). Included in this idea is removing barriers that prohibit or block access because "when access threatens change, standards are always the tools used to resist that change" (Fox, 1999, p. 8).

While technical communicators are ideally positioned to solve communication problems and to determine the best delivery method, those same issues are compounded when they are viewed through the dual lens of accessibility and disability. With the increasing use of wireless, expanding global marketplaces, the increasing prevalence of technology in our daily lives, and the ongoing changes of writing through and with technology, technical communicators need to be acutely aware of issues involved with accessibility and disability.

CONTENTS

The first two chapters approach technical communication and disability studies from a design perspective by looking at two distinct user types, autistic users and low literacy users. In both cases, the authors illustrate the importance of design and the role technical communicators can play in improving design practices. By reviewing current design practices from distinct positions, technical communicators and disability studies scholars will have access to more informed design practices. Elmore (chapter 1) opens the volume by focusing on the autistic user experience. Independence and dependence are social constructions, and research shows that the abled and the disabled define dependence and independence differently. Considering these terms from the perspective of autistics can illuminate the ethical argument for embracing human interdependence and can inform the accommodation of the autistic experience in usability practice from the beginning of the design process for assistive technologies. Many technical communicators possess both the rhetorical theory and the audience-oriented practice needed to change the way assistive technologies are developed for autistics and others with disabilities. However, technical communicators need more research in both areas to support their work. This chapter suggests how the autistic user experience can be accommodated in design, argues the ethical importance for including autistics in the design process for assistive technologies, and explains why technical communicators should lead such developments in the research and practice of designing user-centered technology.

Moving from a specific community to a broader construction of design, Jarrett, Redish, and Summers (chapter 2) discuss design for people who do not read easily. People who already have some familiarity with designing for "at-risk" audiences but who need or wish to reach out to additional audiences or who are interested in knowing (and applying) design solutions are most likely to result in universal accessibility and usability. This chapter looks at issues relating to universal design. The authors combine expertise from disparate areas of study: designing for those who don't read well due to age-related issues, visual disabilities, low literacy skills, and low English proficiency. The chapter explores overlap in research-driven design guidelines for these "at-risk" audiences. We suggest that despite the actual differences in reasons why people do not read easily, the ways in which we can design for them are generally similar and the effect of good design for people who do not read easily is good design for everyone.

What many may not realize is that the rich theoretical work being done in disability studies can improve technical communication practice. Alternatively, for disability studies scholars, seeing the application of theories to another realm may encourage additional research areas.

Meloncon (chapter 3) discusses the opportunities posed by technological embodiments. Technological embodiment erases differences between the able-bodied and disabled by focusing on the dispersal of embodiment through technologies. The remaking of bodies as technological embodiments draws on a long historical malleability designed to make exterior bodies all the same. Our experiences, whether our bodies are "disabled" or not, are relationships between bodies and things and between bodies and technologies. By using the framework of the posthuman developed by Merleau-Ponty (1962/2002), this chapter offers a theory of technological embodiments to put the body back into technical communication, particularly into discussions of audience analysis and ethics. For technical communicators, a body that can be remade through technologies becomes not a cyborg, but rather, a complex user. Reconsiderations of embodiment can have wide-ranging impact on the work of technical communicators.

Moving from theory, we turn our attention to language, specifically metaphors. Chapters 4 and 5 look at metaphors from two distinct identity positions: normalcy and empowerment. Focusing on the metaphors of the "supercrip" and the "beast," these chapters forefront—once again—the importance of paying close attention to the language we use and ramifications of such use. Gutsell and Hulgin make clear that inclusive language means more than being "politically correct," and it involves more than being inclusive of race and gender. By putting the person first, inclusive language enables the physical condition or circumstances to become just one of many characteristics that combine to make that person who he or she is. The "supercrip" is a metaphor used to describe people who have "overcome" their disability. Because this metaphor identifies them as being abnormal or problematic, the solution is for them to "overcome" or to "fix" themselves or to remediate their condition in order to make it possible to participate in daily activities. By moving past the metaphor of "supercrip," inclusive practitioners Gutsell and Hulgin (chapter 4) discuss the ramifications of this consistent metaphor in the discourse about disability and then move the conversation forward by offering a definition of inclusive language that recognizes the full identity of people with disabilities. Their chapter is a much needed summary and reminder that we must be meta-aware of the language we use because that language can be disempowering or empowering, which is seen in a specific example in Arduser's chapter.

Shifting from a larger framework to one focused on a specific community, Arduser (chapter 5) uses critical discourse analysis to examine the use of metaphor by members of a diabetic social networking site. Most research on metaphors associated with disability and chronic illness has been framed from the perspective of the health care community, the media, and other "abled entities," and this research has shown that metaphors that have attached themselves to certain diseases have influenced attitudes toward those who experience the disease. Arduser argues that even though the disease is still framed by the medical community's root metaphor of "control," the way these counter metaphors are used by this particular community empowers people living with the disease. Because the metaphors used within online diabetes narratives can help uncover the conceptual frameworks of people living with diabetes, understanding such patient-generated metaphors can give medical practitioners a clearer understanding of the lived experience of the disease, which can lead to better patient care. This understanding is constructive for both disability scholars and technical communicators. From a disabilities study perspective, paying attention to and understanding counter narratives helps lessen the stigma associated with particular illnesses and disabilities, while an attention to narratives constructed by disabled users also can move technical communicators closer to meeting the goals of universal design and user-centered environments.

With the growth of technical communication programs offering courses and programs online and with an increasing need to offer training and continuing education online, strategies are needed on how to teach about accessibility and disability and how to integrate discussions about it into course work. The next two chapters focus on teaching discuss teaching accessibility in a technical communication classroom and how to make online instruction more accessible. In many courses, students are not taught, or expected, to incorporate accessibility principles into website design or other documents that are posted to the web. Pass (chapter 6) shares her teaching practice to illustrate how to incorporate accessibility instruction into courses on web design. Using an alternate and expanded definition of *disability* means accessibility design is more involved throughout the design and creation process. In using the Kindle 2 reader as a technological example, students gain an understanding of how the effect of on-screen reading impacts design. This discussion about accessibility as a part of web design pedagogy will let the audience visualize teaching accessibility at an advanced level for students in classes that address writing, communication, information technology, and other fields.

Oswal and Hewett (chapter 7) discuss the challenges of online writing instruction. They begin by encouraging those teaching online to move beyond thinking of accessibility in online writing instruction simply as reaching out to students who may geographically dispersed. Instead, they suggest that "accessibility" of online courses should be more than a marginal issue. Rarely do instructors get sufficient or in depth advice on how to make their courses accessible. To address the marginalization of teaching writing online, this chapter discusses both the technological and pedagogical issues inherent in planning a truly accessible course that would meet the needs of all students, and in doing so provides useful guidelines for other forms of online writing instruction such as corporate training and continuing education modules.

Accessibility issues are not confined to a U.S. perspective, thus the strength of the next two chapters are in their international perspective. Both chapters analyze existing disability guidelines. Lewthwaite and Swann (chapter 8) argue that it may be counter-productive to assume that the primary accessibility battles being fought in developed nations are those most important in other regional and local contexts because disability studies itself is not yet a global discipline. By advocating the application of critical disability studies perspectives to engagement with web standards, this chapter encourages a finer distinction and approach to the application of web standards. The authors argue that the creation of web standards, as well as disability studies itself, is controlled by the western majority discipline. Disability and impairment in the majority of the world are, as yet, poorly understood. There are clear and powerful indices between poverty, war, disaster, and famine and the levels and types of disability a particular country will face and prioritize. There are also cultural issues that lead to disablism (relating to stigma, taboo, religion, folklore, etc.) and more latent aversive disablism.

Moving from the accepted and well-defined web standards, Larkin (chapter 9) examines web accessibility statements posted on corporate websites. Accessibility statements are a specific, generic form of corporate communications that falls under the purview of corporate social responsibility. Accessibility statements are criticized for being too technical and jargon filled and for not providing enough details on how to use features included on the website. While there is a need for corporations to include accessibility statements on their websites, it becomes important that those statements are more than formalities that provide little substantial or useful information to the user. As another form of institutional branding, corporate accessibility statements can indicate the level of involvement and commitment to true inclusiveness. When accessibility statements are simply included because of legal constraints, the statements lose their efficacy while also suggesting a corporation's true stance on inclusiveness. After an overview of common features and current practice and usage of accessibility statements, this chapter suggests ways to development a useful accessibility statement.

The final two chapters give resources for understanding disability and accessibility better. The legal terrain of accessibility laws can be confusing.

Furthermore, legal limitations are only part of the picture when creating accessible electronic content. Pappas (chapter 10) offers a much-needed summary of the legal landscape of disability laws for both workplaces and educational institutions. Then the chapter moves into an explanation of the broader benefits of creating accessible electronic content, including the right of citizens to access information as well as the many business benefits. Beyond reducing the risk of disability litigation, accessible content benefits all users, which is a primary area of work for technical communicators. The chapter concludes with ethical implications for technical communication. The volume ends with a series of resources compiled and annotated by Maloney (chapter 11) that can be used as a ready reference or as a starting place to learn more.

RHETORICAL ACCESSABILITY

The word play on *accessibility* and *access ability* is meant to bring to the forefront the common focus on the subject of accessibility between the two fields, while simultaneously emphasizing ability. Whereas Siebers has advocated a position that deconstructs the assumption that levels of ability define who we are and our place in society (2008), *ability* is used here to emphasize the need to meet the abilities of users and audiences, no matter what those abilities are, while understanding the need to promote inclusive access for those same abilities.

This book opens the door for additional research at the intersection of technical communication and disability studies and answers the call to expand our sense of the communities for teaching, research, and practice, as well as expanding the community of audiences and users (Redish, 2002). Linking disability studies and technical communication serves to implicate and to draw greater attention to issues that both fields care deeply about. Beyond accessibility, issues that could benefit from increased attention include:

- **Technology:** This broad topic needs ongoing and more involved exploration. From online access to online discourse and from the documentation that accompanies various technologies to the role of technical communicators in the design process, technology is an area that needs a sustained and variegated approach in research and analysis.
- **Audiences:** Several chapters in this book take on the concept of audience, and as one of the primary tenets of technical communication, this area offers much space and much need for additional research. What would a universal audience mean to technical communicators? How can a universal audience improve design and access for all users? In what ways can we expand our theoretical discussions of audiences to more adequately address audiences with disabilities?

- **Rhetorical analysis of documents:** The large number of guidelines, legal documents, and technical documentation associated with disability and accessibility can provide a rich vein for additional research. From user manuals to analysis of laws to online communities and forums, there is ample opportunity to turn our critical eye to these different forms of discourse, while also offering ways to write for people with disabilities.
- **Usability:** Much more work needs to be done that involves users with disabilities. Universal design offers the promise to improve the range of users for a variety of products and environments. However, we still have a limited understanding of whether the large number of guidelines and suggestions work for users with disability.
- **Teaching and training:** Online teaching and online training will continue to be a major segment of the work we do, but we have only a limited understanding of what is necessary in these arenas to be successful. What are best practices in online teaching and learning and for online training modules? How can we integrate ideas and concepts of accessibility across our curricula? What can students with disabilities tell us to help us meet their needs better? What would be the best usability approaches to determine these answers?

This brief list is by all means not comprehensive since it leaves out conceptions of normalcy, identity, embodiment, and a more thorough and robust engagement with ethics, but it does highlight some important and pressing issues facing the field of technical communication.

This book will advance the field of technical communication by expanding the conceptual apparatus for understanding the intersections between disability studies, technical communication, and accessibility and by offering new perspectives, theories, and features that can emerge only when different fields are brought into conversation with one another. Whereas it could be said that such breadth is at the expense of depth, one of the goals of this book is to start conversations. The chapters that follow do start much needed conversations and, hopefully, will inspire others to pursue the possibilities of the intersection of technical communication and disability studies.

REFERENCES

Carter, J., & Markel, M. (2001). Web accessibility for people with disabilities: An introduction for web developers. *IEEE Transactions on Professional Communication,* *44*(4), 225–233.

Davis, L. (1995). *Enforcing normalcy: Disability, deafness, and the body.* New York, NY: New York University Press.

Dee, J. (2002, October 13). The myth of "18 to 34." *The New York Times Magazine.* Retrieved from http://www.nytimes.com/2002/10/13/magazine/13DEMOGRAPHIC. html

Cheng, K. (2002). What marketers should know about people with disabilities. DiversityInc. Retrieved from http://disability-marketing.com/newsroom/diversityInc.php4

Dolmage, J. (2009). Disability, usability, universal design. In S. K. Miller-Cochran & R. Rodrigo (Eds.), *Rhetorically rethinking usability: Theories, practices, and methodologies* (pp. 167–189). Cresskill, NJ: Hampton Press.

Eurostat. (2009). Prevalence percentages of disability by occupation, sex and age group. Retrieved from http://epp.eurostat.ec.europa.eu/portal/page/portal/statistics/search_database

Fox, T. (1999). *Defending access: A critique of standards in higher education.* Portsmouth, NH: Heinemann-Boyton/Cook.

Goggin, G., & Newell, C. (2003). *Digital disability: The social construction of disability in new media.* Lanham, MD: Rowman & Littlefield Publishers.

Goggin, G., & Newell, C. (Eds.). (2005). Disability studies and technology Part 1 [Special issue]. *Disability Studies Quarterly, 25*(2).

Goggin, G., & Newell, C. (Eds.). (2005). Disability studies and technology Part 2 [Special issue]. *Disability Studies Quarterly, 25*(3).

Huang, J., & Guo, B. (2005). Building social capital: A study of the online disability community. *Disability Studies Quarterly, 25*(2). Retrieved from http://www.dsq-sds.org/article/view/554/731

Human Resources and Skills Development Canada. (2006). *Participation and activity limitation survey 2006: Tables.* Ottawa: Statistics Canada, 2007 (Cat. No. 89-628-XIE - No. 003). Retrieved from http://www4.hrsdc.gc.ca/.3ndic.1t.4r@-eng.jsp?iid=40

Iezzoni, L., & Freedman, V. (2008). Turning the disability tide: The importance of definitions. *Journal of the American Medical Association, 299*(3), 332–334.

Karreman, J., van der Geest, T., & Buursink, E. (2007). Accessible website content guidelines for users with intellectual disabilities. *Journal of Applied Research in Intellectual Disabilities, 20*(6), 510–518.

Linton, S. (1998). *Claiming disability: Knowledge and identity.* New York, NY: New York University Press.

Linton, S. (2010). Reassigning meaning. In L. J. Davis (Ed.), *The disability studies reader* (3rd ed., pp. 223–236). London, UK: Routledge.

Lippincott, G. (2004). Gray matters: Where are the technical communicators in research and design for aging audiences? *IEEE Transactions on Professional Communication, 47*(3), 157–170.

Leuthold, S., Bargas-Avila, J. A., & Opwis, K. (2008). Beyond web content accessibility guidelines: Design of enhanced text user interfaces for blind Internet users. *International Journal of Human-Computer Studies, 66*(4), 257–270.

Mbipom, G. (2009). Good visual aesthetics equals good web accessibility. *SIG Access Newsletter, 93*, 75–93.

Meiselwitz, G., Wentz, B., & Lazar, J. (2009). Universal usability: Past, present, and future. *Foundations and Trends in Human-Computer Interaction, 3*(4), 213–233.

Merleau-Ponty, M. (2002). *Phenomenology of perception* (C. Smith, Trans.). London, UK: Routledge. (Original work published 1962). Retrieved from http://www.disability-marketing.com/newsroom/diversityInc.php4

O'Hara, K. (2004). Curb cuts on the information highway: Older adults and the Internet. *Technical Communication Quarterly, 13*(4), 423–445.

Palmeri, J. (2006). Disability studies, cultural analysis, and the critical practice of technical communication pedagogy. *Technical Communication Quarterly, 15*(1), 49–65.

People's Daily Online. (2006, December 1). Number of disabled Chinese soars as population ages and industrial injuries increase. Retrieved from http://english.peopledaily. com.cn/200612/01/eng20061201_327388.html

Perkins, J., & Blyler, N. (Eds.). (1999). *Narrative and professional communication.* Stamford, CT: Ablex Publishing.

Pescosolido, B. A. (2001). The role of social networks in the lives of persons with disabilities. In G. Albrecht, K. D. Seelman, & M. Bury (Eds.), *Handbook of disabilities studies* (pp. 468–489). Thousand Oaks, CA: Sage.

Physical Disability Australia. (2003). Australian Bureau of Statistics. Retrieved November 30, 2010, from http://www.abs.gov.au/ausstats/abs@.nsf/7d12b0f6763c78caca 257061001cc588/768ee722e31f6315ca256e8b007f3055!OpenDocument

Qureshi, A. (2010). Yahoo India and W3C India jointly host web accessibility conference. *Disability News India, December 2010.* Retrieved from http://www.disabilityindia. com/html/news.html#yiw3c

Redish, J. (2002). Foreword. In B. Mirel & R. Spilka (Eds.), *Reshaping technical communication: New directions and challenges for the 21st century* (pp. vii–xiii). Mahwah, NJ: Lawrence Erlbaum Associates.

Roberts, L., & Pappas, L. (2009). Accessibility—Good business, best practice. *Intercom, November,* 33–34.

Roza, D. (2005). Inclusive education in Russia: A status report. *Disability World, 26.* Retrieved from http://www.disabilityworld.org/12-02_05/news/inclusiveedrussia. shtml

Seeman, T., Merkin, S., Crimmins, E. M., & Karlamangla, K. (2010). Disability trends among older Americans: National health and nutrition examination surveys, 1988–1994 and 1999–2004. *American Journal of Public Health, 100*(1), 100–107.

Siebers, T. (2008). *Disability theory.* Ann Arbor, MI: University of Michigan Press.

Smith, S. (2010). Why you should adopt an accessible content strategy. Content Wrangler. Retrieved from http://thecontentwrangler.com/2010/05/24/why-you-should-adopt-an-accessible-content-strategy/

Spinuzzi, C. (2007). Texts of our institutional lives: Accessibility scans and institutional activity: An activity theory analysis. *College English, 70*(2), 189-2001.

Suddenly Senior. (2002). Senior facts. Retrieved from http://www.suddenlysenior.com/ seniorfacts.html

Theofanos, M. F., & Redish, J. (2005). Helping low-vision and other users with web sites that meet their needs: Is one site for all feasible? *Technical Communication, 52*(1), 9–20.

Titchkosky, T. (2007). *Reading and writing disability differently: The textured life of embodiment.* Toronto, Canada: University of Toronto Press.

Trace Research and Development Center. (n.d.). The graying of the United States—Linear version. College of Engineering University of Wisconsin-Madison. Retrieved from http://trace.wisc.edu/docs/function-aging/graying_linear.htm

United Nations. (2006). Convention on the Rights of Persons with Disabilities. Retrieved from http://www.un.org/disabilities/convention/signature.shtml

United Nations. (n.d.). Human functioning and disability. Retrieved November 30, 2010 from http://unstats.un.org/unsd/demographic/sconcerns/disability/

United Nations Information Service. (2002). United Nations releases new statistics on population ageing. Retrieved from http://www.unis.unvienna.org/unis/pressrels/2002/note5713.html

U.S. Census Bureau. (2008). Americans with disabilities act: July 26. Retrieved from http://www.census.gov/newsroom/releases/archives/facts_for_features_special_editions/cb08-ff11.html

Walters, S. (2010). Toward an accessible pedagogy: Dis/ability, multimodality, and universal design in the technical communication classroom. *Technical Communication Quarterly, 19*(4), 427–454.

Wendell, S. (2006). Toward a feminist theory of disability. In L. J. Davis (Ed.), *The disability studies reader* (2nd ed., pp. 243–256). London, UK: Routledge.

Wilson, J. C. (2000). Making disability visible: How disability studies might transform the medical and science writing. *Technical Communication Quarterly, 9*(2), 149–161.

Wilson, J. C., & Lewiecki-Wilson, C. (2001). *Embodied rhetorics: Disability in language and culture.* Carbondale, IL: Southern Illinois University Press.

World Health Organization. (n.d.). Disabilities. Retrieved from http://www.who.int/topics/disabilities/en/

Zdenek, S. (2009). Accessible podcasting: College students on the margins in the new media classroom. Computers & Composition Online. Retrieved from http:www//bgsu.edu/cconline/prodev.htm

Zdenek, S. (2011). Which sounds are significant? Towards a rhetoric of closed captioning. *Disability Studies Quarterly, 31*(3). Retrieved from http://dsq-sds.org/issue/view/84

http://dx.doi.org/10.2190/RAAC1

CHAPTER 1

Embracing Interdependence: Technology Developers, Autistic Users, and Technical Communicators

Kimberly Elmore

A review of scholarly research on technology development for autistic users reveals that autistic persons either are not involved in the design process or, more commonly, are included as part of an object-centered design process rather than a user-centered one. An analysis of the polarizing themes of competence/ incompetence and dependence/independence present in this research literature supports that some researchers and developers assume that autistic persons are not able to fully participate in a user-centered design process. By approaching my analysis with a "presumption of competence" of autistic persons (Biklen, 2005), however, I found that some of the research literature also includes evidence that autistic users are able to innovate solutions for problems with and express opinions about new technologies. User research techniques and tools applicable to user experience research with autistic persons can also be found in the methods and discussion sections of some research articles. Such evidence supports the plausibility of applying a user-centered design process to the development of assistive technologies for autistic users. However, technical communicators who conduct user research will need to alleviate any potential inhibitions to working with autistic people when advocating for a user-centered design process with technology developers.

Autism spectrum disorder (ASD) comprises a group of pervasive develop-mental disorders that first present in childhood and is medically diagnosed by observed mild-to-profound difficulties with communication, social interaction, restricted interests, and limited repetitive behaviors (American Psychiatric Association, 2000, pp. 69–84). Research released in 2009 found that approximately 1 out of 110 children in the United States has an ASD, according to the Centers for Disease Control (CDC), which estimates that 730,000 children in the United States between the ages of 0 and 21 have an ASD (CDC, 2010). A study of the prevalence of autism in adults in England found that 1% of adults are on the autism spectrum, the same prevalence rate found in children (Brugha, McManus, Meltzer, Smith, Scott, Purdon, et al., 2009, p. 13). These widely publicized numbers of autistic adults and children along with the public relations work of activist organizations, such as Autism Speaks and the Autism Society of America (ASA) in the United States, have increased research attention and funding in the medical, mental health, and education fields in the past decade. Still, little scholarly research has been done on effective methodologies for research and design of assistive technologies for people with autism, and no research is available on how to include autistics as participants in user-centered technology development.

Autistic people share a complex neurodevelopmental condition, but they are a heterogeneous group presenting a spectrum of abilities and disabilities ranging from mild to profound in degree (Francis, Mellor, & Firth, 2009, p. 67; Standifer, 2009, p. i). The medical model, with its drive to quantify observable physical abnormalities and then cure the abnormal condition or ameliorate its physical symptoms, does not adequately describe the autistic experience (Chamak, Bonniau, Jaunay, & Cohen, 2008). Although individuals with autism share difficulties with communication, social interaction, and repetitive or limiting behaviors, each experiences disability differently, not only from others on the spectrum but also over the course of his or her own life. In addition to the variations among individuals, some common elements of autistic experience—such as sensory perception and processing difficulties—are not included in standard definitions of autism or diagnostic criteria because these differences and potential treatments are difficult to identify and measure objectively (Myers & Johnson, 2007, p. 1166). Qualitative research and experience with autistic individuals by occupational therapists, psychologists, and habilitation specialists provide a more complete understanding of common autistic features that vary from person to person and may be disabling:

- Communication difficulties ranging from trouble understanding extra-verbal communication (e.g., gestures, facial expressions, figurative language, and tone) to an inability to speak meaningfully (Myers & Johnson, 2007, p. 1165; Standifer, 2009, pp. 5–6)
- Social interaction problems, including difficulty interpreting and expressing emotion and social signals, establishing and maintaining relationships, and regulating emotions (Chamak et al., 2008, p. 276; Myers & Johnson, 2007, pp. 1165–1166; Standifer, 2009, pp. 6–7)

- Hyper- and/or hypo-sensory perceptions that can make some environments and activities over stimulating, even painful, or cause difficulty perceiving different sensations—even locating one's own body in space (Chamak et al., 2008, p. 274; Myers & Johnson, 2007, p. 1166; Standifer, 2009, p. 7)
- Executive function difficulties that can cause trouble with planning and executing behaviors, especially in new or stressful situations (Gentry, Wallace, Kvarfordt, & Lynch, 2010, p. 101; Standifer, 2009, p. 4)
- Fine motor problems, which may make it hard to grasp small objects, write or type, get dressed, or perform other everyday skills (Standifer, 2009, p. 8)
- Gross motor issues ranging from general clumsiness to difficulty walking (Standifer, 2009, p. 8)

To address these common neurodevelopmental issues that can impair daily function and decrease quality of life for people with autism, a wide range of tools and techniques—which are not necessarily disability-specific—have been developed. Just a few of the types of assistive technologies used by some autistic people are pictorial communication systems, portable communication devices, speech-generating programs, video and/or auditory prompting systems, virtual learning environments, and specially-designed interfaces and utensils. Generally, assistive technologies for autistic people focus on improving communication, social interaction, and the acquisition of new skills. However, all of these issues of disability as well as the social, financial, and environmental "milieu" in which they occur (Scherer, 2005, pp. 128–132) must be considered by technology developers and technical communicators concerned with the autistic user experience as well as by autistic individuals who want the appropriate assistive technologies and services to meet their unique needs and goals. This complexity of each autistic user experience may inhibit technology developers and technical communicators from implementing a user-centered design process for assistive technologies. Davies (2005), a specialist in virtual environments for treatment of brain injuries, remarked that people with intellectual disabilities "are often overlooked in both research and even healthcare funding. One is often given the impression that, in terms of research, this group is considered too complex and diverse in character to tackle, and in terms of healthcare, not necessarily able to make their voices heard" (p. 283). Although technology developers may involve autistic individuals as test subjects for new concepts and designs, publicly available research does not show developers involving these potential users as active participants in the research and development process.

Reliance on a technology-centered design process has failed many users with disabilities. These users abandon approximately one-third of their assistive technologies on average, and the number of users who keep using unsatisfactory technologies because they have no viable alternative is unknown, according to Scherer (2005), a professor of rehabilitative medicine and an expert on the research and development of methods and tools for matching assistive technologies to the needs and goals of disabled users (p. 122). To find out why disabled users abandon assistive technologies and how to increase user satisfaction with and benefit from assistive technologies, Scherer conducted a qualitative study of the adoption and use of assistive technologies and services by four people born with cerebral palsy and four people with spinal cord injuries acquired in adulthood and continued follow-ups with the participants for 18 years. Although these participants were not autistic, the adults with cerebral palsy had difficulty speaking clearly and a couple used the same kinds of assistive communication devices used by autistic people who have speech problems. And as some autistic people have experienced (Biklen, 2005; Selik, 2008), one participant with cerebral palsy whose speech could not be understood was assumed to be mentally retarded throughout his childhood and did not receive assistance to read and write until his late teens (Scherer, 2005, p. 23). This false assumption that the inability to speak intelligibly signals an inability to learn and make decisions about technology use may be one reason why technology developers do not involve people with neurodevelopmental disabilities as participants in the design of assistive technologies. Scherer (2005), in addition to developing techniques to involve people with disabilities in choosing the technologies most suited to their individual needs and goals, argues that

> a major path to ensuring that devices address the tasks intended for them is getting users actively involved in the decision-making process. Involving consumers in the design and field-testing of prototypes of assistive devices helps assure that the devices will produce safe and reliable functional gain, that they are comfortable to use and aesthetically pleasing, and that self-esteem and quality of life are enhanced by their use. (p. 187)

Involving autistic users as full participants in a user-centered design process may seem a daunting task to some technology researchers and developers because they may wrongly perceive autistic differences in cognitive processing and communication as signs of intellectual incompetence that make autistic persons dependent on others for decision-making and unable to actively participate in a collaborative process.

For assistive technologies to be optimally learnable, usable, and desirable for autistic users, autistic people should be part of an interdependent team of designers, users, and technical communicators engaged in a data-driven, user-centered design process. With an understanding of user-centered design,[1] user experience

---

[1] User-centered design (UCD) is a data-driven process that focuses design on meeting the needs of the user through user research and iterative stages of development where each stage examines problems, defines solutions, and implements the solutions (Kuniavsky, 2003, pp. 31–32, 35).

research techniques,[2] and rhetoric, technical communicators are ideal mediators for helping the array of involved stakeholders effectively work together to develop appropriate assistive technologies for autistic people. Complicating the technical communicator's work of conducting user research and helping the design team implement the data throughout the design process, however, is the "user-centered rhetorical complex of technology"—the technological, institutional, cultural, and historical contexts that shape the users, the designers, and the technological artifact or system (Johnson, 1998, pp. 38–39). This user-centered rhetorical complex of technology includes the damaging impact on autistic users and technology development of societal assumptions that autistic people are too complex, too intellectually challenged, and too dependent on others to make their own decisions about technology use. Robert Johnson (1998) explains that foregrounding the rhetorical contexts in which users interact with technology and designers is "a device for audience analysis that technical communicators can use, whether they are operating in the academic or nonacademic world, to study the audience we refer to as users" (p. 40).

In the next two parts of this chapter, I analyze two major rhetorical themes that emerge in the research literature about technology development for autistic users and about autistic perspectives on technology use—the themes of competence/ incompetence and dependence/independence. In the final section, I reflect on the need for technical communicators to mediate these different perspectives on technology use by autistic persons in order to facilitate the inclusion of autistic users in the user-centered design process of new technologies for them.

A REVIEW OF RESEARCH ON
AUTISTIC USERS

Publicly available research on the development of new assistive technologies for autism illustrate how autistic persons are involved in testing high fidelity prototypes during a technology-driven design process rather than included as participants in user experience research as part of a user-centered design process. Yet the need for developing and disseminating techniques and tools for user experience research with autistic persons has grown greatly as the popularity of social media and mobile technologies have revolutionized the ways in which

[2] The user experience (UX) is the perception a user has about a technology as he or she interacts with it, which is influenced by the design of the technology and its interface, the environment in which it is used, and the user's needs and constraints (Kuniavsky, 2003, pp. 43–53). Techniques for researching the user experience include user profiles, surveys, focus groups, and usability tests (Kuniavsky, 2003, pp. 83–437).

autistic individuals can communicate, learn, and interact with others. High-tech assistive technologies for autistic users are now easier to develop, afford, individualize, and carry around and offer multi-sensory choices for communication through unobtrusive devices. A quick search of "autism" in Apple's App Store in November 2010 returned 231 iPhone and 60 iPad applications that were designed to benefit autistic users or their caregivers. Applications available for the iPhone, iPod, or iPad such as Proloquo2Go, MyTalk Tools, AACSpeechBuddy, and the TalkSpeak Button provide visually-driven communication devices with built-in text-to-speech engines that can be used by children and adults with autism, even those with limited fine motor capability. Autistic users have used social media themselves to build a strong autism self-advocacy movement that develops and shares information, support, events, and publicity through such venues as Facebook, Twitter, YouTube, Second Life, individual blogs, group forums, and organizational wikis. One grandparent created the Zac Browser to present appropriate online games, activities, and videos to children with ASDs through a full-screen interface with an icon-based navigational system. Publicly launched in 2008, the Zac Browser quickly gained over one million users from around the world. One problem with this revolution of online assistive technologies for autism is that anyone with some technical know-how can develop an application for autistic users and offer it publicly. Autistic users and their caregivers lose time, energy, and money searching by trial-and-error for potentially appropriate technologies from a plethora of choices that have not been professionally developed through a user-centered process. Davies's (2005) warning about the proliferation of virtual reality applications for users with cognitive disabilities applies here: "The danger is that [developers] may not have the necessary knowledge in good design and issues of usability, nor in the methodologies, collection, and interpretation of results in a scientific and critical manner. We risk, therefore, being overwhelmed by hack-job applications with grand and unjustifiable claims" (p. 283). Technical communicators who are or become part of design teams working on assistive technologies for autistic users can help solve this problem by publishing their experiences with and research on user research techniques, tools, and accommodations in academic and professional venues.

Currently, little research on autistic users and assistive technologies is publicly available in scholarly publications (Davies, 2005, p. 283; Francis, Mellor, & Firth, 2009, p. 66). What does exist provides some insights on how technical communicators can facilitate inclusion of autistic users in the design process of assistive technologies. The technologies studied in the published research are necessarily older than the latest social media and mobile technologies described above due to the time involved in the research and publication process, but my selection represents major types of high-tech devices and applications currently designed for autistic users:

- Social media applications (Bagatell, 2007; Brownlow & O'Dell, 2006)
- Mobile technologies (Bishop, 2003; Gentry et al., 2010; Spence-Cochran & Pearl, 2009)
- Computer-assisted instruction (Stock, Davies, & Wehmeyer, 2009; Van Laarhoven. Chandler, McNamara, & Zurita, 2009; Wehmeyer, Palmer, Smith, Parent, Davies, & Stock, 2006; Whalen, Lidén, Ingersoll, & Lidén, 2007)
- Augmentative and alternative communication (Biklen, Morton, Saha, Duncan, Gold, Hardardottir, et al., 1991; Van Laarhoven & Zurita, 2009; Wert, 2009)
- Virtual reality (Standen & Brown, 2005; Tartaro & Cassell, 2007)
- Robotics (Liu, Conn, Sarkar, & Stone, 2008)

This selection of research overviews the ways autistic people of various abilities and disabilities use technology (Danforth & Naraian, 2007; Standen & Brown, 2005; Stock et al., 2009; Wehmeyer et al., 2006), although it still reflects to some degree the prevalence of research including participants with mild-to-moderate disabilities (Bagatell, 2007; Liu et al., 2008; Van Laarhoven et al., 2009) rather than severe-to-profound disabilities (Biklen et al., 1991; Spence-Cochran & Pearl, 2009). Research on the use of technology by autistic people spans the disciplines of rhetoric (Bagatell, 2007; Brownlow & O'Dell, 2006), psychology (Standen & Brown, 2005; Tartaro & Cassell, 2007), education (Biklen et al., 1991; Bishop, 2003; Spence-Cochran & Pearl, 2009; Van Laarhoven et al., 2009; Wert, 2009; Whalen et al., 2007), engineering (Liu et al., 2008), vocational habilitation (Gentry et al., 2010; Stock et al., 2009; Wehmeyer et al., 2006), and clinical sciences (Danforth & Naraian, 2007). Overall, this representative research illustrates the technologies, disciplines, and methods on assistive technologies for autistic persons. More importantly, however, this research explains research processes in a manner that can help shape the theory of and practice for including autistics in the design process for technologies.

The assumption that autistic people are incapable of contributing expert user knowledge to the design process of new technologies is evident in much of the literature on assistive technology research and development for autistic users. An analysis of the literature reveals that several factors inhibit the adoption of a user-centered approach to assistive technology for autistic users:

- A lack of understanding of the various experiences, preferences, and needs of autistic users

- A distrust in the cognitive ability of autistic people to know and reflect on the technologies they use
- A concern about the difficulty of working with users with social, communication, and behavioral differences
- A fear of developing technology that subjects people with autism to increased dependence
- A lack of appreciation of the value of collaboration with users

These issues need to be openly addressed to improve the user experience of autistic persons and to enable them to participate in technology decisions that affect their everyday lives. Technical communicators who conduct user research will need to alleviate any potential inhibitions regarding working with autistic people when advocating for a user-centered design process with technology developers.

Although a proof of concept study (Liu et al., 2008), pilot studies (Tartaro & Cassell, 2007; Wert, 2009), prototype studies (Stock et al., 2009), and usability tests (Whalen et al., 2007) are among the research methods described in the selected literature for review, only one research team investigated techniques for researching the autistic user experience at the very beginning of the design process (Francis et al., 2009). In the promisingly titled article "Techniques and Recommendations for the Inclusion of Users With Autism in the Design of Assistive Technologies," Francis et al. (2009) discuss their use of a three-round Delphi study with seven psychologists specializing in the treatment of autism to assess the use of four techniques for revealing the user experience at the earliest stage of developing a new assistive technology for off-the-shelf mobile devices, when "input by the user can have the greatest influence on the direction of development" (p. 59). The four techniques—video recording and review,[3]

---

[3] In the video recording and review technique described by Francis et al. (2009) the designer/researcher visits the user at his or her workplace and gathers data through interviews, observations, workplace artifacts, and videotape to determine the user's requirements for a new technology (p. 61). This user research technique is known as contextual inquiry (see Kuniavsky, 2003, pp. 160–181, for a discussion on how to conduct and analyze one). The designer/researcher in this scenario spends two days with the user gathering data and videotaping some interviews to familiarize the user with the designer/researcher and the videographer. On the third day, the designer/researcher and videographer accompany the user through a typical day. After reviewing the data collected, the designer/researcher reviews the videotape and notes with the user for verification. See Francis et al. (2009, p. 65) for a list of specific modifications to the video recording and review technique for autistic users recommended by the study participants.

self-photography,[4] thinking aloud,[5] and role play[6]—had not been used with autistic people participating in user research before but were selected because they have been productively used with autistics for educational and therapeutic purposes. The researchers developed scenarios of an autistic user and a non-autistic designer engaging in the process of using each technique to select a new digital assistive technology for development. The researchers conducted three rounds of online task-oriented questionnaires with each psychologist to arrive at eight general recommendations for interacting with autistic users during the design process, including the following:

- Plan the user research activities to accommodate the cognitive, psychological, and physical needs of each individual participant
- Balance the need to observe the participant in his or her natural environments with the autistic participant's need to avoid distractions or the discomfort of interrupting a familiar routine
- Ensure that the participant fully understands the purpose of the activity so that he or she can actively and comfortably participate
- Prepare to communicate instructions in a clear, step-by-step manner by avoiding abstract language, using visual aids, and checking for participant understanding

The psychologists participating in the Delphi study also had specific recommendations for modifying the four user experience design techniques for autistic participants (Francis et al., 2009, pp. 65–66) but did not choose a single technique as most appropriate. Instead, the researchers suggested matching the technique to

---

[4] The self-photography technique used in the second scenario (Francis et al., 2009, p. 61) requires the user to photographically document his or her daily life and any problematic situations encountered over the course of two weeks. The designer/researcher reviews the photos with the user each week in an unscripted interview, asking the user to talk about the photos of problems and consider how technology might be used to help solve them. See Francis et al. (2009, p. 65) for recommended modifications.

[5] The thinking aloud technique used in the third scenario (Francis et al., 2009, p. 61) should not be confused with the thinking aloud method often used during usability testing. In this scenario, the user and his or her support worker physically walk through a typical day while they talk out loud about what the user is doing. The exercise is recorded by lapel microphones and a videographer following them "at a discreet distance" (Francis et al., 2009, p. 61). See Francis et al. (2009, p. 65) for recommended modifications.

[6] In the role play scenario (Francis et al., 2009, p. 61), the designer/researcher creates dollhouse-like representations of the user's home and workplace and connects them with a map of the places in between. Using these props, the user talks about his or her typical day with the designer/researcher. The session is videotaped for review by both in a follow-up session. See Francis et al. (2009, p. 66) for recommended modifications.

the individual user as educators have found this to be critical in the selection of educational techniques in their work with autistic individuals.

Ironically, Francis et al. (2009) did not involve autistic persons in their selection and development of the four techniques for user experience design they selected. In the methods section they state that to conduct the research with autistic participants would have required them

> to submit users with autism to a series of design exercises with no practical outcome for them. However, because this population has characteristics such as dislike of change and tendency toward anxiety and stress when encountering new situations, working directly with them as users was ruled out on ethical grounds. (pp. 58–59)

However, I question whether developing user research techniques solely on the perceptions that psychologists have of autistic persons can fully predict the needs and preferences autistic users might have for participating in user research. I am also concerned that autistic participants were ruled out rather than accommodated because of cognitive differences. Francis et al. (2009) conducted their research using an "online survey tool" (p. 59), so the psychologists who participated likely used their own computers in a familiar environment. Given these conditions, autistic users could have been recruited for and participated in the same study with little anxiety or stress due to change. Alternatively, another user research method, such as focus groups, could be modified to accommodate the dislike of change or unfamiliarity that causes anxiety for many autistic people. The researchers chose to use a small group of psychologists with "rich experience of the day-to-day activities of the users, a detailed knowledge of the underlying condition, and an understanding of the research process" (Francis et al., 2009, p. 59). Using this sample of convenient participants still provides us with valuable information but misses the opportunity for researchers to better understand the "rich experience" of autistic persons themselves and for autistic persons to participate as expert users in the development of technologies meant to assist them.

Several other research projects have included or planned to include in later iterations autistic participants with severe-to-profound disabilities, illustrating not only that autistic people can test technology designs at various stages of development but also that they can express their opinions about technology, even if they cannot speak. Stock et al. (2009) tested a high-fidelity prototype of an interactive, animated computer simulation for work-based social skills training with 26 teenagers and adults with mild-to-severe cognitive disabilities, including autism. The researchers found that all participants completed the training simulation with no or minimal administrative support and with significantly improved social skills when pre- and post-tests were compared (p. 51). Stock et al. conducted interviews with the participants themselves, as well as with teachers and vocational habilitation staff, to learn whether they were satisfied with using the technology (pp. 51–52). Spence-Cochran and Pearl (2009) studied whether vocational training for five autistic high school students with severe disabilities was more efficient and satisfying when presented as a multimodal application on a mobile touchscreen device than as face-to-face instruction. Before, during, and after the study, participants were asked if they enjoyed using the technology. Each expressed that he or she did, which was verified by onsite observations and interviews with parents and school staff (Spence-Cochran & Pearl, 2009, p. 37). In addition, two of the participants independently figured out how to restart the application to review task instructions when they had difficulty completing a task (Spence-Cochran & Pearl, 2009, p. 40), which demonstrates that people with severe cognitive disabilities can troubleshoot new technologies, even in potentially stressful situations. Although the students' parents and school staff contributed their perspectives on the value, appropriateness, and usefulness of the technology for the students with more reflective detail, the students' opinions and reactions were an essential part of the "social validation" of the technology (Spence-Cochran & Pearl, 2009, p. 36). In these studies, the research methods applied to questions about user experience include accommodations for cognitive disability and, in those cases including minors, for age. One common accommodation is to include parents, caregivers, teachers, therapy staff, and/or support assistants with autistic users as participants in the study. These additional participants may provide both assistive services and familiar interactive relationships to the autistic users, enabling them to better communicate with researchers and to minimize the anxiety of unfamiliar research situations. The minimally described development of the technology reported on in each of these scholarly articles would likely not be considered user-centered design since they include user research only late in the process. However, the researchers do incorporate valuable user experience research with autistic participants, including those with severe cognitive disabilities, whose opinions they consider essential to the success of the technology.

One research and design team created a more user-centered design process by planning from the outset to include autistic users as participants in most of the process by recruiting autistic children with increasing levels of disability for later research stages as the technology became increasingly predictable (Tartaro & Cassell, 2007). This team is developing a virtual life-sized child peer for young autistic users to interact with as they practice storytelling and other social skills. Tartaro and Cassell (2007) summarize results of an early pilot study of the "virtual peer" with non-disabled participants, report on their current pilot study involving an autistic girl with mild disabilities, and describe plans to conduct future pilot studies with autistic children with more severe disabilities. The technology developers explain that "as we build the interfaces for our system, we use an iterative design process that relies on prototyping a system and then continuing to revise the design by having children with ASD interact with the system. This allows us to design an interface that is maximally intuitive to the child, and maximally successful" (Tartaro & Cassell, 2007, p. 249). This research and design team, which applied an iterative development process common to user-centered design, provides us with one model of planning a design process that enables people with mild-to-moderate disabilities as well as those with severe-to-profound disabilities to successfully and meaningfully participate in the process when the representative users span a broad range of disability levels. Davies (2005) calls for "further development of methodologies to allow usability testing and development of usable applications involving users with various cognitive disabilities who are not necessarily able to take part in usability testing in the same manner as able-bodied subjects," but this challenge has still not been fully or formally answered (p. 283). However, the selected literature suggests that design teams can plan ahead for the participation of autistic users early and often in the design process, for example, by involving those with less severe disabilities in the process before those with more severe disabilities (Tartaro & Cassell, 2007), by scheduling practice tasks with participants, test equipment, and scripts (Liu et al., 2008; Van Laarhoven et al., 2009), or by including parents and other members of a participant's support network in assessment (Spence-Cochran & Pearl, 2009; Stock et al., 2009). More research and reporting on research techniques and methods for working with autistic users is needed, and technical communicators can add valuable scholarship on user experience research techniques and methods that support the inclusion of autistic participants in the development of the technologies they use.

Several researchers expressed that user independence is the end goal of assistive technology (Silverman, 2008; Spence-Cochran & Pearl, 2009; Standen & Brown, 2005; Van Laarhoven et al., 2009; Van Laarhoven & Zurita, 2009); however, many autistic users value interdependence over independence. In a landmark study by Biklen et al. (1991), the researchers were able to support the results of a previous study on facilitated communication. Biklen et al. trained 22 nonverbal autistic students in facilitated communication, which enabled the students to demonstrate surprising communication and math abilities. For example, the eight students who used facilitated communication for the first time demonstrated that they could read and some could write in complete sentences, the students' writing did not reveal common problems in the communication of autistics like pronoun reversal, the students who echoed the speech of others could type the ideas they wanted to communicate at the same time, and the students were able to express their personal feelings. The revelation of communication and other intellectual abilities in non- or low-verbal students caused the researchers to rethink "prior assumptions about autism, communication, independence, and interdependence, and the education of students with and without disabilities" (Biklen et al., 1991, p. 161). Several students revealed a preference for interdependence—such as that needed in facilitated communication—rather than complete physical independence. One student who became very proficient in typing with a minimal touch on the elbow from a facilitator, typed "I AM QUITE HAPPY RTO BE DEP [dependent] ON PEP [people] MUCH OF THE TIME" because it created a closer relationship between her and her facilitator (Biklen et al., 1991, p. 175). Another student explained that she wanted to make her own "big choices" and be "reasonably accepted" but that society's view of independence was "too dreadfully frightening and so I do not make a big effort to achieve this" (Biklen et al., 1991, p. 175). Reindal (1999) explains these differing definitions in reference to independent living: professionals view (physical) independence as the ability to perform self-care activities while the disabled view (mental) independence as the ability to make life decisions and follow through with them even if they need physical help to do so.

Critiques of the ideal of able-bodied independence and an exploration of the benefits of interdependence for autistic and non-autistics are also found in the literature of assistive technologies for autistic users. In a literature review of research on autism in the social sciences, Silverman (2008) writes, "Individuals with autism whose life histories suggested the most resilience and best overall quality of life were often those who, rather than being independent, benefitted from accommodations in their surroundings and a complex network of social and family supports" (p. 328). Among the literature she reviews, one researcher advocates a "partnership model" in working with autistics to determine treatment, and another group of researchers who worked with autistic adults to assess services promotes participatory research (Silverman, 2008, pp. 328–329). Scherer (2005) explains that

> It may seem a contradiction in terms, but *Independent Living* can focus as much on interdependence as it does on independence. In addition to peer assistance, persons with disabilities acknowledge the important role of educators and rehabilitation professionals in their attainment of an autonomous lifestyle. A supportive family is also important—especially when family members provide care and act as personal assistants. (p. 79)

Furthermore, Scherer (2005) emphasizes that the end goal of assistive technology should be to improve quality of life, which is not achieved by independence from assistance but by interdependence with others (p. 191). Autistic users must be included in the conceptualization and design of the assistive technologies meant to benefit them because it is their goals that should be addressed by user-centered design, and if they are not included in the design process, researchers cannot know what these goals are. User-centered design need not require independent participation from autistic participants. Technical communicators can help technology developers understand that autistic users are competent to participate in the design process and make accommodations or modifications[7] to user experience research techniques to enable their participation, which is an essential part of the user-centered design process.

Facilitating the inclusion of autistic users with a wide range of disability levels in a user-centered design process can benefit technology developers and the general public by contributing to our understanding of universal design and the development of universal design features. Universal design is a process of designing new technologies and environments that are fully accessible to the widest possible audience, including those with disabilities (Connell et al., 1997; Thatcher et al., 2006, p. 591).[8] Wehmeyer et al. (2006), who conducted a meta-analysis to evaluate the effectiveness of technology to help people with cognitive disabilities meet work objectives, were also interested in whether the inclusion of universal design features in work-related technologies improved their effectiveness for helping this population meet work objectives. A wide range of assistive technologies—such as audio prompting, video-assisted training, and alternative communication on mobile devices and personal computers—was represented by the 13 studies analyzed. The researchers calculated the percentage non-overlapping data (PND) scores for each of the 95 unique treatment cases included in the 13 studies. The PND measures the effectiveness of a treatment, with a score below 80% indicating a questionable treatment, 80%–99% a fair treatment, and 99% a highly effective treatment. The mean PND score for all 95 cases was 93%, indicating that the treatment outcomes of work-related technology use for people with cognitive disabilities were generally fair. The effectiveness for people with mild-to-moderate disabilities (PND = 94%) was similar to that for those with severe-to-profound disabilities (PND = 92%). When the cases were categorized into a group that used technology with no reported universal design features ($n = 40$) and a group that used technology with more

---

[7] Accommodations are changes to the research environment, conditions, or tools that enable users with disabilities to participate in the same research tasks as able-bodied users—for example, replacing fluorescent lights with special lighting, permitting typed rather than verbal responses, allowing additional time to complete tasks, or reducing the number of items per page. Modifications are a different, and generally less preferred, type of change to user research to help disabled users participate. Modifications are changes made to the research tasks that allow for a reduced level of participation from disabled users than that expected from able-bodied users. Choosing a more basic task and reducing the scope of the task are examples of modifications.

[8] The concept of universal design is based on "The Principles of Universal Design," a set of seven principles—design for equitable use, flexible use, simple and intuitive use, perceptible information, tolerance for error, low physical effort, and size and space appropriate for approach—developed by "a working group of architects, product designers, engineers and environmental design researchers" at the Center for Universal Design at North Carolina State University (Connell et al., 1997). See the website for the Center for Universal Design for a copy of the principles and accompanying guidelines and additional information about universal design (http://www.ncsu.edu/www/ncsu/design/sod5/cud/about_ud/udprinciples.htm).

than one universal design feature ($n = 41$), the researchers found that technologies that incorporated universal design features (PND = 97%) were more effective in helping people with cognitive disabilities meet work-related objectives than technologies without universal design features (PND = 91%). The idea that universal design features make technologies equally available to all users is demonstrated by the explosion of developers using iPod, iPhone, and iPad platforms to build applications for autistic users. In a practitioner's guide for using video iPods to teach autistic users life skills, Van Laarhoven and Zurita (2009) explain that touchscreen systems help autistic users access icon-based interfaces, managerial functions like calendars and timers, and other operations even with limited fine motor capabilities. They also note that "iPod technologies appear to conform to several principles recommended for universally designed products "iPod technologies appear to conform to several principles recommended for universally designed products . . . which not only increases accessibility for individuals with disabilities, but also provides convenience for the vast majority of consumers" (Van Laarhoven & Zurita, 2009, p. 23). Just as improved universal design has made touchscreen technology desirable for autistic users, the continued research and development of universal design features with autistic users can improve technology use for everyone—an example of the benefits of interdependence between the nondisabled and the disabled to develop technology.

THE EXAMPLE OF ONE AUTISTIC USER

Analyzing the example of how one exceptional autistic user, Baggs (2007), interacts with technology and her statements of how the competence/incompetence and dependence/independence of autistic people are constructed by rhetorical perspective supports the position that autistic people can and should be participants in the design of assistive technologies. Baggs (2007), an autistic adult without functional spoken language, thoughtfully portrays her autistic experience in a collection of YouTube videos. The first part of her most popular video, "In My Language," illustrates without exposition how she communicates nonverbally with her environment through sound, touch, smell, and taste in a manner that might startle a non-autistic audience. Her "interpretation" of her "native communication" in the second part of the video—which she relates by typing her thoughts and having them read aloud by a voice synthesizer—is, as she explains, "a strong statement on the existence and value of many different kinds of thinking and interaction in a world where how close you can appear to a specific one of them determines whether you are seen as a real person or an adult or an intelligent person" (Baggs, 2007). Baggs (2007) explains that people with cognitive disabilities who think differently than able-bodied persons and use assistive technology to help them communicate and organize their interactions with others "are considered non-persons or non-thinking." Her capabilities are often unnoticed because of a prevalent assumption that autistic people with no functional speech or with speaking difficulties lack intelligence; in fact, until recently, most researchers in the autism field incorrectly accepted that the majority (70%–80%) of autistic children are also mentally retarded (Edelson, 2006, pp. 66, 73). In a qualitative study of seven severely autistic people, all but one of whom use assistive and augmentative communication (AAC) devices, Biklen (2005) concluded that professionals should have a "presumption of competence" of autistic persons and develop an "intimate contact with the person [that] allows one to dispense with the fault-finding, deficit-seeking framework of the professional diagnostician" and find ways of interacting that help autistic people express their knowledge and opinions (pp. 260–261). Most of the seven participants in Biklen's (2005) study were labeled mentally retarded in childhood and all but one use AAC devices, but each wrote a chapter for Biklen's study that illustrates his or her intellectual competence and ability to communicate.

In addition to identifying the incorrect assumption that speaking difficulties reflect intellectual incompetence, Baggs, in the documentary "Positively Autistic," warns against the assumption that assistive technologies and services make her more dependent, and so less competent, than people without disabilities:

> Nobody is truly independent. Why is it that some kinds of dependence are so invisible to people that they are called independence while other kinds are considered dependence and considered something awful for it? Why is it that I am not considered to live independently because I cannot cook for myself, but other people are considered to live independently if they can't fix their computer? (as recorded in Selik, 2008)

Technological assistance for non-disabled people is considered normal—and therefore is mundane and "invisible"—whereas assistive technology for autistic people, like Baggs's voice synthesizer, is not considered normal and marks the autistic person in society as dependent. Independence and dependence are social constructions, and Baggs's questions can help us recognize the dichotomy as unrealistically polarizing.

Considering these terms of dependence/independence from Baggs's perspective can also illuminate the ethical argument for embracing human interdependence and can inform the accommodation of the autistic experience throughout the design process for assistive technologies. As Reindal (1999) argues, "When the human condition is viewed as one of interdependency and vulnerability, this leads to an understanding of independence as 'partnership' . . . [and] independence becomes a two-way responsibility and not solely an individual ability" (p. 364). Including autistic members as part of a design team and recognizing autistic users as able "practitioners," "producers," and "citizens" (Johnson, 1998, p. 46) will require technical communicators to accommodate autistic differences in their user experience research[9] and to persuade designers of the value of making such accommodations despite the initial planning, scheduling, and budgeting flexibility needed for such accommodations.[10] Many technical communicators possess both the rhetorical skills and the audience-oriented practice that can help change the way assistive technologies are developed for autistics and others with disabilities from object-centered to user-centered. One argument that technical communicators can make with colleagues who are doubtful that cognitively disabled people can actively participate in the design process is that the need for assistive technology can itself wrongly mark a person as dependent on others for making decisions about technology use.

According to the Technology-Related Assistance of Individuals with Disabilities Act (1988), an assistive technology (AT) device is any device or system that improves the functional abilities of a disabled person. The device or system may be commercially available to the general or disabled population and may be adapted or customized for individual use (Scherer, 2005, pp. 36–37). Technologies may be low-tech (e.g., a picture schedule or a special pen grip), mid-tech (e.g., a portable schedule with interchangeable pictures representing different activities), or high-tech (e.g., a text-to-speech application or an electronic ACC device). As shown in "Positively Autistic" (Selik, 2008), Baggs coordinates an array of assistive technologies and services to help her make videos like "In My Language," live in her own apartment, and advocate for autistic people. Baggs briefly demonstrates how her AAC device turns her thoughts typed on a keyboard into synthesized speech. Baggs uses a power wheelchair but moves her chair with her feet when filming with a hand-held digital camera to better control the shot. She uses standard software and freeware programs to transfer her video to a computer, edit and caption the movie, and then convert the finished piece to a file to post on YouTube. Low-tech devices Baggs uses may include the plastic hanger on the back of her wheelchair, which she might use to reach for certain objects, and the small metal bands she wears on each knuckle of each finger of her hands, perhaps to better feel the position of

---

[9] Practical suggestions for working with autistic adults and children in interview, testing, and informal research situations can be found in the writings of habilitation and education specialists, such as Bellini and Ehlers (2009), Standifer (2009), and Van Laarhoven and Zurita (2009).

[10] For more information on how to convince corporate leaders and design team members of the value of user-centered design, see Kuniavsky (2003, pp. 505–527). See Thatcher, Burks, Heilmann, Henry, Kirkpatrick, Lauka, et al. (2006) for information on how to involve people with disabilities in the design process (pp. 22–26) and for arguments on the value of addressing accessibility issues from the beginning and throughout a design process to ensure that the design is "effective, efficient, and satisfying for more people, especially people with disabilities, in more situations" (pp. 26–49). Although Thatcher et al. (2006) discuss the accessibility of the web in particular, many of their general suggestions for creating accessible design can also be applied to the design of other technologies.

her hands as she types. Assistants help Baggs with daily living activities, like doing laundry, cooking meals, organizing medications, and reminding her to brush her teeth. With her abilities to teach herself new technologies, communicate her experience purposefully to others, coordinate systems and people, and troubleshoot problems (Selik, 2008), Baggs has deftly pulled together a variety of assistive technologies and services to increase her quality of life and achieve her goals. Although Baggs is in some ways an exceptional case, the knowledge and skills she needs to choose and manage the technologies she uses illustrate that she is a highly competent user of technologies and can clearly express and act on her opinions. With accommodations, she would be able to participate in user experience research and her contributions would be valuable to a design team. By accommodating autistic people in user experience research, persuading technology developers of the need for user-centered design, and publishing the results of the user-centered research techniques and methods they develop, technical communicators can apply their expertise to involve disabled users in the design and development of assistive technologies created for them.

THE TECHNICAL COMMUNICATOR AND
USER-CENTERED TECHNOLOGY

User experience research would benefit from the incorporation of ideas from disability studies, such as the view of disabilities as human differences in abilities that should be accommodated in society to the benefit of all. Methods of inquiry in the sciences and the humanities are often borrowed from each other, although they are not always understood completely by the borrowing discipline, which can obscure the analysis of research results and misdirect the production of new knowledge and technologies. For example, Danforth and Naraian (2007) studied the underlying assumptions about autism found in the autistic-mind-as-computer metaphor often found in clinical studies to determine if the metaphor is a viable means for generating new and useful theories for autism researchers. Their analysis examined a common use of the concept of programming to refer to input of various components of educational plans, including early intervention, to be processed by the autistic brain to produce the target behavioral output. Agents for this process include parents, teachers, and service providers who implement the program. Student behavior is thus mechanically controlled to produce the desired output. These desired behaviors must then be maintained by the student-machine. Based on their study, Danforth and Naraian (2007) became concerned that the focus on output from the autistic user ignores the internal, inaccessible variables of human cognition. Further, the autistic-mind-as-machine metaphor limits learning to a passive, uni-directional transmission model, which does not support active, higher order thinking by autistic students. This limiting view of the learning potential of autistic people also points to a prevalent view among researchers that they are "enigmatic, mysterious, and even bizarre"

(Danforth & Naraian, 2007, p. 288) and unable to actively participate in research and development. The "subjectivities of students, families, and adults with autism are rarely sought as a strategy to expand the professional knowledge base . . . [resulting in] the reification of dominant social norms as conceptualized by the professionals" (Danforth & Naraian, 2007, p. 288). Danforth and Naraian (2007) call for new productive metaphors for autism that can generate "theories bearing sufficient complexity, flexibility, fecundity, and richness to drive research to improved understandings of persons with autism" and provide specific concepts and practices for autism professionals to benefit autistic children and their families (p. 289). Technical communicators can help design and development teams can analyze user experience research with autistic people in a manner that does not limit the significance of results with inappropriate metaphors or heuristics, encouraging developers to consider the participation of autistic users in the development of technologies from a perspective more productive to innovative design. Drawing on their understanding of research methods in the sciences and the humanities, technical communicators can also develop and test new user experience research tools and techniques with autistic users that will enable autistic people to more actively participate in user research throughout the design process of new assistive technologies for autism. Technical communicators can also add to the scholarship on user research and usability techniques by grounding their development of new tools and techniques in theory and practice and publishing their knowledge for others to apply.

In addition, technical communicators can bridge the divide between the knowledge-bases of the sciences and the humanities to facilitate productive dialogue between technology developers and autistic users. An interdependence model of the user-centered technology design process would require technical developers to depend on the expert experiential perspectives of the autistic users they design for and would require autistic users to depend on the engineering and clinical expertise of technology developers to shape the kinds of assistive technologies that will increase their quality of life. Embracing these dependences can liberate both groups from the limitations of their necessarily circumscribed perspectives on living with autism and designing technology, and the technical communicator can reveal to them the limitations and possibilities of both by orchestrating the dialectic between the two. In *Claiming Disability*, Linton (1998) criticizes the divide of disability studies between the clinical sciences and the humanities, which sabotages the study of disability (p. 93). She states that new multidisciplinary fields that draw on research from the sciences, social sciences, and humanities "rarely produced merging across the divide between the liberals arts and the applied fields" (p. 78), which weakens our understanding and accommodation of disability. The current work of research clinicians and technology developers on assistive technologies for autism is important and necessary and is born, I believe, from a desire to help autistic people and their families. Technical communicators, however, can help bring autistic people into the design process as participatory members in decisions about how assistive technologies should be designed, making user-centered design possible.

Also inhibiting the adoption of user-centered design with assistive technologies for the developmentally disabled is a fear that technologies are proliferating out of control, taking away our ability to choose and shape a social life world with science and technology. For example, Scherer (2005) is concerned that assistive technologies designed to increase the disabled person's independence from people rather than facilitate interdependence with people can produce a dependence on technology that actually decreases his or her quality of life (pp. 194–198). Echoing this concern, Cromby and Standen (1999) argue that assistive technologies that extend one's subjectivities, such as communication devices, allow the body to be permeated by technology, creating new tensions between technology, identity, culture, and the body. Those with cognitive disabilities may become dependent on such new technologies, which can further marginalize them and drain financial resources: "in a sense, people with disabilities would become hostages to the machines that help them" (Cromby & Standen, 1999, p. 108). To such fears about our dependence on technology, Mesthene (1967/2003) responds that neither uncritical acceptance of technology as a blessing nor renouncement of it as a curse helps us deal with the philosophical issues of technology and human development that must be addressed in order to wisely shape our technology use as well as our technologies. Even when they argue that technology is deterministic, philosophers of technology such as Ellul (1964/2003) and Jonas (1979/2003) point to the human potential to master technology by thinking critically about it and choosing to respond accordingly. User experience research and user-centered design can help us think critically about our development of assistive technologies and ensure that they increase quality of life rather than a faulty valorization of able-bodied independence. Johnson (1998) proposes that this area of ethics is the domain of the technical communicator who studies technologies from a user perspective (p. 156) and helps make the invisible use and "know how" of everyday technology visible and valuable (p. 11). This is a "radical act," writes Johnson (1998), in opposition to the dominant perception that the expertise and value of technology is held by the designers and developers of technology to whom we have surrendered our democratic rights and responsibilities (pp. 10–11). Technical "rhetoricians" are needed to participate in the development of technologies for autism from a critical stance gained through their knowledge of the multidisciplinary field of disability studies, their practice of user experience research with autistic participants, and their advocacy for user-centered design.

The vital role of technical communicators in the design of assistive technologies for autism is to help technology developers and autistic users embrace their interdependence in the user-centered design process. Johnson (1998) argues for recognition of the user as practitioner, producer, and participatory citizen who should be involved in the process of shaping everyday technology focused on human concerns. This recognition should not be denied autistic users because of concerns that they are not intellectually able to make decisions about the technologies they use or fears that they are vulnerable to dependence on technology. Continued user experience research on autistic users of technology, the support networks they use, and the environmental milieu they live in is needed. In addition, user experience research techniques and tools need to be developed to accommodate the full participation of autistic users in the user-centered design process. Although this might cost businesses more in the short term, Johnson (1998) points out—as have proponents of user-centered design and universal design—that these costs will be recouped by greater user satisfaction and accessibility and by the valuable knowledge gained from users for future development (p. 149). For autistic users, technical communicators not only must "get involved with actual people and situations" (Johnson, 1998, p. 161) but also must adapt their skills for the benefit of a previously neglected and vulnerable audience. "The end of user-centered theory is only complete when coupled with the end of social action" (Johnson, 1998, p. 156), and the technical communicator's ethical responsibility is to realize this connection.

REFERENCES

American Psychiatric Association. (2000). *Diagnostic and statistical manual of mental disorders* (4th ed.). Washington, DC: Author.

Bagatell, N. (2007). Orchestrating voices: Autism, identity and the power of discourse. *Disability & Society, 22*(4), 413–426.

Baggs, A. M. (Producer). (2007, January 14). In my language. *YouTube.* Video retrieved from http://www.youtube.com/watch?v=JnylM1hI2jc

Bellini, S., & Ehlers, E. J. (2009). Video modeling interventions for individuals with autism spectrum disorders: A practitioner's guide to implementation and use of technology. *Assistive Technology and Autism Spectrum Disorders: Researched-Based Practice and Innovation in the Field* [Special issue]. *Assistive Technology Outcomes and Benefits, 5,* 56–69.

Biklen, D. (2005). *Autism and the myth of the person alone.* New York, NY: New York University Press.

Biklen, D., Morton, M. W., Saha, S. N., Duncan, J., Gold, D., Hardardottir, M., et al. (1991). "I amn not a utistivc on thje typ" ("I'm not autistic on the typewriter"). *Disability & Society, 6*(3), 161–180.

Bishop, J. (2003). The Internet for educating individuals with social impairments. *Journal of Computer Assisted Learning, 19*(4), 546–556.

Brownlow, C., & O'Dell, L. (2006). Constructing an autistic identity: AS voices online. *Mental Retardation, 44*(5), 315–321.

Brugha, T., McManus, S., Meltzer, H., Smith, J., Scott, F. J., Purdon, S., et al. (2009). *Autism spectrum disorder in adults living in households throughout England: Report from the adult psychiatric morbidity survey 2007.* The Health and Social Care Information Centre. Retrieved from http://www.ic.nhs.uk/webfiles/publications/mental%20health/mental%20health%20surveys/APMS_Autism_report_standard_20_OCT_09.pdf

CDC. (2010, May 13). Autism Spectrum Disorders (ASDs). Retrieved from http://www. cdc.gov/ncbddd/autism/index.html

Chamak, B., Bonniau, B., Jaunay, E., & Cohen, D. (2008). What can we learn about autism from autistic persons? *Psychotherapy and Psychosomatics, 77*(5), 271–279.

Connell, B. R., Jones, M., Mace, R., Mueller, J., Mullick, A., Ostroff, E., et al. (1997). *The principles of universal design: Version 2.0.* The Center for Universal Design, North Carolina State University. Retrieved from http://www.ncsu.edu/www/ncsu/design/sod5/cud/about_ud/udprinciplestext.htm

Cromby, J., & Standen, P. (1999). Cyborgs and stigma: Technology, disability, and subjectivity. In A. J. Gordo-López & I. Parker (Eds.), *Cyberpsychology* (pp. 95–112). Florence, KY: Taylor & Frances/Routledge.

Danforth, S., & Naraian, S. (2007). Use of the machine metaphor within autism research. *Journal of Developmental and Physical Disabilities, 19*(3), 273–290.

Davies, R. (2005). Commentary on Standen, P. J., & Brown, D. J., Virtual reality in the rehabilitation of people with intellectual disabilities: Review. *CyberPsychology and Behavior, 8*(3), 283–284.

Edelson, M. G. (2006). Are the majority of children with autism mentally retarded? A systematic evaluation of the data. *Focus on Autism and Other Developmental Disabilities, 21*(2), 66–83.

Ellul, J. (1964/2003). On the aims of a philosophy of technology. Reprinted in R. C. Scharff & V. Dusek (Eds.), *Philosophy of technology: The technological condition* (pp. 182–190). Malden, MA: Blackwell Publishing.

Francis, P., Mellor, D., & Firth, L. (2009). Techniques and recommendations for the inclusion of users with autism in the design of assistive technologies. *Assistive Technology, 21*(2), 57–68.

Gentry, T., Wallace, J., Kvarfordt, C., & Lynch, K. B. (2010). Personal digital assistants as cognitive aids for high school students with autism: Results of a community-based trial. *Journal of Vocational Rehabilitation, 32*(2), 101–107.

Johnson, R. R. (1998). *User-centered technology: A rhetorical theory for computers and other mundane artifacts*. Albany, NY: State University of New York Press.

Jonas, H. (1979/2003). Toward a philosophy of technology. Reprinted in R. C. Scharff & V. Dusek (Eds.), *Philosophy of technology: The technological condition* (pp. 191–204). Malden, MA: Blackwell Publishing.

Kuniavsky, M. (2003). *Observing the user experience: A practitioner's guide to user research*. San Francisco, CA: Morgan Kaufmann Publishers.

Linton, S. (1998). *Claiming disability: Knowledge and identity*. New York, NY: New York University Press.

Liu, C., Conn, K., Sarkar, N., & Stone, W. (2008). Online affect detection and robot behavior adaptation for intervention of children with autism. *IEEE Transactions on Robotics, 24*(4), 883–896.

Mesthene, E. G. (1967/2003). The social impact of technological change. Reprinted in R. C. Scharff & V. Dusek (Eds.), *Philosophy of technology: The technological condition* (pp. 617–637). Malden, MA: Blackwell Publishing.

Myers, S. M., & Johnson, C. P. (2007). Management of children with autism spectrum disorders. *Pediatrics, 120*(5), 1162–1182.

Reindal, S. M. (1999). Independence, dependence, interdependence: Some reflections on the subject and personal autonomy. *Disability & Society, 14*(3), 353–367.

Scherer, M. J. (2005). *Living in the state of stuck: How assistive technology impacts the lives of people with disabilities* (4th ed.) Brookline, MA: Brookline Books.

Selik, L. (Producer). (2008, October 27). Positively autistic. *CBC news: The national.* Documentary film retrieved from http://www.cbc.ca/thenational/indepthanalysis/story/2009/10/06/national-positivelyautistic.html

Silverman, C. (2008). Fieldwork on another planet: Social science perspectives on the autism spectrum. *BioSocieties, 3,* 325–341.

Spence-Cochran, K., & Pearl, C. (2009). A comparison of hand-held computer and staff model supports for high school students with autism and intellectual disabilities. *Assistive Technology and Autism Spectrum Disorders: Researched-Based Practice and Innovation in the Field* [Special issue]. *Assistive Technology Outcomes and Benefits, 5,* 26–42.

Standen, P. J., & Brown, D. J. (2005). Virtual reality in the rehabilitation of people with intellectual disabilities: Review. *CyberPsychology and Behavior, 8*(3), 272–282.

Standifer, S. (2009). *Adult autism and employment: A guide for vocational rehabilitation professionals.* Columbia, MO: Disability Policy & Studies, School of Health Professions, University of Missouri. Retrieved from http://www.dps.missouri.edu/Autism/Adult%20Autism%20&%20Employment.pdf

Stock, S. E., Davies, D. K., & Wehmeyer, M. L. (2009). Design and evaluation of a computer-animated simulation approach to support vocational social skills training for students and adults with intellectual disabilities. *Assistive Technology and Autism Spectrum Disorders: Researched-Based Practice and Innovation in the Field* [Special issue]. *Assistive Technology Outcomes and Benefits, 5,* 43–55.

Tartaro, A., & Cassell, J. (2007). Using virtual peer technology as an intervention for children with autism. In J. Lazar (Ed.), *Universal usability: Designing computer interfaces for diverse user populations* (pp. 231–262). New York, NY: Wiley.

Thatcher, J., Burks, M. R., Heilmann, C., Henry, S. L., Kirkpatrick, A., Lauke, P. H., et al. (2006). *Web accessibility: Web standards and regulatory compliance.* New York, NY: Apress.

Van Laarhoven, T., Chandler, L. K., McNamara, A., & Zurita, L. M. (2009). A comparison of three prompting procedures: Evaluating the effectiveness of photos, AAC, or video-based prompting for teaching cooking skills to young children with developmental disabilities. *Assistive Technology and Autism Spectrum Disorders: Researched-Based Practice and Innovation in the Field* [Special issue]. *Assistive Technology Outcomes and Benefits, 5,* 1–17.

Van Laarhoven, T., & Zurita, L. M. (2009). Using video iPods to teach life skills to individuals with autism spectrum disorder: Background research and creation of video-based materials. *Assistive Technology and Autism Spectrum Disorders: Researched-Based Practice and Innovation in the Field* [Special issue]. *Assistive Technology Outcomes and Benefits, 5,* 18–25.

Wehmeyer, M. L., Palmer, S. B., Smith, S. J., Parent, W., Davies, D. K., & Stock, S. (2006). Technology use by people with intellectual and developmental disabilities to support employment activities: A single-subject design meta analysis. *Journal of Vocational Rehabilitation, 24*(2), 81–86.

Wert, B. Y. (2009). A comparison of verbal prompting and video self-modeling on the spontaneous request behaviors of young children with autism spectrum disorders. *Assistive Technology and Autism Spectrum Disorders: Researched-Based Practice and Innovation in the Field* [Special issue]. *Assistive Technology Outcomes and Benefits, 5,* 70–81.

Whalen, C., Lidén, L., Ingersoll, B., & Lidén, S. (2007). Evidence-based computer-assisted instruction for autism spectrum disorders. In J. Lazar (Ed.), *Universal usability: Designing computer interfaces for diverse user populations* (pp. 263–297). New York, NY: Wiley.

Zac Browser (Version 1.5) [Software]. (2009.) People CD. Retrieved from http://www.zacbrowser.com/

http://dx.doi.org/10.2190/RAAC2

CHAPTER 2

Designing for People Who Do Not Read Easily

Caroline Jarrett, Janice (Ginny) Redish, and Kathryn Summers

Reading is a complex process involving a wide range of physical, mental, and environmental elements, any one of which can become a point of interruption or interference for effective reading.

A substantial literature explores the causes and implications of various contexts that contribute to reading difficulty. Issues that can make reading difficult include

- Physical problems related to vision or motor control
- Cognitive problems, such as aphasia due to a stroke, congenital cognitive impairments, dyslexia, and memory loss from aging
- Low literacy due to poor schooling, lack of practice, limited access to reading materials, lack of exposure to a culture of literacy, and other factors
- Reading in a nonnative language

Even skilled readers may experience moments when they have difficulty reading due to causes such as

- Lack of time
- Fatigue
- Stress
- Lack of necessary background knowledge
- Technological limitations (e.g., reading on a mobile phone or PDA)
- Environmental challenges (e.g., reading in a crowded or noisy room or with too little light)

What do we know about these problems? How different are the problems that come from different causes and different situations? Despite those differences, are there common solutions—ways of changing text that help many groups of people who have difficulty reading?

Those questions are the topic of this chapter and of a project called Design to Read (www.designtoread.com). In this chapter, we first describe the research methodologies that gave us insights into the problem. We then describe the Design to Read project and elaborate on some of the specific findings from research on reading difficulties. From several Design to Read workshops where experts in different types of problems shared information, we found that common solutions are indeed possible. In the last section, we give guidelines for some of these common solutions.

RESEARCH METHODOLOGIES

We find relevant information for understanding the problems of people who have difficulty reading through at least four research methodologies:

- Experimental studies, usually done at universities
- Exploratory studies, done both inside and outside universities
- Formative evaluations, done with specific groups on specific products
- Case studies of individuals with a specific disability

Researchers tend to work mainly with others who are focusing on the same methodology and same population. Meeting with, writing for, and talking with others in the same field helps to advance knowledge and increase depth of that field. But this means that those researchers may know little about other populations who face similar challenges. One of our goals in the Design to Read project and in this chapter is to bring together information across these potential silos and to encourage further cross-silo information sharing.

Experimental Studies

Traditional research in cognitive psychology investigates one specific condition, often through single-variable, hypothesis-testing studies. The goals of this research may be to identify causes and effects of the condition and to see the effect of specific changes that might mitigate the challenges faced by one specific special population.

To ensure appropriate experimental conditions, these studies often need to be narrowly focused and carried out under tightly controlled circumstances in university settings. While that research may lead to increased depth of knowledge about a specific condition, it doesn't always result in practical methods that communication professionals can use as they try to create products that will serve multiple categories of readers.

However, these experimental, academic studies can inform other research methodologies by suggesting both underlying reasons for the problems that people experience and possible solutions for those problems.

Exploratory Studies

Not all research is hypothesis testing. Some of the best insights into how people with different conditions cope with reading problems come from more exploratory studies that are based on observing people without constraining what they do in the controlled conditions of an academic experiment (e.g., Theofanos & Redish, 2003).

While experimental studies are primarily quantitative, exploratory studies are usually both qualitative and quantitative. The quantitative work in exploratory studies, however, is usually reported only with descriptive statistics, not tested for statistical significance.

An interesting exception to this was a UK study (Disability Rights Commission, 2004) that created a large team of participant observers: people with a variety of disabilities trained to record their naturalistic interactions with websites. Each of these people worked with several websites. Thus, the study tested a large number of websites in real settings. The result of this study was a very depressing picture of the state of accessibility of UK websites at that time.

Formative Evaluation

Most usability work is formative evaluation: small-scale studies involving short sessions with a small set of users (Barnum, 2011; Krug, 2010; Rubin & Chisnell, 2008). Typically, the focus of usability studies is on developing a specific product that will work effectively across a wide range of potential users.

In a formative evaluation usability study, the researchers usually present users with a proposed interface, give them tasks to complete, and observe and record the users' actions through methods such as simple note-taking, eye-tracking, keystroke recording, or videotaping for later analysis. Tasks typically include both open-ended—or user-driven—tasks and scripted tasks that the moderator assigns.

Researchers may also try to capture the reasoning behind users' actions by asking questions and having users think out loud as they work. Specific problems that the researchers observe become the basis for suggested revisions to the product. When time and budget allow, the team then tests a revised version of the product to see how well the changes worked and what problems remain.

Because of the small sample size, most formative evaluation usability studies are qualitative with only a few simple quantitative results reported (such as how many participants were able to complete a task successfully).

Formative evaluations are driven by the desire to create a workable outcome, generally with corporate or institutional (as opposed to academic) sponsorship. Because they relate to products under development, most of these studies are proprietary. Often, the results and any potentially generalizable learnings are not publicly available.

Occasionally, an enlightened organization will allow its staff or consultants to publish their studies in academic forums and sometimes even to use sample sizes that approach those typical of experimental studies. We have been fortunate to work with organizations in this category, and we are also grateful to Fidelity Investments for their work (e.g., Tullis & Chadwick-Dias, 2003).

Unfortunately, few formative evaluations include people with special needs. They could and should include users with different needs. By doing so, formative evaluations could help teams find solutions and accommodations that would greatly broaden the range of people who might buy and use the product. And that is good for the business's profits.

Case Studies

Disability studies are often intensive case studies. Like formative evaluations, case studies usually involve a small number of participants—sometimes the heartfelt description of a single user's experience (e.g., Slatin & Rush, 2002). Unlike formative evaluations, case studies usually involve extended observations.

A case study may extend to a larger number of users, sometimes moving into the territory of exploratory studies; but case studies are inherently qualitative.

The Techniques Compared

Experiments typically examine only one or a few factors of a reading experience with a large number of participants and primarily quantitative results. The other methods typically involve every aspect of the reading experience with a much smaller number of participants. Only rarely do exploratory studies, formative evaluation studies, and case studies lead to more quantitative comparative studies to validate or confirm their conclusions. All these approaches can give us useful information about the behavior of specific groups of readers—and about strategies to help those specific people overcome challenges.

THE DESIGN TO READ PROJECT

The Design to Read project seeks to bring together researchers who wish their work to have practical value and practitioners who wish to base their practice on research—specifically in the area of designing for people who do not read easily. It also seeks to help researchers make connections across methodologies and populations.

Our hope is that through this collaboration, we can find similarities across multiple categories in what works best for helping people who do not read easily. By looking beyond causes of specific disabilities and identifying similarities in behaviors, responses, and performance across causes and contexts, we believe we can derive design guidelines that apply across populations and environments.

The recommendations in this chapter represent just such a set of findings, drawing on a wide variety of types of research studies and practitioner experience.

WHAT MAKES READING DIFFICULT?

Reading is a complex process that starts with identifying marks on a page—or dots on a screen—as text. Reading ends, for the skilled reader, with a grasp of the meaning. A skilled reader can also decide to skim over the text, picking when to read closely.

Many factors can disrupt this process: from the physical level (e.g., a pale gray, small, complicated font on white background) to the cognitive level of making sense of complex sentences written in unfamiliar language (e.g., typical legalese).

Less skilled readers often misrecognize words, substituting a more familiar word for the word on the page. Then they try to make sense of sentences with words that don't really fit together. They may struggle through words letter by letter, but usually they take shortcuts. Their skimming and scanning sometimes becomes random; they read any segment they alight on and thus create confusion for themselves rather than understanding.

To the extent that readers are trying to extract meaning from what they read, they must work even harder. In order to understand something, readers try to make sense out of the words and images by putting them together into a verbal representation and a visual representation, which they must then connect to what they already know and have stored in long-term memory. Readers acquire, or learn, information only if they successfully

- build a coherent mental model of the information being processed,
- connect this model of the information to other information that they already know in order to make a coherent structure, and
- put the connected model into long-term memory.

That's a lot of "ifs." Clearly, reading is hard work and takes a lot of effort and concentration.

COGNITIVE, EMOTIONAL, AND PHYSICAL
CHARACTERISTICS THAT AFFECT READING

Looking at four particular groups who often struggle with reading—people with lower literacy skills, people who are older, people who are under stress, and people who must rely on screen readers (programs that read text from the screen)—reveals several broad categories of potential reading challenges. In this section, we explore three of those categories: cognitive, emotional, and physical.

Cognitive Challenges

Everyone has a limited working memory. But for those who do not read well, low-level information processes use up the working memory resources that might normally go into high-level cognitive processes, such as building meaningful representations to make sense of the material and making connections to long-term memory. This diversion of resources has serious consequences for cognition:

- Reading speed goes down.
- Comprehension goes down. Words and visuals are likely to be interpreted very literally.
- The ability to separate the important from the unimportant goes down.
- The ability to make inferences, understand relationships, and make connections goes down.

For example, we all tend to face cognitive impairments as we age. Older adults may have less ability to divide attention between tasks. Switching attention between tasks may become a relatively slow and laborious process. Older adults' visual search performance (their ability to scan a visual field in order to locate a particular object or feature) is likely to go down. Working memory capacity decreases, and the time required to access long-term memory increases (Park & Holzman, 1992).

Age isn't the only reason for cognitive challenges. Even people who are not old may have less cognitive capacity when reading because they are trying to deal with something else at the same time. For example, they may be reading a screen while also trying to respond appropriately to an angry customer on the telephone.

A similar effect occurs under stress. McGrath (1976) defines stress as the interaction between a perceived demand, the person's perceived ability to respond to the demand successfully, and the person's sense of urgency with regard to the demand. Psychological stress occurs when individuals have an urgent demand that they feel unable to respond to successfully (Lazarus, 1966, 1990; Lazarus & Folkman, 1984).

Stress affects the ability to reason logically, do visual search tasks, and keep track of changing information (MacDonald & Labuc, 1982). Effects of stress also include reduced memory (Burger & Arkin, 1980; Cohen & Weinstein, 1981) and increased errors (Larsson, 1989; Reid, 1948; Villoldo & Tarno, 1984). When people feel threatened, they consider fewer alternatives, consider these alternatives less systematically, and look or scan for information and for options less systematically (Keinan, 1987).

People under stress pay less attention to cues outside their immediate locus of attention, which means paying attention to a smaller portion of the visual field. They scan their environment less (Easterbrook, 1959). Anxiety redirects cognitive resources toward the perceived threat and away from the task (MacLeod, 1996). Intense stress can lead to the phenomenon referred to as tunnel vision: a complete or nearly complete focusing of attention on the task that appears to be most related to the threat. The result can be a literal constriction of vision. Unfortunately, if information that is deemed peripheral turns out to be related to task success, performance goes down.

The effects of stress on memory are particularly important for reading because the goal of reading is often to get and keep information. Researchers don't completely understand the mechanics of how stress affects memory, but research shows that stress is likely to disrupt both the encoding and the rehearsal of information (Staal, 2004).

Stress doesn't seem to affect long-term memory, but it does make our access to long-term memory less efficient. It also seems to draw off some of the capacity of working memory because some of our attention is going toward the stressor or even toward our own reaction to the stressor. Reduced working memory capacity has serious consequences for cognition for all readers, as we noted above—and impaired access to long-term memory is likely to disrupt the process of connecting new information to what is already known.

Stress also affects our ability to commit new information to memory. We may have more intense memories of the stressor, but we are less likely to remember other information, thus disrupting our encoding processes.

Emotional Challenges

People who don't read well may have low self-confidence, especially when faced with a task that requires learning, a situation that feels like a test, or even a situation that simply feels new. Older adults are sometimes more vulnerable to frustration, anxiety, and self-blame. People under stress are sometimes more vulnerable to the effects of failure or error.

As a result, these readers may experience "learned failure." Previous bad experiences damage their confidence that the information is available or that they can find the information. When faced with difficulties, they may give up quickly. Therefore, we should write so readers succeed quickly in what they're trying to do.

Conversely, if people feel able to exert some control over a problem, they experience less stress. Thus, giving readers control over elements of the reading experience—such as the contrast of text/background, text size, and the density of information on a page—is likely to have positive effects. Also, because appraisal affects performance (Staal, 2004), a visual design that *seems* easier or less demanding is likely to improve people's performance.

Physical Challenges

Except for those who must rely on screen readers, people read in a series of short saccades (abrupt, rapid movements of the eyes from one place to another) and fixations (focus of the eyes on a particular location for visual processing), with occasional regressions (backing up to refixate on a previous word or phrase).

Readers with lower literacy skills are likely to read with more fixations and longer fixations (trying to figure out what they're reading), and they often read with more regressions (Rayner, 1998).

Older readers also tend to have longer fixations (Rayner, 2009), as they try to compensate for age-related vision effects such as reduced acuity, reduced contrast discrimination, and increased sensitivity to glare (Kline & Schieber, 1985). Older readers may also experience reduced color perception, especially in the green/blue/violet range (Werner, Peterzell, & Scheetz, 1990).

Implications of the Three Challenges

These cognitive, emotional, and physical challenges mean that people who don't read well face severe difficulties in

- using search engines to find desired content,
- navigating to desired information on individual web sites, and
- reading and understanding content when (or if) they find it (Becker, 2004; Birru, Monaco, Charles, Drew, Njie, Bierria, et al., 2004; Kodagoda & Wong, 2008; Summers & Summers, 2005).

As information gets longer and more complex, cognitive load increases. For technical communicators and user experience designers, this means that every field added to a form increases the cognitive load and creates potential for error, every additional page in an interaction is an opportunity for users to think they have succeeded when they have not, and every additional piece of text may potentially trigger skipping. And as cognitive load increases, more and more users will give up or settle for an outcome that they may or may not realize is less than satisfactory.

Another important effect of these challenges for readers with lower literacy skills, some readers who are older, and readers under stress is that their effective field of view is especially narrow. Processing the text itself takes so much cognitive attention that they become less able to pay attention to cues about what might be coming up or to remember where they came from. As they move through page content, they are not looking ahead or behind. They are not likely to notice any content above, below, or to the sides of their focus of attention.

Readers who are using a screen magnifier literally have a narrow field of view. They can see only what the magnifier focuses on. Much of what is around the magnified text is literally obscured.

Readers who must rely on screen readers have an even more narrow "field of view." They can "see" only what the screen reader is currently reading aloud. They have no access to information above, below, or to the side.

This narrow field of view has implications for the design and content of online reading materials. We must design material that supports sequential processing. Pages must make sense independently. Headings must make sense out of context. Even adjacent paragraphs should be as independent as possible. If readers must remember one paragraph to make sense of the next paragraph, some people who do not read well are likely to come away with misinformation.

COPING STRATEGIES AND READING BEHAVIORS

In usability tests of complex tax forms, we observed that readers who had low knowledge of the tax domain, often associated with lower literacy and lower education, read more pages of the instructions and read them more carefully but had far less success in filling out the forms. They tried, and failed, to absorb large chunks of information that were irrelevant to them, whereas higher-knowledge, more confident readers skipped to the relevant sections. We observed that the low-knowledge users started by trying to read every word even if was not relevant. They tired easily. Then, they began to skip or flap about in the document, and they gave up or arrived at the end of the document without extracting the appropriate information from the material.

By combining research with different special populations, we can identify similar behaviors and issues across groups. Some specific behaviors that have been observed across groups in usability studies are listed in Table 1. The table includes behaviors that may seem contradictory, but that's reality. People both read excessively in places and skip in other places.

Over-Thorough Reading

Reading takes a great deal of concentration and effort for lower-literacy users. Most lower-literacy users can't grasp the structure of the page at a glance by

Table 1. Coping Strategies and Reading Behaviors of
Three Groups of Web Users

People who don't read well due to literacy challenges	People who rely on screen readers	Older adults
Over-thorough reading	Over-thorough listening	Over-thorough reading
Skipping	Skipping	—
Hopping from link to link	Hopping from link to link	Cautious clicking
Satisficing early	Time-consuming persistence, worry that more information needs to be found	Tendency to seek help and information from peers or advisors or through the phone

reading headings and subheadings. In some cases, they compensate by reading every word on the page so they don't miss the answer.

Similar over-thorough reading has been reported for older adults, people who have less web experience, and people who lack necessary domain-specific knowledge. These people are more likely to read all the information on a page carefully before moving on.

Some readers who depend on assistive technology know that it is easy to miss key content or key links, so they carefully listen to all the content on every page before choosing any links or performing any actions (Coyne & Nielsen, 2001). Similar behavior has been reported for older web users (Chadwick-Dias, McNulty, & Tullis, 2003).

Over-thorough reading can be a problem in several ways. At the simplest level, the reading task takes longer and is potentially more frustrating. Readers become more likely to get bogged down or to give up. If the delays caused by thorough reading are severe enough, the delays themselves place additional demands on working memory and readers become less successful at making cognitive connections.

Sometimes, over-thorough reading means *obsessively* thorough reading. People read extraneous content like footers, side panels, or administrative information about the site owners or the website (Summers & Summers, 2005). This extraneous information competes with the relevant information for attention and processing, reducing overall comprehension and retention.

Skipping Chunks of Text

When confronted by long, dense pages of text, some lower-literacy users simply skip chunks of text (Summers & Summers, 2005). Ironically, they sometimes then skip over the very content they are trying to find—even if the target content is appropriately signaled by a heading, a well-chunked paragraph, or a bulleted list.

This skipping is clearly not the same as the more purposeful and successful scanning behaviors that more literate readers use. For example, on longer pages with multiple paragraphs, lower-literacy readers sometimes skip over headings and lists and land in the middle of a paragraph.

Similarly, because listening to a page or moving through a magnified page can be agonizingly slow, some people with vision loss try to skip ahead. But because they cannot see what they are skipping, they sometimes skip over the content or link they want (see Table 2).

Many people who listen to assistive software know how to tell it to read them only the links on a page or to read only the headings on a page. They are scanning with their ears just as sighted users scan with their eyes. If the links and headings are not useful signals to the content they are seeking, they may entirely miss that the relevant content is, in fact, on the page (Theofanos & Redish, 2003).

Hopping from Link to Link

Some low-literacy web users try to minimize how much reading they have to do by focusing on finding links instead of reading content. They report that they are hoping to arrive at more focused information. They skip from link to link throughout a site, sometimes ignoring page content completely. Relying on this

Table 2. Triggers for Skipping

Summers and Summers (2005) found that for web users who don't read well, skipping seemed to be triggered most often by the following:	Coyne and Nielsen (2001) found that for web users who rely on screen-reading technology, skipping seemed to be triggered most often by the following:
• long paragraphs of dense text	
• long sentences with complex syntax	• long strings of parameter descriptions associated with page formatting (such as scripting), tables used to format content, or long lists of mostly irrelevant links
• long pages requiring scrolling	
• numbers in the text	
• tables with lines	
• difficult, long, or unfamiliar words	• long paragraphs of dense text
• parenthetical text	• parenthetical text

strategy, they sometimes land on pages with their desired content but fail to recognize it. Research has found that these web users have very low rates of task success (Summers & Summers, 2005).

In contrast, older adults are sometimes very cautious about clicking on links. They are reluctant to click unless they are sure they have found what they want (Tullis & Chadwick, 2003). Instead, they spend time and effort thinking about links that they could otherwise spend reading and understanding page content.

We can help both link-hoppers and cautious clickers by taking care when writing links. Every link is a potential distraction, so every link must be appropriate and relevant to the tasks that people need to complete on the page.

Headings require similar care. A good, informative set of headings helps both skilled readers and people who do not read well, while Bartell, Schultz, and Spyridakis (2006) found that simply inserting headings at arbitrary intervals can hurt reading performance even for skilled readers.

Web users who rely on screen readers also need a page title that is read first by a screen reader so that they can immediately identify page content.

Early Satisficing

Any reader may end up satisficing: deciding consciously or subconsciously to "make do" with whatever meaning they have gleaned from the material even though they have not gotten the full meaning (see Simon, 1957). Highly-skilled readers tend to satisfice when they have a good enough sense of the material to meet their goals. People who do not read easily often satisfice too early, when they've struggled as much as they feel they can but have not yet met their goals.

For the stressful tax forms, readers with a good understanding of the domain have an overall sense of whether they have completed the relevant areas. Readers with low domain knowledge stop when they feel overwhelmed, whether or not they have dealt with all the relevant areas. This can lead to filing incomplete forms or failing to file altogether because the task is simply too hard. The U.S. Document Design Center reported these problems in the early 1980s (Holland & Redish, 1982). More than 20 years later, a UK National Audit Office report identified similar issues (National Audit Office, 2003). And our current experience of usability testing of forms shows that the problems continue.

HELPING ONE GROUP HELPS OTHERS

Fortunately, research shows that improvements that are aimed at a particular special population (for example, older adults or low-literacy readers) will help members of other groups as well.

In general, expert readers (not surprisingly) also prefer information that looks easy to read, gets to the point quickly, and provides plain language explanations of unfamiliar terms and concepts. Expert readers also sometimes skip over long blocks of text because they feel overloaded with information. So adaptations that increase accessibility for at-risk groups help expert readers as well.

For example, a study at Fidelity Investments (Chadwick-Dias et al., 2003) tested a website with younger and older adults and found that the older adults had significantly more problems and lower performance on a set of tasks. They then created a prototype that fixed the older adults' problems. As expected, the performance of the older adults improved. Additionally, however, the performance of younger adults also improved.

Another study (Summers & Summers, 2005), this time focusing on low literacy adults dealing with information about medicine, found similar results. After testing the original website with low literacy and high literacy readers, the researchers revised the site to meet the needs of low literacy readers and tested again. The changes helped the low literacy readers immensely. The changes helped the high literacy readers even more (see Table 3).

Research has also shown that designing information and interactions to address the needs of specific populations makes economic sense for businesses. In another study (Summers, Summers, & Helm, 2008), the researchers worked on a form that patients used to request help paying for prescription medicine. The goal of the research was to make the form work for older adults and people with lower literacy skills. The new form resulted in fewer skipped fields and more correct information (see Table 4).

After the new form had been in use for three months, the number of actual applications that required expensive follow-up had gone down by 36%.

Table 3. Helping Low-Literacy Web Users Helps
High Literacy People Too

	Site 1	Site 2	Improvement
Time on Task (minutes: seconds)			
High-literacy users	14:19	5:05	+182%
Low-literacy users	22:16	9:30	+134%
Average time-on-task	17:50	6:45	+164%
Success Rate (tasks completed successfully)			
High-literacy users	68%	93%	+37%
Low-literacy users	46%	82%	+77%
Average success rate	59%	89%	+52%
Subjective Satisfaction			
High-literacy users	3.73	4.58	+23%
Low-literacy users	3.54	4.38	+24%
Average subjective satisfaction	3.67	4.51	+23%

Table 4. Making Forms Work for Older Adults
and Lower Literacy Readers

	Old	New	% Change
Average errors per form	6.6	3.4	48%
Average skipped fields per form	7.7	3.5	54%
Time on task	10:45	12:24	−15%
Acceptable applications (number that did not need follow-up)	3	22	633%

SIX GUIDELINES THAT MAKE INFORMATION EASIER FOR EVERYONE

In a previous article for *User Experience*, the magazine of the Usability Professionals' Association, we focused on six guidelines that make information easier for everyone (see Jarrett, Redish, Summers, & Straub, 2010). These guidelines are sufficiently helpful to include here as well. The foundational principle for these guidelines is that simplicity in organization, language, and design helps everyone.

Following these guidelines can help everyone deal more easily with what you write:

- Develop the information from bite to snack to meal.
- Show the structure with an informative title, headings, and links.
- Break up the information with short sections, paragraphs, sentences, and lists.
- Write in plain language, with common words and active verbs.
- Design for visual clarity.
- Provide feedback and guide interaction.

Develop the Information from Bite to Snack to Meal

With scientific journal articles, readers frequently start with the abstract and then jump to the conclusion. They want the main point first, even though it is physically at the end of the article. We should all learn to lead with the conclusion (the key message). This means inverting the writing style we learned in school.

Leading with the key message is, in fact, called the inverted pyramid style. The top of the article is where you have the most readers. Readers drop off as the article continues. If you draw this readership as an upside down pyramid (most readers at the broadest part of the pyramid), you will see why you also want your key message at the broadest part—where you have the most readers.

Different readers want different levels of detail. You can provide those levels in one article—going from the key message to more details to even more details. On a website, you can provide those levels with layering—going from the title as link to a short article to a full report or different pages of details.

The concept of "bite, snack, meal" comes from Rudick and O'Flahavan (n.d.) of E-write (www.ewriteonline.com). For people who have trouble reading, the "bite" may be all they need—if the bite conveys the key message. With a little more effort, they may take in the "snack"—a few sentences or short paragraphs or set of relevant questions and answers. That leaves the "meal" for those who need the details or have the time, stamina, or ability to read in depth (see Figures 1 and 2).

The concept of bite, snack, meal fits well with the inverted pyramid style of writing as well as with the linear style from key message to details that Summers and Summers (2005) found works best for low-literacy readers.

A linear reading path collects all the content about a particular topic into a single broad category, which is then presented in a set of linearly organized pages. It starts with the information that is most important, most general, and most simple. It then moves into information that is more complex and more specific.

We break the paths into logical chunks, based on a logical series of questions that people might ask. Therefore, the content on each page feels like it belongs together and appears in a logical sequence. At the same time, site navigation can provide non-linear access to pages in the reading path, allowing more expert users to navigate directly to the information they want.

These linear reading paths allow web users to access content with a minimum of wayfinding. Wayfinding relies heavily on both reading ability and the ability to keep information in working memory for comparison. That makes it difficult for readers with lower literacy skills, older adults, and readers experiencing stress.

Linear reading paths raise the success rate of most web users because the paths pull *all* the information about a category into a single area. Once users get to the right broad category, the path itself leads them to task success.

Linear reading paths also help because once readers find a path that interests them, they do not have to interrupt their reading or working to figure out how to move forward to more information.

Other research has confirmed the value of designs that encourage people to focus on one thing at a time. Allowing for more linear cognitive processing increases the success rate of people experiencing any form of cognitive impairment (Detterman, Gabriel, & Ruthsatz, 2000; Salthouse, 1985). Making task demands sequential rather than concurrent increases the success rate of people under stress (Dutke & Stöber, 2001).

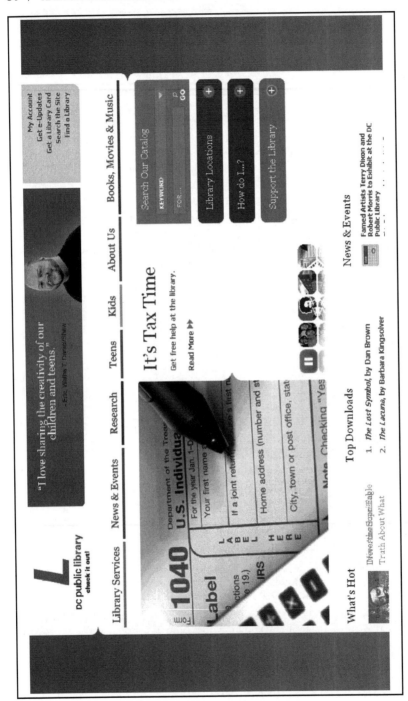

Figure 1. The homepage of the Washington, DC, public library offers a bite: Renowned artists exhibit at library.

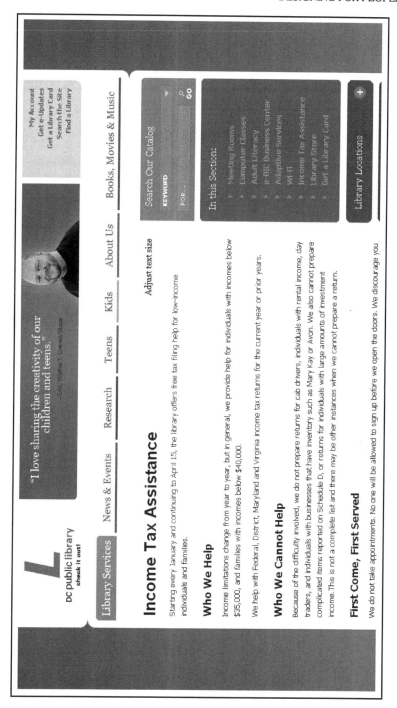

Figure 2. Clicking through brings more, starting with a snack of the key message, which adds a little more information about the art and the exhibit. That's followed by more details: the meal.

Show the Structure with an Informative
Title, Headings, and Links

When you have organized your messages into bite, snack, meal, the next step is to clearly signal that structure to your readers with an informative page title supported by good headings and links.

On the web, cute titles don't work. The title may appear as a link with no further description. That link has to entice the people who need it to click on it—and not entice people for whom it is not relevant.

One of the authors of this chapter named a column "Piggy in the Middle." Who would know that this is about whether to use an even or odd number of response categories in a survey? In hindsight, it's no surprise that it gets few hits. In contrast, a column in the same series called "Sentence or Title Case for Labels?" clearly signals its content and achieved 100 times as many visitors.

Many web users hop from link to link, so make sure that those links are meaningful. Write the links with words your site visitors are thinking of . Don't use "click here" or "more." Imagine someone listening to assistive software and hearing only "click here," "more," or "read more." Write "more about [topic]" instead. (See Redish, 2007, for more on this and other guidelines for clear writing on websites.)

Break Up the Information with Short
Sections, Paragraphs, Lists, and Sentences

Long, dense pages are a problem for everyone. In school, we were all taught that a paragraph has to have at least three sentences. Not so on the web or even in a print article. A one-sentence paragraph may be fine. A question heading with a short answer—or even a fragment of an answer—may be fine.

Keep paragraphs and sentences short. It isn't "dumbing down" to write simply. It's respecting your low-literacy readers' needs. It's respecting how busy your high-literacy readers are.

Lists make information easy to grasp. Numbered lists make instructions obvious and easy to use.

Figure 3 is a page from the site www.direct.gov.uk about who can get government money for taking care of another person.

Write in Plain Language, with Common
Words and Active Verbs

We all read and understand simpler, more common, and less abstract words faster. Lengthy, complex, or unfamiliar words may impress readers; but unless the writing is intended for a specialized audience with a shared technical vocabulary, these words may hinder communication more than they help it.

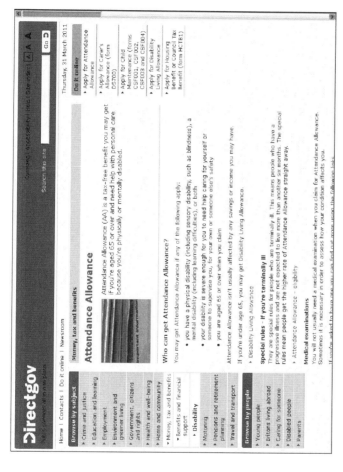

Figure 3. Part of a webpage that is designed for people to read easily—note the bite at the top; clear headings that connect to questions site visitors have; the conversational tone, talking directly to the site visitor; active voice; one-sentence paragraphs; and bulleted lists. This page manages to convey useful information to people who may not read easily. It does assume that the people reading it know some specific terms like "Attendance Allowance." That is likely to be true, even for low-literacy and second-language readers. If they are coming to this page, they are likely to be involved in a situation where one or more of those named allowances apply. The context they live in is the context the content refers to.

Research many years ago showed that when readers have to deal with passive sentences with hidden actions, they have to spend the mental energy to tell themselves the story—to translate into active, action sentences (Flower, Hayes, & Swarts, 1983).

- Passive sentence—hard to read: "All applications must be filed ahead of the Physical Damage Filing Deadline, 15 June 2011."
- Active verb—a bit easier: "You must file your application ahead of the Physical Damage Filing Deadline, 15 June 2011."
- Common words, active verb, no jargon—even easier: "You must send us your application before 15 June 2011."

Design for Visual Clarity

We've already mentioned several aspects of visual clarity: contrast, type size, and density of information.

For those who don't read well, the text also needs to stand out clearly from the other elements on the page. Readers must be able to focus on the key message without being forced to ignore other visual or text elements that are fighting for their attention.

People with any form of cognitive impairment are likely to have trouble separating the important from the unimportant (Gazzaley, 2009). Visual design should help readers so that they can focus on processing and understanding the message.

The best layout is often radically simple, incorporating content that is designed to support a linear reading path, and presented using a straightforward, uncluttered design that guides readers along that path. Labels for the fields in forms should appear above or to the left of their fields to support linear progress through the form.

Visual design can support cognitive processing in other ways as well. A design strategy that can help less skilled readers to approximate the behavior of more skilled readers is to manipulate the spacing between letters and inside words because grouping letters into familiar chunks helps less skilled readers. Manipulating the spacing between words to group words into meaningful clusters also helps less skilled readers.

The Readability widget (www.readability.com) by Arc90 conveniently automates this process, as Figures 4 and 5 illustrate.

Provide Feedback and Guide Interaction

On the web, people must often read in order to do. For example, text may help readers understand what to do next; explain the results of actions; or help readers avoid, discover, and recover from errors.

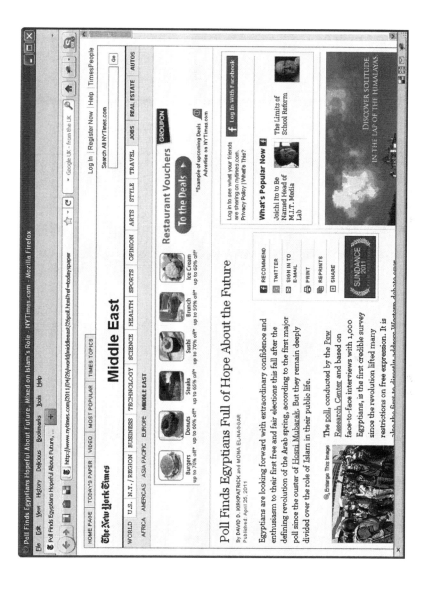

Figure 4. A typical page from the *New York Times* website.

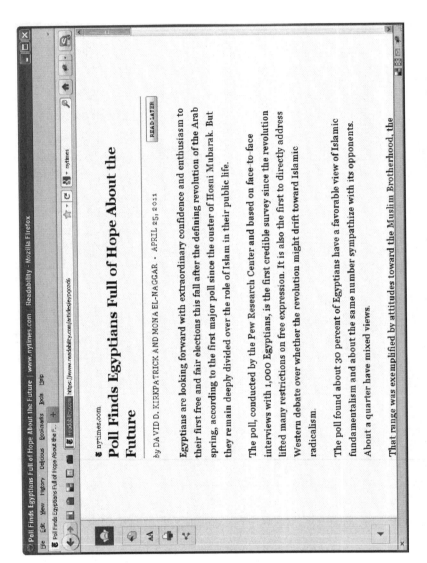

Figure 5. The page from the *New York Times* with the readability widget applied.

Unnecessary diversions distract readers and make their tasks more difficult. Links are fundamental to the web, but they should help readers who are in the wrong place get to the right place rather than distracting and enticing readers from a good path they are on or from useful information they are reading.

Usability research shows that, many times, readers who leave a webpage don't come back to that page (Summers & Summers, 2005). Links must support the site's goals and the readers' goals as exit points for readers to use when they have finished getting what they need from a particular webpage.

Similarly, processes should not feel circular to web users. Even if web users must repeat a step, they should feel that they are making steady progress. At the same time, they need to feel in control of the process. Giving web users "Next" and "Back" buttons during a specific process and allowing them to preview the next part of an interaction can give them a sense of control and make it easier for them to move through the process.

It's also important to help users understand the results of their actions, with simple language and clear design. Where you put those results matters. Display results within the user's current focus of attention. When possible, give immediate feedback for users' actions. Build results into the reading path.

Preventing errors and helping people recover from errors can mean success or failure in many interactions. Visual design can prevent some errors. If the visual design of form fields helps guide input, web users will be less dependent on successfully reading the text labels. When you provide a linear interaction path and remove distractions, web users are much more successful at recovering from errors. Removing visual distractions frees up cognitive resources for error correction—dramatically increasing success rates (Summers, Langford, Wu, Abela, & Souza, 2006).

One successful approach is to show fields that need correction by themselves on a new page. Putting fields that have errors and their associated error messages on their own page helps web users by taking away distractions. It also helps programmers and content providers make sure all fields that need attention are treated similarly and appropriately and that visual signaling of fields that need attention is complete and consistent. It also helps content providers use error messages effectively. Because the error message appears alone on the page with the field that it relates to, it is easier for content providers to focus attention on making the error message helpful and specific. Thus a commitment to putting errors on a new, separate page makes it more likely that developers and content providers will be successful at helping users be successful.

WE CAN'T SOLVE EVERYTHING FOR EVERYONE THE SAME WAY

In this chapter, we have focused on similarities in solutions across different groups of people who do not read easily. We realize, however, that the overlap in behaviors, issues, and solutions from group to group is not complete. Solving all the problems for one group may still leave difficulties for others.

- Alt-text is still needed for those who listen to assistive software, no matter how much we simplify the page design and content.
- Some short and simple words may be problematic for dyslexics.
- Specific technical words may be "plain language" to people in that technical field but cause difficulties for other readers.

Even within a specific population, individuals differ. For example, different types of aphasia represent losses of different abilities.

Older adults vary greatly along several dimensions, as Chisnell and Redish (2005) have shown. These dimensions include aptitudes for using technology, attitudes toward technology, and physical abilities.

Even after incorporating all the changes that we recommend in this chapter, there is still a need to let web users adjust sites for type size, contrast, speech, and other features, as the BBC and some other sites do. (See http://www.bbc.co.uk/accessibility/, http://www.mobilitymotoringprogram.com/accessibility.mob, and http://www.webaim.org/.)

At times, optimal solutions for different user groups will pull in different directions. However, we should strive to find ways to meet most needs for most people. For example, web users with total vision loss typically rely on screen readers. Screen readers cannot read graphics; instead, they read the associated alt-text. An optimal page for blind web users, therefore, has minimal graphics. But readers with low literacy skills often benefit from simple informational graphics. In this case, we can provide those simple informational graphics for our low-literacy web users while helping our blind web users by writing useful alt-text for the graphics.

A FINAL THOUGHT

In this chapter, we discussed many reasons why people do not read well, described four research methods that contribute to our knowledge, explored some specific research findings, and offered guidelines that practitioners can use to help design for all those diverse audiences. We are in the early stages in our Design to Read project. We hope you will join us. We welcome researchers to share their studies with any of the four research methods, practitioners to share their experience designing for people who do not read easily, and people who have experienced difficulty reading to share their personal experiences.

REFERENCES

Barnum, C. (2011). *Usability testing essentials: Ready, set . . . test!* Burlington, MA: Morgan Kaufmann.

Bartell, A. L., Schultz. L. D., & Spyridakis, J. H. (2006). The effect of heading frequency on comprehension of print versus online information. *Technical Communication, 53*(4), 416–426.

Becker, S. A. (2004). A study of web usability for older adults seeking online health resources. *ACM Transactions on Computer-Human Interaction, 11*(4), 387–406.

Birru, M., Monaco, V., Charles, L., Drew, H., Njie, V., Bierria, T., et al. (2004). Internet usage by low-literacy adults seeking health information: An observational analysis. *Journal of Medical Internet Research, 6*(3), e25.http://www. jmir.org/2004/3/e25/

Burger, J. M., & Arkin, R. (1980). Prediction, control, and learned helplessness. *Journal of Personality and Social Psychology, 38,* 482–491.

Chadwick-Dias, A., McNulty, M., & Tullis, T. (2003). Web usability and age: How design changes can improve performance. *Proceedings of the 2003 conference on universal usability* (pp. 30–37) New York: ACM. Retrieved from http://dl.acm.org/citation.cfm?id=957205.957212&coll=DL&dl=GUIDE&CFID=52406706&CFTOK EN=11693941

Chisnell, D., & Redish, J. C. (2005). Who is the "older adult" in your audience? *Intercom, January,* 10–14.

Cohen, S., & Weinstein, N. (1981). Nonauditory effects of noise on behavior and health. *Journal of Social Issues, 37*(1), 36–70.

Coyne, K. P., & Nielsen, J. (2001). *Beyond ALT text: Making the web easy to use for users with disabilities.* Fremont, CA: Nielsen Norman Group.

Detterman, D. K., Gabriel, L. T., & Ruthsatz, J. M. (2000). Intelligence and mental retardation. In R. J. Sternberg (Ed.), *Handbook of intelligence* (pp. 141–158). Cambridge, MA: Cambridge University Press.

Disability Rights Commission. (2004). *The web: Access and inclusion for disabled people.* Retrieved from http://hcid.soi.city.ac.uk/research/Drc.html

Dutke, S., & Stöber, J. (2001). Test anxiety, working memory, and cognitive performance: Supportive effects of sequential demands. *Cognition and Emotion, 15*(3), 381–389.

Easterbrook, J. A. (1959). The effect of emotion on cue utilization and the organization of behavior. *Psychological Review, 66,* 187–201.

Fisk, A. D., Rogers, W., Charness, N., Czaja, S. J., & Sharit, J. (2004). *Designing for older adults: Principles and creative human factors approaches.* London, UK: Taylor & Francis.

Flower, L., Hayes, J. R., & Swarts, H. (1983). Revising function documents: The scenario principle. In P. Anderson, J. Brockmann, & C. Miller (Eds.), *New essays in technical and scientific communication: Research, theory, and practice* (pp. 41–58). Amityville, NY: Baywood.

Gazzaley, A. (2009). The aging brain. *User Experience, 8*(1), 10–13. Retrieved from http://www.usabilityprofessionals.org/upa_publications/user_experience/past_issues/2009-1.html

Holland, V. M., & Redish, J. C. (1982). Strategies for reading forms and other documents. In D. Tannen (Ed.), *Proceedings of the Georgetown roundtable on language and linguistics: Text and talk* (pp. 205–218). Washington, DC: Georgetown University Press.

Jarrett, C., & Gaffney, G. (2008). *Forms that work: Designing web forms for usability.* Burlington, MA: Morgan Kaufmann.

Jarrett, C., Redish, J. C., Summers, K., & Straub, K. (2010). Design to read: Guidelines for people who do not read easily. *User Experience, 9*(2), 10–12.

Keinan, G. (1987). Decision making under stress: Scanning of alternatives under controllable and uncontrollable threats. *Journal of Personality and Social Psychology, 52*(3), 639–644.

Kline, D. W., & Schieber, F. (1985). Vision and aging. In J. E. Birren & K. W. Schaie (Eds.), *Handbook of the psychology of aging* (pp. 296–331). New York, NY: Van Nostrand Reinhold.

Kodagoda, N., & Wong, W. (2008). Effects of low & high literacy on user performance in information search and retrieval. *Proceedings of the 22nd British HCI Group Annual Conference on People and Computers: Culture, Creativity, Interaction—Volume 1.* Swinton, UK: British Computer Society. Retrieved from http://dl.acm.org/citation. cfm?id=1531514.1531538&coll=DL&dl=GUIDE&CFID=52406706&CFTOKEN= 11693941

Krug, S. (2010). *Rocket surgery made easy: The do-it-yourself guide to finding and fixing usability problems.* Berkeley, CA: New Riders.

Larsson, G. (1989). Personality, appraisal and cognitive coping processes and performance during various conditions of stress. *Military Psychology, 1,* 167–182.

Lazarus, R. S. (1966). *Psychological stress and the coping process.* New York, NY: McGraw-Hill.

Lazarus, R. S. (1990). Theory-based stress measurement. *Psychological Inquiry, 1*(1), 3–13.

Lazarus, R. S., & Folkman, S. (1984). *Stress, appraisal, and coping.* New York, NY: Springer.

MacDonald, R. R., & Labuc, S. (1982). *Parachuting stress and performance* (Memorandum 82m511). Farnsborough, England: Army Personnel Research Establishment.

MacLeod, C. (1996). Anxiety and cognitive processes. In I. G. Sarason, G. R. Pierce, & B. R. Sarason (Eds.), *Cognitive interference: Theories, methods, and findings* (pp. 47–76). Mahwah, NJ: Lawrence Erlbaum Associates.

McGrath, J. E. (1976). Stress and behavior in organizations. In M. D. Dunnette (Ed.), *Handbook of industrial and organizational psychology* (pp. 1351–1395). Chicago, IL: Rand McNally.

National Audit Office. (2003). *Difficult forms: How government agencies interact with citizens.* Retrieved from http://www.nao.org.uk/publications/0203/how_government_ agencies_intera.aspx

Park, S., & Holzman, P. S. (1992). Schizophrenics show spatial working memory deficits. *Archives General Psychiatry, 49,* 975–982.

Quesenbery, W. (2006). More alike than we think. UXmatters. Retrieved from http:// www.uxmatters.com/mt/archives/2006/03/more-alike-than-we-think.php

Rayner, K. (1998). Eye movements in reading and information processing: 20 years of research. *Psychological Bulletin, 124*(3), 372–422.

Rayner, K. (2009). Eye movements and attention in reading, scene perception, and visual search. *Quarterly Journal of Experimental Psychology, 68*(2), 1457–1506.

Redish, J. C. (2007). *Letting go of the words: Writing web content that works.* Burlington, MA: Morgan Kaufmann.

Reid, D. D. (1948). Fluctuations in navigator performance during operational sorties. In E. J. Earnaley & P. B. Warr (Eds.), *Aircrew stress in wartime operations* (pp. 63-73). New York, NY: Academic.

Rubin, J., & Chisnell, D. (2008). *Handbook of usability testing: How to plan, design, and conduct effective tests.* Indianapolis, IN: Wiley.

Rudick, M., & O'Flahavan, L. (n.d.). The bite, the snack, and the meal: How to feed content-hungry site visitors. Retrieved from http://ewriteonline.com/articles/2011/11/bite-snack-and-meal-how-to-feed-content-hungry-site-visitors/

Salthouse, T. (1985). *A theory of cognitive aging.* Amsterdam: North Holland.

Simon, H. A. (1957). *Models of man: Social and rational.* New York, NY: John Wiley & Sons.

Slatin, J. M., & Rush, S. (2002). *Maximum accessibility: Making your web site work for everyone.* Boston, MA: Addison-Wesley.

Staal, M. A. (2004). *Stress, cognition, and human performance: A literature review and conceptual framework.* NASA: Ames Research Center.

Summers, K., Langford, J., Wu, J., Abela, C., & Souza, R. (2006). Designing web-based forms for users with lower literacy skills. *Proceedings of the American Society for Information Science and Technology, 43*(1), 1–12. doi: 10.1002/meet.14504301174

Summers, K., & Summers, M. (2005). Reading and navigational strategies of web users with lower literacy skills. *Proceedings of the American Society for Information Science and Technology, 42*(1). doi: 10.1002/meet.1450420179

Summers, K., Summers, M., & Helm, C. (2008). *PAP application usability and lessons learned.* Center for Business Intelligence Patient Assistance Programs, Baltimore, MD.

Theofanos, M. F., & Redish, J. C. (2003). Guidelines for accessible and usable web sites: Observing users who work with screen readers. *Interactions, 10*(6), 38–51.

Tullis, T., & Chadwick-Dias, A. (2003). *Web usability and age* [PowerPoint slides]. Fidelity Center for Applied Technology. Retrieved from http://assets.aarp.org/www.aarp.org_/build/templates/research/oww/Fidelity-March4.ppt

Villoldo, A., & Tarno, R. L. (1984). Measuring the performance of EOD equipment and operators, Naval Explosive Ordnance Disposal Technology Center, Technical Report T-270, AD-B083850L. San Francisco, CA: Frederick Burk Foundation Research Center.

Werner, J. S., Peterzell, D. H., & Scheetz, A. J. (1990). Light, vision, and aging. *Optometry & Vision Science, 67*(3), 214–229.

CHAPTER 3

Toward a Theory of Technological Embodiment

Lisa Meloncon

The lived body is a *how*, not a *what*.
(Aho & Aho, 2008, p. 33)

In 1974, the *Six Million Dollar Man* premiered on network television. Air Force Colonel Steve Austin was almost killed in a plane crash, but as the episode opens, the viewer hears the narrator, "We can rebuild him. We have the technology. . . . Better than he was before. Better, stronger, faster" (Bennett, 1974–1978). Colonel Austin receives a series of bionic parts—an arm, both legs, and one eye; thus, he becomes one of the first cyborgs—an amalgamation of body and machine—born in U.S. popular culture. Haraway's (1991) cyborg was initially conceived to critique traditional representations of the feminine, but it is now more widely used as a mechanism to theoretically discuss the relationships between people and machine. For this chapter, "the *cyborg* reflects the dynamic synergy of individual, technologies, and the contexts they share, a flexible and simultaneous emphasis that previous names for ages, eras, and periods could not provide" (Inman, 2004, p. 14).

Two years later, the *Bionic Woman* began as a spin-off from the *Six Million Dollar Man* series (Bennet & Siegel, 1976–1978). Played by Lindsey Wagner, the bionic woman was Jaime Sommers, a pro tennis player. After a devastating parachuting accident, Jaime Sommers, too, was made "better, stronger, faster." Her surgery replaced one ear, one arm, and both legs with bionic counterparts. Bodies, like Jaime Sommers's, that fall outside of the realm of the "normal" are often stigmatized as deformed, grotesque, crippled, or retarded. Historically, narratives and descriptions of these bodies focus almost exclusively on the single part that is deficient or not "normal," such as the hunchback, the one-armed

67

man, or the village idiot. But for Jamie Sommers there was not a single part to emphasize. She did not look freakish; she looked normal. It was only in moments of dramatic distress, such as a fight scene with a known enemy, when an injury may reveal the technology beneath her skin.

Jaime Sommers helps to explain, in part, what I mean by technological embodiments. Most simply defined, "embodiment is all the many and various ways that we (self and other) accomplish relations to being in possession of the bodies that we are" (Titchkosky, 2007, p. 13). When embodiment incorporates technology, the body and its actions become technologically embodied. As an iconic cultural symbol, Jamie Sommers reflects the merging of bodies and technologies and the shifting of the lived body toward technological embodiment. Jamie Sommers also represents the idea of Aho and Aho's (2008) epigram. He newly bionic body was not a "what." Instead, her newly bionic body reflected "how" she was going to live and how her body and its meaning had changed to one that was technologically embodied. "We tend to think of our body as a given, but its meaning evolves all the time" (Hacking, 2007, p. 93), and Jaime Sommers body evolved to become a way to a both/and compromise. She is both human and inhuman. She is both abled and disabled. She is embodied and technologically embodied. She illustrates the impact of technologies on the making and remaking of bodies, no matter whether those bodies are classified as abled or disabled.

By destabilizing categories of the body, technological embodiment erases differences by focusing on the dispersal of embodiment through technologies. Working within the framework of the posthuman and Merleau-Ponty's (1962/2002) notion of embodiment, this chapter discusses the ways theories of technical communication can be enhanced through technological embodiments. For the technical communicator, a malleable body that can be remade through technologies is more than a manifestation of cyborg, but rather the manifestation of a complex user, which can have wide ranging impacts on some of the most basic work of technical communication.

POSTHUMANISM AND EMBODIMENT

Posthumanism owes much to the work of Hayles (1999), who famously declared we have never been human, and it is a "general category for theories and methodologies that situate acts and texts in the complex interplays among human intentions, organizational discourses, biological trajectories, and technological possibilities" (Mara & Hawk, 2010, p. 3). This scholarly trajectory moves in and out of multiple fields, including technical communication and disability studies. While the scholarship on posthumanism in technical communication is growing (see Mara & Hawk, 2010), my concern is to make more visible the connection between technological possibilities and human intentions by drawing on the work of "body studies" (Hawhee, 2004, p. 10). Coming from a variety of fields (e.g., Butler, 1993; De Lauretis, 1989; Foucault, 1994; Scarry,

1987), body studies place the body "in direct relations with the flows or particles of other bodies or things" (Grosz, 1994, p. 168). In other words, body studies ensure that posthumanism doesn't forget about the living, breathing body since "the body and its specific behavior is where the power system stops being abstract and becomes material. The body is where it succeeds or fails, where it acceded to or struggled against" (Fiske, 1992, p. 162).

Speaking of not forgetting the living, breathing body, technical communication is almost guilty of that very thing. The field has too long assumed an unproblematic and disembodied body. There are only a few instances where technical communication scholars directly take up the issue of embodiment (Haas & Witte, 2001; Sauer, 2003). The idea of embodiment "is contextual, enmeshed within specifics of place, times, physiology, and culture, which together compose enactment," and it is "akin to articulation in that it is inherently performative, subject to individual enactments" (Hayles, 1999, pp. 196–197). The explicit claim to action and performance, which is an important part of embodiment, connects embodiment to phenomenology.

Phenomenology provides "an opening, a space, for things to reveal themselves differently from what we are accustomed" (Aho & Aho, 2008, p. 12), and it does so because it "inquires into *how* we are engaged participants in a shared world" (Aho & Aho, 2008, p. 25). A key to understanding the "how" is through the body's engagement and experience with the world. Since we gather and obtain knowledge beyond the physical limitations and restrictions of our bodies, our bodies are often extended into different locations. For example, we can smell things from some distance away; we can extend our understanding of our world by touch. Even disabled bodies are extended through assistive devices or by the idea that one sense grows stronger in the absence of others (e.g., a person without sight is much more sensitive to sound).

The French phenomenologist Merleau-Ponty has been highly influential in his work on the body and embodiment.[1] In one of his key texts, *Phenomenology*

---

[1] Readers may be thinking throughout this section of other philosophical works that discuss the body, such as those by Foucault's *Discipline and Punish* and the body and technology corpus of Don Ihde or Andrew Feenburg. Additionally, readers may also bring to mind the work of disability scholars, such as Tom Shakespeare, or the interdisciplinary work of Graham Pullin's *Design Meets Disability* or the work by systems theorists, such as Niklus Luhmann, Humerto Maturnara and Francisco Varela, and Gregory Bateson. In thinking of "things" as extensions of self, one may see a direct relationship to Bruno Latour's actor-network theory, which emphasizes all objects—both human and non-human—as important actants nodes on the network. Even though actor-network theory can be usefully applied to the large idea discussed here, my focus is solely on a single point in the network, the interaction between human and technological things. All of these works have influenced the information presented here, but the length of this chapter prohibits an in-depth engagement with these works and others like them. Rather, I take all of this work as a starting point to be more inventive than evaluative.

of Perception (1962/2002), Merleau-Ponty takes to task Cartesian dualism: "In fact every habit is both motor and perceptual, because it lies, as we have said, between explicit perception and actual movement" (p. 175). Thus, he remakes the body by merging it once again with the mind. Here he recombines the mind (perceptual) with the body (motor) because the body is a "nexus of living meanings" (Merleau-Ponty, 1962/2002, p. 175). Merleau-Ponty (1962/2002) uses the example of a blind man learning to use a cane. When he is learning to use the cane, the man is experiencing a motor habit. But the cane is also an example of a perceptual habit.

> Once the stick has become a familiar instrument, the world of feelable things recedes and now begins, not at the outer skin of the hand, but at the end of the stick. . . . the stick is no longer an object perceived by a blind man, but an instrument *with* which he perceives. It is a bodily auxiliary, an extension of the bodily synthesis. (Merleau-Ponty, 1962/2002, pp. 175–176)

This example illustrates the ways in which a tool—a cane—had become part of the body. The blind man could feel and guide himself through the everydayness of life, no longer aware of the cane itself but of the world the cane revealed. Using Merleau-Ponty's (1962/2002) concept of extending the body through a specific tool as a foundation, let us shift to a more specific everyday example.

Vignette

One course that regularly falls into my teaching rotation is technical and scientific writing, which is the service course populated primarily for engineers. I've always enjoyed teaching this course, and as a teacher with a reputation for being hard, I rarely encounter classroom management problems, including the unauthorized use of mobile phones. However, recently I had a particularly flagrant violation: a student, let's call him Robert, was texting during another student's presentation. I was quite surprised. Robert was an excellent student—came to class prepared, offered thoughtful comments, asked probing questions, and put forth full effort on the assignments. I was unable to catch up to him after class, so I sent an email asking him to see me the next day.

During the course of our conversation, we both had a revelation. His revelation was that he had no memory of texting during class. I asked him to pull up the list and see whether I had imagined it. There right in front of him was the day and time, clearly indicting him. He was dumbfounded. How could he not remember? My revelation was in his reaction. His phone had truly become an extension of his body.

Much like the blind man with the cane, Robert experienced the world, in part, through what appeared on his phone. Rarely do we remember every movement our bodies make during the day. Did I hold the coffee pot in my left hand or my right as I filled my cup? How did I get into the car or open the door? Which hand did I use when I pointed to the board in class? For my student, his mobile phone had become an unconscious extension of who he is and how he interacts in the world. "It is meaningless to imagine a human being as a biological entity without the complex network of his or her tools—such a notion is the same as, say, the goose without feathers" (Zizek, 2004, p. 19). It was so commonplace for Robert to respond to a text message—no matter what he should be or was doing—that he had no memory of it. He literally had no recollection of what his right hand was doing with his network of tools.

TECHNOLOGY AS TOOLS AND HUMANS AS TOOL-BEINGS

The idea of the human body being a tool-being moves through modern philosophers of technology (e.g., Feenburg, 2002; Idhe, 2001), with its roots going back to Heidegger (1997). The instrumental nature of technology means that human bodies exist as tool-beings that use a variety of equipment, or technology, to move through each day. In "The Question Concerning Technology," Heidegger (1997) discusses modern technology as a tool or an instrument that compels things to be revealed or "enframed" as resources. From our mobile phones to our cars to our computers to our pens, each one of our tools works with a series of other tools. "Technologies are never distinct objects: they are only experiences in relation to other entities arranged in complex constellations to form particular environments" (Hawk, 2007, p. 171; see also Slack & Wise, 2006, chap. 10). Geographer Nigel Thrift pushes Hawk's concept of technologies as part of relationships even farther. Thrift (2008) insists that the body interacts with other things:

> It could be argued that the human body is what it is because of its unparalleled ability to co-evolve with things, taking them in and adding them to different parts of the biological body to produce something which, if we could see it, would resemble a constantly evolving distribution of hybrids with different reaches. . . . The human body is a tool-being. (p. 10)

By incorporating this view of technology and our interaction with it, we move beyond thinking about just the "thingness" of the technology. Instead we have to think through the many contingencies within a culture and situation that create the technology and its uses. Thinking of a technological culture removes the either/or problems of selecting technological determinism or cultural determinism (or any range of position in between) by focusing on the connections, the articulations between the technology, the culture in which the technology is created, and the corresponding uses of the technology. The articulation of a technical culture implies that it is the articulations that matter because they incorporate a range of practices, representations, experiences, and affects. This means that agency remains at the forefront of the equation. The encounter between person and technology in the act of doing something is not reduced to the division between technology and human, nor are technology and human set in opposition. In considering technology in this way, I am much more interested in the relationship, the merging of technologies and users and in understanding what that relationship means for our understanding of ourselves, our bodies, and, ultimately, the work we do.

Foucault (1988) acknowledged he developed a greater interest in the "history of how an individual acts upon himself" (p. 19). He identified his major objective as "to sketch out a history of the different ways in our culture that humans develop knowledge about themselves" (Foucault, 1988, pp. 17–18). One of the techniques he offers is

> technologies of the self, which permit individuals to effect by their own means or with the help of others a certain number of operations on their own bodies and souls, thoughts, conduct, and way of being, so as to trans-form themselves in order to attain a certain state of happiness, purity, wisdom, perfection, or immortality. (Foucault, 1988, p. 18)

It is significant to note Foucault's choice of wording. To begin, *technologies* is plural, which signifies that at any given moment more than one technology can be used to act upon the self. Also, *technologies* is a non-specific signifier. Foucault never defines what a technology is, nor does he even specify what kinds or types of technologies should be used to "effect" aspects of the self. Technologies of the self is a technical enterprise enacted upon a body by a body and is at once a practice and a theory. In Foucault's (1998) explanation, he provides examples from ancient Greece and Rome and then from the days of early Christianity. These wide ranging examples from years gone past are significant because they prompt one to ask, "What type of self are we dealing with today? What understanding of the self motivates our practices and norms our ideas of what it means to be an individual who makes her own choices? And in our highly technological society, how do the gadgets of our everyday life relate to us, to who we are?" (Dumitrica, 2008, pp. 132–133). Taking technologies of the self to a new embodied level, the following two vignettes begin to answer these questions. Inserting technologies as a third object in the relationship of body and world means that existing relationships are altered and complicated, and it also means "becoming able to add, not subtract, means learning how to get access, not renouncing the possibility of access" (Stengers, 2005, p. 5).

Vignette

Jarle, the team captain of the national skydiving team, broke his neck. Now he does many things that abled people do, which he demonstrates as he maneuvers in his wheelchair. The story proceeds with Jarle showing a visitor around his customized, technologically advanced house that contains an environmental control system that he can control either through a device mounted on his wheelchair or through a suck-and-blow system from his bed. For Jarle, he maintains control over his life because his body

> *must remain attached to a set of ordered relations between elements such as cables, infrared beams and apparatuses, transmitters and receivers, the electricity network and its cables, a computer, a software program in which the many possibilities are programmed, a fuse box the size of a wardrobe, switches, remote controls. (Moser, 2006, pp. 370–382)*

Disability studies is rife with stories such as Jarle's in which technological advancements and assistive technologies have radically transformed the way people with disabilities live and interact. These narratives of "normalcy" enabled through technology illustrate Merleau-Ponty's (1962/2002) embodiment in ways he probably never imagined. But all of these technologies are extensions of Jarle's body and enable him to interact in ways that he could not without them. A careful and critical reader can already recognize the problems embedded within this narrative—problems of technological failure, the limits of the health care system, the need for someone to also monitor the situation, the large costs involved, and, of course, whether this is independence or not, just to name a few of the issues this story invokes. "We all have and are a body. But there is a way out of this dichotomous twosome. As part of our daily practices, we also do (our) bodies. In practice we enact them" (Mol & Law, 2006, p. 45). Although a further explication of these problems is outside the scope of the present, Jarle's story highlights the promise and the peril of technological embodiment for people with disabilities. For Jarle, he enacts his body through technology. Jarle's technological embodiments are one extreme of the spectrum where bodies and technologies merge into one. Now let us consider Nathan.

Vignette

Nathan's day begins like so many others. He wakes to his alarm and listens to the news while he is in the shower. He dresses for work (in a shirt made with nanotechnology) and goes to the kitchen, where his coffee is already made. While he drinks his coffee, he turns on his laptop to check the weather online, turns the TV on for the children, and then checks his work email on his mobile device. His wife reminds him of an appointment, which he enters into his phone's calendar, and then he syncs his laptop and phone.

While not a life-defining necessity for him, as it is for Jarle, Nathan too is technologically embodied; he is constantly connected. Much like Nathan, most of us would find it difficult to imagine going an entire day without technology, much of which no longer enters our consciousness as separate from our lives, until it goes wrong, of course.

> *If Zizek (2004), Thrift (2008), and others are right about tools and bodies— and I believe they are—this merging together of biology and the mechanical/ technical is as natural as any other process. Thinking of technology as an extension of biology helps to blur the boundaries of what is considered a normal body, which is of primary concern to disability studies. Taking this view eliminates the physical bodily differences between people—those with and without disabilities—and forces the makers of technologies to recognize that technological embodiments are paramount to the success of any system.*

> > *Successful technology developments will come from those who recognize the importance of tools and social systems that support human goals, control, and responsibility. Users want the sense of mastery and accomplishment that comes from using a tool to accomplish their goals. (Shneiderman, 2002, p. 237)*

> *One of the goals of looking at technological embodiments is to level the playing field between abled bodies and disabled bodies. We are all posthuman. Think about specific technologies attached to the body, such as sophisticated mind controlled prosthetics, pacemakers, or insulin pumps. Think about technologies that aid the body, such as self-help books, canes, or insulin pumps. Think about ways in which our bodies are dispersed, such as multi-player online games, training simulations for doctors and pilots, the Xbox Kinect, or virtual global conferencing. In both large and small ways, technologies are changing the way we view and act out our own bodies.*

AN EXAMPLE OF THEORY TO PRACTICE: AUDIENCE ANALYSIS

Sometimes theory is accused of being too abstract, too far from practice. This notion of technological embodiments is one that technical communicators cannot ignore, especially for one of the key functions we perform—audience analysis. While the field discusses users, audiences, and readers, the discussions often fail to move past an idealized disembodied user toward an embodied user. "We brandish expressions like 'user advocate,' 'user-centered design,' and 'ease of use' with the understanding that one of our main goals is to write and design documents with the target audience in mind" (Blakeslee, 2010, p. 199). Technical communication teachers are quite familiar with standard exercises in audience analysis. Many popular textbooks provide checklists to complete. But what these linear and one-dimensional checklists do not adequately address is the three-dimensional, embodied mode of audience.

One of the benchmark works in audience analysis is Johnson's (1998) work on "user-centered" technology. As one of the first technical communication scholars to deploy this term, Johnson (1998) advocates adopting a user-centered approach to documentation, which he defines as "a thorough form of audience analysis that is aimed at designing documentation that fits what a user actually does, not necessarily what we think he or she should do" (p. 136). User-centered designed assumes that technologies are a medium for doing different things and that the goal of using the technology is to make the technology seamless with the user's activities.

Although much scholarship in technical communication draws on Johnson's (1998) work, it has not been without critique. Spinuzzi (2000) feels that the user-centered approach "hides that fact that technical communicators actually do try to marginalize, inhibit, and discourage certain types of users and assign circumscribed roles to those readers" (p. 215). Spinuzzi's (2000) critique carries additional weight when viewed through the lens of disability studies. To date, technical communicators have made the "normal" body the focus of the user-centered experience. We forefront the user, a person who operates something, but rarely do we embody this user because the emphasis is on the operation, the success or failure of it, rather than on the embodied person. And too often audiences that do not interact in "normal" ways are discounted from consider-ation. If information has lost its body, as Hayles (1999) has suggested, those of us who work in communicating information to audiences need to pay more attention to the idea of embodment. Audiences (or users) all have bodies, no matter whether that body is abled or disabled.

With the rise of dynamic systems, Albers (2003) claimed that the importance of audience analysis would increase. In the years since, this claim has come to pass as systems of all shapes and sizes and in all kinds of industries have increases in complexity. The recent work *Usability of Complex Information Systems*, by Albers and Still (2011), advances the premise that increasingly complex systems need to be evaluated in new ways. If systems are more complex, then how users interact with those systems is more complex as well. Our theories of audience analysis have not kept pace. The field needs an understanding of a complex user that ensures the user is embodied. "Disability studies demands a shift from the ideology of normalcy, from the rule and hegemony of normates, to vision of the body as changeable, unperfectable, unruly, and untidy" (Davis, 2002, p. 39). Technical communicators can also benefit from this shift toward the actual users rather the idealized user.

Vignette

Matt has been working at his new job as an information architect and content developer for about six months. He's just been made the lead on a new web project that has two parts: updating the client's public website and reorganizing and enhancing the client's intranet, which is run through a custom-built content-management system. One of Matt's first tasks is to create a series of personas and a task analysis. Matt's personas could be used as models for others because they are detailed, specific, and incorporate almost every conceivable scenario—except he never once considers whether any of the potential users are people with disabilities. His client: Goodwill Industries.

A three-dimensional audience analysis that expands the characteristics of the user and helps to embody it is sorely needed. This three-dimensional model of audience analysis would include specific questions about disability or, at the very least, a greater awareness that one out five users is disabled. A three-dimensional model would better account for the technological embodiment between user, text, technology, space, and author. Pushing embodiment ever farther, this would address the idea that our bodies are not a constant of "always disabled or always able-bodied" but that our bodies and "our abilities change depending on the context" (Pullin, 2009, p. 91). These added dimensions help to embody audience analysis. "The thinking here is that technology potentially makes our writing accessible to a much broader audience than before—potentially to all Internet users or to anyone who can access an online document" (Blakeslee, 2010, p. 201), but only if those users can truly access the information. If technical communicators continue to only imagine an ideal user of the system in ideal circumstances, then technical communicators, consciously or unconsciously, are ensuring that people with disabilities— either temporary or more permanent—will always be marginalized, inhibited, and discouraged. It takes only a slight shift, possibly to technological embodiments, to understand that audience analysis needs to expand to incorporate a three-dimensional view of the user, a user with a body that is "changeable, unperfectable, unruly, and untidy." (Davis, 2002, p. 39)

A CONSIDERATION OF THEORY TO PRACTICE: ETHICS

In presenting this theory of technological embodiment, one must also consider the ethical dimensions of it. Consider Oscar.

The May 2007 headline in the *New York Times* read "An Amputee Sprinter: Is He Disabled or Too-Abled?" (Longman, 2007). The story is focused on Oscar Pistorius, a South African sprinter who has set records for Paralympic athletes. He is a double amputee who competes wearing a "pair of j-shaped blades made of carbon fiber and known as Cheetahs" (Longman, 2007, para. 3). He became a focus of international attention when he attempted to become part of the 2008 South African Summer Olympic Team—the regular, able-bodied team. Pistorius's dream was cut short when the International Association of Athletics

Federation, the governing body of Olympic and amateur sports, declared that "his prosthetic racing blades give him a clear competitive advantage"(Associated Press, 2008, para. 1).

This chapter started with an image of Jaime Sommers, a fictional cyborg. In Oscar Pistorius, we have returned to a similar twenty-first century techno-body, but it is real. With it a whole series of ethical questions arise: What is the definition of a body? Who has the right to define a foot, since Pistorius has known only a prosthetic as a foot? (He received his first prosthetics as a toddler.) Are his Cheetahs feet or prosthetics? What are the limits of technology? And, the ever confounding question, who is disabled? Or how do we define abled?

At the heart of any ethical inquiry is the fundamental question, how should one live? In advanced societies, a closely allied question is that of what decisions should be regulated. When placed alongside technology and bodies, these questions become more vexing, more troublesome, which means technical communicators who are often tasked with writing and communicating about many of these technologies must be diligent in both asking and answering ethical questions.

Another ethical dimension to consider is the creation of a "technological ghetto at the margins of consumer and political culture" (Ott, Serlin, & Mihm, 2002, p. 21). According to historians Ott, Serlin, and Mihm (2002), bionics and cyborgs have become mainstream in large part because they are "divorced from disability." Complicating this "technological ghetto" even more is the "line between assistive and prosthetic technology." Both assist with access to day-to-day living, and "since all useful technology is assistive, it is peculiar that we stipulate that some devices are assistive while others need no qualifications" (Ott et al., 2002, p. 21). Why is it that certain technologies have few stigmas while others have more? If any technological embodiment assists, then they should all be classified the same. Devices that aid daily activities have always existed, so why should there be a needless perpetuation of a hierarchy of assistive devices?

> The issue, then, is not first and foremost whether new, digital, ICT-based technologies will revolutionize the lives and situation of disabled people, but rather whether they will revolutionize the way we conceive of and make distinctions between abled and disabled people in the first instance. (Moser, 2006, p. 389)

At its heart, this is a question of ethics. Ethical questions will not fade into the background, nor will they cease being complicated and complex. From biopolitics to genetics to increased surveillance to definitions of technologies and disability to nano-size infiltration of advanced technologies into every aspect of our lives, ethics should remain central to any discussion of technological embodiments. Both technical communicators and disability studies scholars have the knowledge and ability to enter into these discussions and provide a "humanistic" view to ethical questions. OR: We are in a good position to emphasize the human in posthuman.

LOOKING TO THE FUTURE

Jaime Sommers, Jarle, Robert, Oscar Pistorius, Nathan, Matt, and any person who interacts with and acts through technology all provide examples of technological embodiment and the importance of this concept to technical communication. This brief foray into theoretical dimensions of technological embodiments is an experiment into alternative ways of thinking about technologies, bodies, and the work we—technical communicators and disability scholars alike—do. Theory is sometimes criticized for being disconnected and abstracted from anything practical. The multiple examples—vignettes—presented in this chapter serve as an attempt to connect the theoretical dimensions of technological embodiment to actual practices, such as audience analysis. Admittedly, I have only scratched the surface of the practical application and, more so, have only initiated a limited exploration of the theory of technological embodiment, and in the process, I have asked many more questions than I have answered.

If we could do a better job of addressing the embodiments of users, the limitations of their actual bodies would be diminished. If all bodies, both abled and disabled bodies, need technologies to function, then all bodies immediately become the same. "What is striking about the history of the Internet, its contemporary forms, and future visions, is that disability is both highly visible and curiously invisible in its digital landscape" (Goggin & Newell, 2003, p. 110). If disability is a gap that needs to be addressed in Internet studies and technical communication, the first step would be to remember that disability is not a deficit or "something less." By attempting to level the playing field between abled and disabled through technological embodiments, I hope to place the emphasis on improving our practices to better serve all users, which would mean the inclusion of disability as a category of diversity to be considered when designing new technologies or writing about existing ones.

In the everydayness of technical communication, its usefulness rests in foregrounding the necessity to proceed with caution, to actually consider the myriad ethical dimensions embedded in every technology embodiment. And in this creation, what are the limits of surveillance? When does our body not belong to us? If the face is obscured, is the technological image of our body no longer human and, thus, no longer ours? Shifting to a related area, what roles should technical communication and disability scholars play in ongoing concerns over Internet privacy, particularly the increase in the numbers of technologies designed to be placed in the home?

Technological embodiment, as manifested in the "latest add-on, the fastest computer, or even a more expansive application of universal design" will do nothing for anyone until we fully appreciate that "whatever we do we have the opportunity to disable or enable" (Goggin & Newell, 2003, p. 154). And this is the area where technical communication and technical communicators can intervene. What we can learn from the first decade of the twenty-first century is that the work of technical communicators and disability studies scholars needs to find a greater synergy because what stands for technological embodiments will become only more complicated and more important. "To speak of embodiment is to form some knowledge of it, and how we know our embodied reality acts upon how we orient toward disability" (Titchkosky, 2007, p. 13). Understanding that we are all embodied, and all technologically embodied, should ensure that we more consciously, directly, and ethically orient ourselves in ways that make sure people with disabilities are granted more accessibility. Since technical communicators play vital roles in the development, deployment, and documentation of many technologies and systems, it's past time to consciously orient ourselves toward and with disability.

As I conclude, let me offer a caveat to this discussion. I am not advocating for the erasure or loss of the uniqueness of bodies. The raced, sexed, disabled, aged, and other body categories are important and vital—they bleed, rejoice, and, yes, even use technologies. But I do want to offer the suggestive idea that technical communicators have to consider the corporeal body in light of technological embodiment. Our society has evolved to the point that few users are outside the reach of technologies and the impact of those technologies on their everyday lives. We can no longer ask the basic question, how will the user interact with thing X? Rather, the question needs to be, how does this technologically embodied user imagine thing X as part of himself or herself and what does it mean to all of us?

REFERENCES

Aho, J., & Aho, K. (2008). *Body matters: A phenomenology of sickness, disease, and illness*. Lanham, MD: Lexington Books.

Albers, M. (2003). Multidimensional audience analysis for dynamic information. *Journal of Technical Writing and Communication, 33*(3), 263–279.

Albers, M., & Still, B. (2011). *Usability of complex information systems: Evaluation of user interaction*. Boca Raton, FL: CRC Press.

Associated Press. (2008, January 14). IAAF rules Pistorius' prosthetics give him unfair advantage. *ESPN*. Retrieved from http://sports.espn.go.com/oly/trackandfield/news/story?id=3195563

Bennett, H. (Executive producer). (1974–1978). *The six million dollar man* [Television series]. Burbank, CA: American Broadcasting Company (ABC). Retrieved from http://www.imdb.com/title/tt0071054/quotes

Bennett, H., & Siegel, L. E. (Executive producers). (1976–1978). *The bionic woman* [Television series]. Burbank, CA: American Broadcasting Company (ABC), seasons 1–2. New York, NY: National Broadcasting Company (NBC), season 3.

Blakeslee, A. (2010). Addressing audiences in a digital age. In R. Spilka (Ed.), *Digital literacy for technical communication: 21st century theory and practice* (pp. 198–229). New York, NY: Routledge.

Butler, J. (1993). *Bodies that matter: On the discursive limits of "sex."* New York, NY: Routledge.

Davis, L. (2002). *Bending over backwards: Disability, dismodernism & other difficult positions.* New York, NY: New York University Press.

Davis, L. (2005). Disability: The next wave or twilight of the Gods? *PMLA, 120*(2), pp. 527-532.

De Lauretis, T. (1989). *Technologies of gender.* New York, NY: Palgrave.

Dumitrica, D. (2008). You are your iPod! In D. E. Wittkower (Ed.), *iPod and philosophy icon of an epoch* (pp. 129–142). Chicago, IL: Open Court Publishing.

Feenburg, A. (2002). *Transforming technology: A critical theory revisited.* Oxford, UK: Oxford University Press.

Fiske, J. (1992). Cultural studies and the culture of everyday life. In L. Grossberg, C. Nelson, & P. Treichler (Eds.), *Cultural studies.* New York, NY: Routledge.

Foucault, M. (1988). *Technologies of the self: A seminar with Michel Foucault.* L. Martin, H. Gutman, & P. Hutton (Eds.). Amherst, MA: University of Massachusetts Press.

Foucault, M. (1994). *The birth of a clinic: An archaeology of medical perception.* New York, NY: Vintage Books.

Goggin, G., & Newell, C. (2003). *Digital disability: The social construction of disability in new media.* Lanham, MD: Rowman & Littlefield Publishers.

Grosz, E. (1994). *Volatile bodies: Toward a corporeal feminism.* Bloomington, IN: Indiana University Press.

Haas, C., & Witte, S. (2001). Writing as embodied practice: The case of engineering standards. *Journal of Business and Technical Communication, 15*(4), 413–457.

Hacking, I. (2007). Our neo-Cartesian bodies in parts. *Critical Inquiry, 34*(1), 78–105.

Haraway, D. (1991). *Simians, cyborgs, and women: The reinvention of nature.* New York, NY: Routledge.

Hawhee, D. (2004). *Bodily arts: Rhetoric and athletics in ancient Greece.* Austin, TX: University of Texas Press.

Hawk, B. (2007). *A counter-history of composition: Toward methodologies of complexity.* Pittsburgh, PA: University of Pittsburgh Press.

Hayles, N. K. (1999). *How we became posthuman: Virtual bodies in cybernetics, literature, and informatics.* Chicago, IL: University of Chicago Press.

Heidegger, M. (1977). *The question concerning technology and other essays.* (W. Lovitt, Trans.). New York, NY: Harper Torch Books.

Ihde, D. (2001). *Bodies in technology.* Minneapolis, MN: University of Minnesota Press.

Inman, J. (2004). *Computers and writing: The cyborg era.* Mahwah, NJ: Lawrence Erlbaum Associates.

Johnson, R. (1998). *User-centered technology: A rhetorical theory for computers and other mundane artifacts.* Albany, NY: State University of New York Press.

Longman, J. (2007, May 15). An amputee sprinter: Is he disabled or too-abled? *New York Times.* Retrieved from http://www.nytimes.com/2007/05/15/sports/othersports/15runner.html?pagewanted=1

Mara, A., & Hawk, B. (2010). Posthuman rhetorics and technical communication. *Technical Communication Quarterly, 19*(1), 1–10.

Merleau-Ponty, M. (2002). *Phenomenology of perception.* (C. Smith, Trans.). London, UK: Routledge. (Original work published 1962.)

Mol, A., & Law, J. (2006). Embodied action, enacted bodies: The example of hypoglycemia. *Body and Society, 10*(2), 43–62.

Moser, I. (2006). Disability and the promise of technology: Technology, subjectivity, and embodiment within an order of the normal. *Information, Communication & Society, 9*(3), 373–395.

Ott, K., Serlin, D., & Mihm, S. (Eds.). (2002). *Artificial parts, practical lives: Modern histories of prosthetics.* New York, NY: New York University Press.

Pullin, G. (2009). *Design meets disability.* Cambridge, MA: MIT Press.

Sauer, B. (2003). *Rhetoric of risk: Technical documentation in hazardous environments.* Mahwah, NJ: Lawrence Erlbaum Associates.

Scarry, E. (1987). *The body in pain: The making and unmaking of the world.* Oxford, UK: Oxford University Press.

Shneiderman, B. (2002). *Leonardo's laptop: Human needs and the new computing technologies.* Cambridge, MA: MIT Press.

Slack, J. D., & Wise, J. M. (2006). *Culture and technology: A primer.* New York, NY: Peter Lang.

Spinuzzi, C. (2000). Exploring the blind spot: Audience, purpose, and context in "product, purpose, and profit." *ACM Journal of Computer Documentation, 24*(4), 213–219.

Stengers, I. (2005). *A constructivist reading of process and reality.* London, UK: Goldsmiths.

Thrift, N. (2008). *Non-representational theory: Space, politics, affect.* London, UK: Routledge.

Titchkosky, T. (2007). *Reading and writing disability differently: The textured life of embodiment.* Toronto, Canada: University of Toronto Press.

Zizek, S. (2004). *Organs without bodies: Deleuze and consequences.* New York, NY: Routledge.

http://dx.doi.org/10.2190/RAAC4

CHAPTER 4

Supercrips Don't Fly: Technical Communication to Support Ordinary Lives of People With Disabilities

Margaret Gutsell and Kathleen Hulgin

> The most destructive aspect of the media's use of Supercrips
> is that the Supercrip image kicks real issues off the table.
> (Haller, 2000, para. 12)

We have all heard stories lauding the deaf high school student who plays softball or the man who uses a wheelchair yet manages to sail a boat. While the inspirational disabled person, a dominant image portrayed in popular culture, seems positive, it interferes with inclusive living. Prodigious achievement is praiseworthy in anyone, yet the focus on people considered to have a disability as courageous or super-achieving eclipses the fact that most of them simply desire ordinary lives (Shapiro, 1993). Rather than "overcoming" their individual characteristics, they are concerned with countering the social barriers that interfere with everyday activities. Instead of being raised to some kind of hero status, they would prefer to be included in the life of a community by addressing challenges such as inaccessible or unavailable transportation, limited employment opportunities, inaccessible affordable housing, or unreliable wheelchairs. The focus on disability as an individual pathology to be overcome, is grounded in cultural notions of normalcy (Davis, 1995) and associated ideas about what action should be taken when perceived deviation occurs.

The supercrip metaphor is used to describe the most current example of how language perpetuates negative images and minimally valuable roles for individuals. Shapiro (1993) explains how views of the disabled as pitiable poster children preceded this image, yet both are rooted in adherence to social norms that produce deviation. Deviation from socially desirable norms is considered problematic, even tragic. Furthermore, the concept of disability locates the problem inside of the individual, who is lauded for overcoming it. A person's achievements are viewed as spectacular because she has something wrong with her that the rest of us don't have to live with and manage. This manner of metaphorically representing people is tied to exclusive thinking and practice. This and other metaphors often occur in media and public relations materials, technical manuals, and medical communications, thus having significant impact.

In this chapter, we use a constructionist approach to examine how notions of disability and the inherent concept of normalcy are created and can be reconstructed through the language system. Davis (1995) noted, "the consideration of disability . . . rather than being a marginal and eccentric focus of study, goes to the heart of issues about representation, communication, language, ideology, and so on" (p. 124). We use the supercrip metaphor as a beginning point for understanding language and the representation of disabilities, and its connection to cultural meaning and the associated challenge to support inclusion through technical communication. The ultimate purpose is to develop technical communication that supports ease in the everyday life of those who experience disability.

LANGUAGE AND THE CONSTRUCTION OF DISABILITY AND EXCLUSION

Language is a wonderful cultural invention. It allows us to communicate with one another in a quick, presumably concise manner. Words just pop out of our mouths. They fly off our fingertips at a keyboard. They appear in bulleted form on a printed page or computer screen, and we scan them in a heartbeat to understand. We adopt words and phrases and their associated meaning from immersion in a particular context, typically without conscious consideration. We are supposed to feel a particular way about a person or topic, so we just draw the phrase out of our hat that describes what we've always known. Rarely do we actually stop and ask ourselves a question about what the various messages we are communicating might be. If and when we do, we may be greeted with the accusation that we're just being politically correct, a phrase that has come to mean something close to "ridiculously and unnecessarily picky."

Language is, indeed, powerful. As understood from cultural theory, language represents socially constructed conceptual maps or images. Hall (1997) explains, "We are able to communicate because we share broadly the same conceptual maps and thus make sense of or interpret the world in roughly similar ways" (p. 21). Meaning depends on the relationship constructed between things in the world—people, objects, and events, real or fictional—and the conceptual system. The meaning is not in objects, people, or things themselves, nor is it in the word. Rather it is socially generated, with codes or social conventions fixing meaning. As Hall (1997) argues, it is not the material world that conveys meaning and value: it is the language system and how we choose to use it to represent our concepts.

Foucault (1969/1972) further argues that the ultimate importance of understanding the social construction of cultural concepts and language is not simply in terms of meaning but within a framework of power relations. He describes language and meaning as more directly shaped within various disciplines over time and in terms of power. He refers to this discipline specific knowledge as discourse. Discourses gain authority as part of the establishment of disciplines that produce and reproduce shared ways of thinking, social practices, and structures. While new discourses develop over time, those that have been institutionalized for periods of time have significant impact over our world.

The construction of social norms necessarily leads to the existence of deviancy. Specifically, the notion of disability is defined and enforced through a number of culturally dominant discourses. The most influential of these has been medical discourse through which disability has been shaped and identified as a pathology located within an individual to be treated, remediated, or cured (Longmore & Umansky, 2001; Oliver, 1990). This notion is so entrenched in our culture that it is taken for granted. The power of the medical model lies in its grounding in the mechanistic world view or positivist science, which seeks knowledge and progress through examination and control of parts, separated from the whole. This approach drives most disciplines in our culture, including technical communication. In the remainder of this section, we will discuss disability related language and the use of the supercrip image as rooted in these limiting ideologies.

The medical model dominates early writings, which refer to people with single-word labels or group labels like "the feeble-minded" or "deaf and dumb." Words that assigned roles—such as *patient, resident,* and *ward*—were established (Linton, 1998). The focus of earlier researchers on disability was typically oriented toward developing programs or teaching strategies that would remediate or treat individual pathology, with the goal of bringing individuals closer to societal notions of normal. Members of the various groups of people identified as having disabilities were very often the subjects of experimental medical interventions, and where these were deemed unsuccessful in moving members of the group toward identified normalcy, efforts to segregate the groups and minimize their entrance into larger society were described in some texts as justifiable.

In the 1940s and 1950s, writers began to represent individuals with certain physical or cognitive difference as pitiable or requiring charity. Phillips (1990) explains how this representation was driven by the failure of medicine to cure polio. If medical science could not cure the condition, individuals were considered damaged goods, objects of pity, unless they could personally overcome it, as promoted through the supercrip image.

The pity approach has successfully been used to raise dollars for and provide justification for service organizations and research. It also reinforces the notion that certain conditions are tragic and emphasizes the needs of the person rather than his or her abilities and contributions. Failure to represent positive characteristics of and roles occupied by people considered to be disabled can result in minimal expectations about them as neighbors, coworkers, and community members. The intense focus on inabilities to experience circumstances, relationships, conditions, and rewards generally connected with successful self-sufficiency also negates the possibilities of healthy interdependence, accommodation, or accessible design.

Consider the simple description that is usually associated with a person using a wheelchair. He or she is either described as being wheelchair bound or confined to a wheelchair. The language immediately evokes an image of a suffering human being who is tethered to a chair, unable to move or to do anything else those who are free from chairs can enjoy. The reaction of readers or listeners to this phrase is to expect that the confined, bound person is an invalid (dissect what that compound word means) with very limited capacity. Such images and assumptions are evident, as reported by contemporary bloggers who talk about how young children ask them how it feels to sleep in their wheelchairs. Now the in-valid person not only has to manage the different tasks involved in working from a seated position but also has to teach colleagues and neighbors that he or she is a contributing and active member of the community. It may seem inconceivable when people who use wheelchairs describe them as "freedom machines."

Disability rights advocates have challenged representations of abnormality. One of the most influential leaders, Judith Heumann, has used her roles within the federal government and international organizations to promote a shift away from viewing disability as an individual pathology and toward social change. She states, "dis-ability only becomes a tragedy for me when society fails to provide the things we need to lead our lives—job opportunities or barrier-free buildings, for example. It is not a tragedy to me to be living in a wheelchair!" (Shapiro, 1993, p. 20). As consciousness has been raised, language has changed, and representations of disability are less explicitly oppressive. For example, "people-first language" has been adopted as a principle for referring to people in terms of their characteristics or circumstances rather than in terms of disability labels (e.g., "person who uses a wheelchair" rather than "wheelchair bound").

Oppression on the basis of disability, however, is now more likely to occur through subconscious or unconscious responses. Young (1990) explains shifts in cultural oppression based on Giddens's (1984) three levels of human response: discursive consciousness, practical consciousness (e.g., habitual behavior or emotional responses), and the basic security system (identity). As discrimination has become culturally unacceptable, Young (1990) argues that we avoid explicit expressions. Yet we continue to distance ourselves from the threat of identification with the undesirable through unconscious aversion—a form of practical consciousness. In other words, oppression continues in ways that are unintentional and less overt, such as distancing and avoidance. This is further complicated by the personal nature of these responses, for which we are typically not held socially responsible. More recent language, including increased usage of the supercrip image, represents a shift from overt discrimination, yet it continues to oppress.

Those who are uncomfortable or unfamiliar with how to write about or for people who have disabilities often try to avoid offending anyone or otherwise saying something wrong by using what they view as pleasant euphemisms to describe what a person does differently or how a person interacts with the world. Common phrases include "physically challenged" and "differently abled." These efforts seem to communicate the discomfort or embarrassment with bold highlights. If disability is just one characteristic of a whole person that simply exists, then using language that is geared toward softening or disguising the characteristic sends confusing messages at best. Often writers collectively group people who have disabilities into a category called "people with special needs." This designation is particularly problematic because it was developed and is most often used in educational settings, where it applies to children. Inadvertently treating adults with disabilities as children continues to reinforce the expectation that persons who have disabilities may not negotiate the challenges common to adults and will not make the contributions typically anticipated of adult competence.

As noted above, the practice of elevating a person's accomplishments by seeing them as occurring in spite of a disability has been identified and criticized by disability activists as the supercrip metaphor (Shapiro, 1993). This approach may reflect an unconscious aversion or help the writer feel more comfortable by minimizing the irrational fear of contagion or guilt associated with not being personally connected with someone who has a disability. While by all appearances this compliments the person and recognizes abilities and achievements, it also communicates the expectation that abilities, strength, and contribution are not typically what is expected of such a person. In the published obituary for Harriet McBryde Johnson—an acclaimed legal scholar, writer, and disability rights advocate—her hometown paper reported she had achieved all of this despite having significant disabilities, *The Post and Courier* (2008, June 5).

The phrase "despite a disability" communicates that the problem is the fault of the person, who has something wrong with him or her. This problem causes suffering and creates obstacles to normal life, which is assumed to be reasonably challenge-free, with the typical person being able to do almost anything life requires independent of other people or specialized equipment. In our daily hustle and bustle lives, we find it difficult to imagine how we might manage if we were not able to run and catch a bus or quickly jump in the car to pick up children. So when we meet someone who has a visible disability and is successfully managing the same kinds of life tasks and demands, we think of them as achieving wonders. Because the problem resides in the person being abnormal with a disability, the solution is for the person to overcome, to "fix" himself or herself, or to remediate his or her condition in order to make it possible to participate in daily activities. When we write or talk about such a person, then, we consistently use language like "despite a disability" or "overcoming obstacles to have a normal life," evoking the supercrip metaphor and not examining what this language conveys. As Wilson (2000) explains, the legacy of discrimination resonates in the metaphor.

Unless the roots of exclusionary language are examined, new and more positive concepts will be eclipsed by or tangled up in them. For example, the concept of universal design, which originated in the field of architecture, has been more broadly defined with the initiative to create buildings, products, and environments that are accessible to all. The continued use of language that dramatizes difference, however, eclipses the concept of universal design while fostering fascination with such notions as extreme home make-over, as represented by the popular TV show which portrays accessibility as that which requires extraordinary measures. Concepts of abnormality and individual pathology, and the history of discriminatory practices with which they are tied, continue to be reproduced through common discourse. If the supercrip metaphor is eliminated and those who are identified as having disabilities no longer have to be fixed or personally overcome their conditions, the way we approach the concepts and practices of universal space and product design, technical communication, and, ultimately, inclusion are fundamentally altered.

While the use of certain disability related language and its consequences may not be intentional, this does not alleviate responsibility for change. Refraining from language that dramatizes a simple condition, such as using a wheelchair, can ameliorate huge barriers. And putting the person first—so that the physical condition or circumstances become just one of many characteristics that combine to make that person who he or she is—changes our perspective. If we write and talk about a "person who uses a wheelchair," we've merely stated a fact and there is room to avoid the stuck, immobile, in-valid image. Change, however, requires more than adopting inclusive language. In fact, the effort to develop inclusive practices has been plagued by change that can be characterized as old wine in new bottles (Hulgin, 2004; Slee, 1993). Inclusion requires the recognition of and conscious participation in meaning-making as a social process, characterized by ongoing questioning and flux. This is distinctly opposed to understanding knowledge and the material world as objective, fixed, and atomistic (or able to be understood apart from context). Technical communicators have a significant opportunity and responsibility to create inclusive everyday experience through language, but this must involve critical examination of identities and approach.

IDENTIFICATION, CONTEXTUALIZATION, AND INCLUSION

The process of technical communication involves a sizing up of an audience, in relation to a particular product or content, and the efficient conveyance of standardized information. This process is typically driven by unquestioned assumptions of positivist science and mechanism. According to positivist science, as noted above, knowledge and the knowledge seeking process are governed by objectivity, distanced observation, and standing above or outside of the object of knowledge. The gaze of modern scientific reason is also a normalizing gaze (Foucault, 1977). In the words of Young (1990):

> It is a gaze that assesses its object according to some hierarchical standard. The rational subject does not merely observe, passing from one sight to the other like a tourist. In accordance with the logic of identity the scientific subject measures objects according to scales that reduce the plurality of attributes to unity. Forced to line up on calibrations that measure degrees of some general attribute, some of the particulars are devalued, defined as deviant in relation to the norm. (pp. 125–126)

The processes of distanced assessment, stripping away context, and normalization are at the root of defining people with certain characteristics as abnormal and failing to account for the situational and social factors that influence their competence. Technical communication is typically based on assumptions of a standard of competence and a fixed notion of the product or content. These standards are determined by culturally dominant groups that project their values, experience, and perspective as normative and universal.

Technical communicators must be careful not to fall into the trap of seeing disability as a problem that, by definition, should be overcome or fixed. The fact that some people cannot access certain documents or move about online in the same way as others does not mean they have a problem or that something internal to their skills needs to change. Instead, good design principles and good technical documentation should continue to interrogate the best ways to maximize interfaces for as many users as possible, including those with disabilities. Instead of certain characteristics being seen as problematic, they should be seen as a benchmark for ensuring quality and accessible design. Titchkosky (2007) states:

> Rather than investing time and energy in shoring up the differences between ability and disability, the right to representation might better serve as a growing sense of ambiguity. In the space between, in the dynamics of becoming interested in how self and other might be mutually constitutive, we have the chance to read and write disability differently. The reading and writing of disability into a time and space imagined as non-disabled has much to teach us about the social organization of normal senses of embodiment required by a certain way of relating to whatever is regarded as not normal, different, out of the ordinary. (p. 39)

Technical communicators can draw many parallels in these sentiments and can probably see similarities to approaching characteristics classified as disability as normal, much as we approach a variety of users for most systems. Environmental features, product specifications, and social expectations can and do minimize the negative impact of physical, sensory, and cognitive characteristics for all of us.

Most of us will experience something currently termed a disability at some point in our lives. This may heighten the threat to our identities, a fear that, as noted above, Young (1990) argues is at the root of contemporary oppression. Through dominant discourse, disabled people are identified as belonging to a different group, not the typical group. Phrases such as "the disability community" or "self-advocates" are used to refer to them.

The impact of "othering" on the basis of disability has a significant effect on individuals who are identified as such. Immersion in dominant ideology has led to the unconscious internalization of an identity, which marks them as lacking an attribute necessary to be fully human. For some, this experience has involved forms of self-oppression including self-punishment, denial, and passing. Disability leaders, such as Swain and Cameron (1999), have actively reclaimed their identity as disabled, which they characterize as a coming out process. They explain how disabled people must work to integrate a sense of difference into a healthy self-concept, despite stigmatization from our dominant culture. This involves rejecting the assumption that treatment or cure, rehabilitation or therapy or control, pity or compensation is always the appropriate response. They define *disability* as the disadvantage or restriction of activity caused by a contemporary social organization that takes no or little account of people who have physical impairments and thus excludes them from participation in the mainstream of social activities.

In his book *Disability Theory*, Siebers (2008) writes about identity as well: "This book theorizes disability as a minority identity . . . that must be addressed not as a personal misfortune or individual defect but as the product of a disabling social and built environment" (p. 3). While critics of Siebers (2008) may view him as too political and extreme, his stance to insist "on the pertinence of disability to the human condition, on the value of disability as a form of diversity, and on the power of disability as a critical concept for thinking about human identity in general" (p. 3) cannot be easily discounted.

One promising avenue for building common identification arises from the challenge of responding to increased aging in our culture. As our lives change, older people remain much the same as they have been and refuse to take on the identity of the different group, fighting fiercely to belong with the same group they have been part of for years.

Some older adults working to integrate a changing identity may refer to themselves as handicapped, sounding apologetic as they explain their status. Regardless of the absolute truth, most younger people who have disabilities maintain the belief that the word *handicap* is derived from the only reasonable employment choice available to people with disabilities several centuries ago— begging with their caps in hand. The word, at worst, reinforces the incompetence of people and, at best, casts them as beggars for valued roles (e.g., employee, policy-maker) in communities. For this reason, many self-advocate groups have been working to abolish the word *handicap* in signage and government-funded publications. This means in many communities that parking spaces designated for persons who need close proximity are labeled "accessible parking" and restrooms are identified as "accessible to all." This approach focuses on the characteristics of space rather than on any perceived inability of the user. Focusing on space, location, and product features represents a major shift in thinking from segregating users based on skill toward functionally labeling and describing items and concepts to the broadest group of end users. The change in focus forces a more inclusive orientation that has the potential to transcend even the notion of accessibility as it is usually understood to address physical features such as slope, width, or height. The inclusive orientation is silent to any specific personal characteristic, thus daring architects, product designers, and technical communicators to consider the wide range of people who might be among the end user group.

A number of other inclusive designs have been developed in the area of communication, which is of critical importance given common challenges such as reliance on websites to gain information. Only recently have pharmacists begun to create large print information about medications and their side effects. Just this past year the Federal Social Security Administration actually communicated with disability applicants and recipients who were identified as blind or visually impaired to let them know that they were now entitled to receive documents in alternate formats, including Braille, large print, and electronic versions.

Focusing on the specific details of how to universally design materials so that they can be accessed by the widest range of people in the widest range of circumstances goes beyond the scope of this chapter. In this chapter, it is our intent, however, to suggest a broader and deeper approach that involves a shift from distanced analysis and a narrow standard of competence in which difference is viewed as a deficit to be overcome. We argue for an approach in which technical communicators take the responsibility to gain an experiential knowl-edge of the range of situations and perspectives to which they are responding, assume competence on the part of their audience, and adopt a strategic framework that asks the guiding question, what will it take to avoid barriers and support success, with full acceptance of diverse characteristics? (Biklen & Burke, 2006).

We describe this approach as one that is inclusive. The word *inclusion* offers the best description of both the manner in which the technical communicator engages in the work of designing and producing materials as well as the wide-ranging definition applied to the user group. This goes beyond the traditional method of thinking "who is most likely to read this" to imagining "who knows who might want or need this information." The inclusive approach is positive and welcoming. It is the opposite of exclusive and powerfully equalizes the status of all users. Because committing to inclusion involves recognizing a full range of users whose characteristics, strengths, and needs are part of the total user group, the practice of inclusive communication urges communicators to meet the challenge of meaningfully engaging and effectively answering questions or providing clarification for everyone.

A context based approach has been advanced by technical communication scholars Vico (1990) and Praetorius (2004) and is especially critical in view of disability issues. They build upon Geertz (1992) and argue for promoting practical knowledge by moving away from declarative statements and toward consideration of what it takes to avoid negative consequences that are caused by everyday problems. In the context of product engineering, for example, a watch that is designed to speak the time for someone who can no longer read the face of the watch employs an unrelated placement of buttons to set the watch features rather than using a clockwise arrangement and button-pressing process with which the watch user might already have some familiarity. The complexity of the design and associated strategy adds yet one more barrier to the common tasks of checking and managing time. Other scenarios include the possibility that someone who bought a product five years ago was reading standard print, but when he needs to refresh his understanding of how to use one of its features this afternoon, the print is too small. Likewise, the woman watching a demonstration of a food preparation product on the manufacturer's website might remain confused about whether she can use the product to do what she needs because the video is too small or because she can't hear the cook, who is moving too fast, and there is no captioning available.

Technical communicators must refrain from approaching their audiences in a standardized and mechanistic manner, separate from relevant contexts; rather, they must write in a manner that best connects with their users' common sense, from a pragmatic perspective. This would involve using descriptive language to refer to user characteristics (and only those characteristics related to the context under consideration) rather than relying on disability labels. Rather than focusing solely on the audience, focus on situations. Consider how typical settings, materials, interactions, and tasks might be rethought and reorganized for success. Use scenarios, metaphors, and narratives to construct and promote a common sense and avoid barriers to successful everyday life. Scenarios turn a declarative sentence into action and situate it in context. Metaphors are easy to relate to. Narratives provide the opportunity for vicarious experience.

Far from being the charitable thing to do, this approach to technical communication is a matter of respect that promotes solution finding and the quality of everyday life for people who have disabilities as well as for everyone else. Because supercrips don't fly, efforts to develop and deliver information that are inclusive of the neighbors, workers, and volunteers who interact with the environment differently simply makes sense.

REFERENCES

Biklen, D., & Burke, J. (2006). Presuming competence. *Equity & Excellence in Education, 39*(2), 166–175.

Davis, L. (1995). *Enforcing normalcy: Disability, deafness, and the body*. New York, NY: Verso.

Foucault, M. (1969/1972). *The archaeology of knowledge*. (A. S. Smith, Trans.). New York, NY: Harper and Row. (Original work published 1969.)

Foucault, M. (1977). *Discipline and punish: The birth of the prison*. New York, NY: Pantheon.

Geertz, C. (1992). Common sense as a cultural system. *The Antioch Review, 50*, pp. 221–241.

Giddens, A. (1984). *The constitution of society*. Cambridge, MA: Polity Press.

Hall, S. (1997). The work of representation: Representation, meaning, and language. In S. Hall (Ed.), *Representation: Cultural representations and signifying practices*. London, UK: Sage Publications.

Haller, B. (2000). False Positive. *The ragged edge*. http://pages.towson.edu/bhalle/rag-article.html

Hulgin, K. M. (2004). Person-centered services and organizational context: Taking stock of working conditions and their impact. *Mental Retardation, 42*(3), 169–180.

Linton, S. (1998). *Claiming disability: Knowledge and identity*. Albany, NY: New York University Press.

Longmore, P., & Umansky, L. (Eds.). (2001). *The new disability history: American perspectives*. New York, NY: New York University Press.

Oliver, M. (1990). *The politics of disablement*. Basingstoke, UK: Macmillan.

Phillips, M. J. (1990). Damaged goods: The oral narratives of the experience of disability in American culture. *Social Science & Medicine, 30*(8), 849–857.

Praetorius, P. (2004). Technical communicators as purveyors of common sense. *Journal of Technical Writing and Communication, 32*, 337–351.

Shapiro, J. (1993). *No pity: People with disabilities forging a civil rights movement*. New York, NY: Crown Publishing Group.

Siebers, T. (2008). *Disability theory*. Ann Arbor, MI: University of Michigan Press.

Slee, R. (1993). The politics of integration—New sites for old practices. *Disability, Handicap & Society, 8*, 351–360.

Swain, J., & Cameron, J. (1999). Unless otherwise stated: Discourses of labeling and identity in coming out. In M. Corker & S. French (Eds.), *Disability discourse* (pp. 68–78). Buckingham, UK: Open University Press.

Titchkosky, T. (2007). *Reading and writing disability differently: The textured life of embodiment*. Toronto, Canada: University of Toronto Press.

Vico, G. (1990). On the study of methods of our time [Excerpt]. In P. Bizzell & B. Herzberg (Eds.), *The rhetorical tradition: Readings from classical times to the present* (pp. 711–727). Boston, MA: Bedford/St. Martin's.

Wilson, J. C. (2000). Making disability visible: How disability studies might transform the medical and science writing classroom. *Technical Communication Quarterly, 9*, 149–161.

Young, M. (1990). *Justice and the politics of difference*. Princeton, NJ: Princeton University Press.

http://dx.doi.org/10.2190/RAAC5

CHAPTER 5

The Care and Feeding of the D-Beast: Metaphors of the Lived Experience of Diabetes

Lora Arduser

Recent narrative research in medicine suggests that narratives can strengthen the patient-provider relationship (Pearson, McTigue, & Tarpley, 2008) and make providers more empathic (Charon, 2006). This research tends to focus on merging the singular experience of a patient's illness into generalized medical standards of care, but it also affords the opportunity for counter-narratives that present "an alternative voice from that offered in the standard biomedical account" (Hurwitz, Greenhalgh, & Skultans, 2004, p. 9). Narrative self-representations of people with disabilities and chronic diseases often challenge the more prominent narratives apparent in the medical community and media, and these acts empower people living with disabilities or illnesses in a way they cannot achieve in the narratives constructed by others on their behalf (Mitchell & Snyder, 2006; Sontag, 1978).

Two such counter-narratives can be found in the metaphors used in threaded discussions of an online diabetes social networking site. The first one is an alternate mapping of the much-used military metaphor. The second is the characterization of diabetes as a beast. In this chapter, I draw on critical metaphor analysis to analyze these metaphors and argue that, while the disease is still framed by the medical community's root metaphor of "control," these counter metaphors empower the members of the community.

Because these metaphors can help uncover the conceptual frameworks of people living with diabetes, understanding such patient-generated metaphors can give medical practitioners a clearer understanding of the lived experience of disease, which can lead to better patient care. From a disability studies perspective, paying attention to and understanding counter-narratives helps lessen the stigma associated with particular illnesses and disabilities (Couser, 2010; Linton, 2006). An attention to narratives constructed by disabled users also can move technical communicators closer to meeting goals of universal design and creating user-centered environments.

METAPHOR AND DISABILITY STUDIES

While metaphor's history as a linguistic device in poetry and prose is long and uncontested (Davis, 1992; Richards, 1936), more recently metaphors have been studied as concepts that help people understand things outside of a person's own direct experience (Baynton, 2006; Lakoff & Johnson, 1980). This movement led to the study of metaphors as being conceptual as well as linguistic (Lakoff & Johnson, 1980). Lakoff and Johnson's (1980) theory of conceptual metaphor relied on mapping one idea from a "source" domain of experience to another idea in a "target" domain. For example, in the metaphor DISEASE IS A WAR, the source domain is WAR and the target domain is DISEASE. By making this connection, the speaker creates the idea of disease for his or her audience as something that must be fought against and is possible to win against.

Searle (1979) and Black (1979) both focused on this role of the audience in their work with discourse metaphors. Discourse metaphors, unlike conceptual metaphors, are created through the interaction of speaker and audience and accepted by a group. Kovecses (2008) argued that Lakoff and Johnson (1980) portrayed metaphor construction as a straightforward, singular process within a culture. Such universality leads to common understanding, which was the ultimate goal of Lakoff and Johnson's theory. Kovecses (2008), on the other hand, defined culture as a more fractured concept that includes larger and smaller groups with shared understandings. Such a definition invites an analysis of metaphor in specific discourse. The metaphors created *for* people with disability or illness tend to try to express the experience of "other" and such representations "are more ugly than sublime, more degrading than elevating, more exploitative than consoling" and function to create "layers of stigma, rejection, fear, and exclusion that attach to particularly dreaded diseases" (Scheper-Hughes & Lock, 1986, p. 137).

Studying metaphors *in situ*, however, can create an environment in which self-constructed metaphors are valid self-representations rather than aberrations. This *in situ* approach addresses the need to center the disabled experience (Linton, 2006). Because these narratives are tales of power struggles over the language used to refer to disabilities and "have been used to arrange people in ways that are socially and economically convenient to the society" (Linton, 2006, p. 161), they can help move linguistic representations of self into the social realm and have empowering consequences (Siebers, 2006).

STUDY METHODS

The project[1] described in this chapter undertakes a critical analysis (Cameron & Low, 1999; Charteris-Black, 2004) of the metaphors embedded in the discourse of an online diabetes community called TuDiabetes (www.tudiabetes.org). Critical metaphor analysis attempts to "reveal covert (and possibly unconscious) intentions of language users" (Charteris-Black, 2004, p. 29) and has similar goals to both critical discourse analysis and disability studies in altering social order. Analysis generally starts from research questions that examine prevailing social problems (Zdenek & Johnstone, 2008) and highlights the perspective of "those who suffer most" (Van Dijk, 1986, p. 4). As such, it is seen as emancipatory.

Disability studies scholars also have argued that their work is designed to alter the social order and that this work takes place by reassigning the meaning attached to a term that has become "a linchpin in a complex web of social ideals, institutional structures, and government policies" (Linton, 2006, p. 162). One way to reassign meaning is through an analysis of text in which people with a disability or illness have taken control of their own representation by creating and choosing their own metaphors. Examining the metaphors they construct and use, rather than those constructed for them by the media or medical community, "re-constitutes the patient as a subject; that is as someone who has the sense of power to signify about his or her illness condition" (Radley, 1993, p. 121). Using metaphor as the unit of examination in critical discourse analysis examines how social order is altered through language use by identifying, interpreting, and explaining the metaphors being used. Identification is concerned with identifying whether a metaphor occurs in a text (Cameron & Low, 1999). Interpretation identifies the relationships between the source domain and the target domain, and explanation analyzes the way the metaphor takes on meaning within the situation it occurs (Charteris-Black, 2004).

The first phase—identification—was complicated for this study by three factors: the high level of activity on the TuDiabetes site, the fact that the site has no archive or site map, and, most importantly, the fact that any word could be a metaphor (Charteris-Black, 2004, p. 35). To begin the identification phase of analysis, I first used the general site search tool to look for the following metaphors: battle, war, storm, and journey. Battle, war, and storm were derived

---

[1] This project was classified as exempt by the University of Cincinnati IRB. The author has worked in consultation with the site organizer and founder, Manny Hernandez, on a number of research projects related to the website.

from Hanne and Hawken's (2007) research on metaphors used for illness in feature stories published in *The New York Times* from September 1, 2005, to May 31, 2006. These metaphors are often used in the news media for diabetes. The journey motif was added because it appears in diabetes educational literature. After deleting texts that used these words literally, I examined 824 texts containing these metaphors that were posted between July 2009 and December 2010. In the process of re-reading the texts in the analysis phase, I also added one more keyword—beast—and its synonym—monster—when it became apparent these terms were a metaphor in the community. This metaphor appeared in 136 texts, bringing the total number of texts analyzed to 960.

Because it is possible for any word to be a metaphor, for the second stage of analysis—interpretation—I followed the principle that a word has to be in a context that has semantic tension or incongruity to be considered a metaphor (Charteris-Black, 2004). To interpret the metaphors in the threaded discussions, I follow the mappings of the source and target domains by examining the metaphors in the context in which they were embedded. For example, in the texts I examined, "war" was often used in reference to the wars in Iraq or Afghanistan. Similarly, "storm" often appeared in the context of literal weather events, and "journeys" sometimes referred to trips and vacations. Examining this context made it clear if these words were being used in their literal sense or as a metaphor for the experience of living with diabetes.

In this stage of analysis I was also able to identify a common root metaphor by employing a simple concordance software program. Concordance software is a qualitative text analysis tool most typically used in discourse analysis to compare the incidence of key words, but it also can be used to examine the linguistic context in which words appear and, therefore, can be helpful in uncovering themes that may be "hidden from view in an ordinary reading of the text" (Seale, 2003, p. 305).

The third stage of critical metaphor analysis—metaphor explanation—requires the researcher to identify the discourse function of metaphors. These functions establish metaphors' ideological and rhetorical motivation and are drawn from evidence within the text (Charteris-Black, 2004). For this stage of analysis, I limited my analysis to one particular new mapping for the metaphor DIABETES IS WAR and one new metaphor, DIABETES IS A BEAST.

METAPHORS IN A DIABETES ONLINE COMMUNITY

The term *online community* has a variety of meanings, but for this chapter, an online health community is defined as "a group of individuals with similar or common health related interests and predominantly non-professional backgrounds (patients, healthy consumers, or informal caregivers) that interact and communicate publicly through a computer communication network" (Eysenbach,

Powell, Englesakis, Rizo, & Stern, 2004). According to the Pew Internet & American Life Project, 86% of Internet users living with disability or chronic illness have looked online for information (Fox, 2007), and those with chronic conditions are more likely than other e-patients (Internet users who have looked online for health information) to report that their online searches affected treatment decisions, their interactions with their doctors, their ability to cope with their condition, and their dieting and fitness regimen (Fox, 2008).

As of July 31, 2009, when this case study was undertaken, the TuDiabetes online community had 10,189 members from around the world. As of December 4, 2010, this number had grown to 17,755. Members include people with type 1, type 2, type 1.5, and gestational diabetes as well as friends and family members of people with the disease (often referred to on the site as type 3s). Along with being a large community, TuDiabetes is an active one. Table 1 shows the activity on two of the major areas of interaction on the site: discussion forums and blogs. Discussion threads on the forums generate anywhere from zero to 11,870 responses. A comparison of the numbers of threads or topics added within a single week illustrates a level of consistent activity on the site.

IDENTIFICATION: METAPHORS USED IN THE COMMUNITY

The identification stage of analysis uncovered metaphors that have been used by the media to refer to illness as well as a new metaphor for diabetes—the beast (see Table 2). Since Sontag's (1978) essay about her own cancer experience was published, most metaphors used for illness in the media have not changed. For example, at the time of her writing, the language of cancer treatment evolved from military metaphors. In 2009, Williams Camus found that among the 15 conceptual metaphors he examined in 37 articles from *The Guardian,* the most frequent was CANCER IS WAR. Over time we have seen a change in what Sontag (1978) called the "master illnesses" (p. 72), however. Hanne and Hawken's (2007) study of metaphors, for example, concluded that while metaphoric constructions of the diseases Sontag wrote of (cancer and HIV/AIDS) still appear, they attract "far fewer, and less alarmist, metaphors" (p. 94) than those used in the articles they analyzed from *The New York Times* about avian flu and diabetes.

Within medical discourse about chronic illness, metaphors have tended to focus on three primary constructions: the body as a machine (Lupton, 2003; Segal, 2005), the warfare/military metaphor (Lupton, 2003; Segal, 1997), and medicine as business (Segal, 1997). Specifically within diabetes care, metaphors often tend to characterize the disease as a journey as well. One example of this metaphor is in Conversation Maps, an educational tool produced by Merck Pharmaceuticals as a part of the U.S. Diabetes Conversation Map® Program (Merck, 2010). In educational sessions that use these maps, educators act as

Table 1. Number of Discussion Forum Topics
and Blog Posts

Discussion forums	Nov. 27, 2010	Dec. 4, 2010
General Diabetes Topics	3144	3186
Introduce Yourself	67	68
Type 1 Diabetes Forum	2984	3005
Type 2 Diabetes Forum	966	970
Insulin Pump Users Forum	1150	1150
LADA (Type 1.5) Diabetes Forum	114	114
New to Diabetes?	749	749
Free, Unused, Non-Expired, Non-Prescription Diabetes Supplies	16	16
Continuous Glucose Monitoring Forum	402	402
Foods, Recipes, and Eating Habits for Diabetics	450	450
Pre-Diabetes Forum	34	34
Treatment, Cure	343	343
Children with Diabetes Forum	131	131
Diabetes News Forum	424	424
Gestational Diabetes, Diabetes and Pregnancy	20	20
Type 3 Diabetes Forum	16	16
Diabetes, Sports, and Fitness Forum	110	110
Alternative Ways of Treating Diabetes	37	37
TuDiabetes Tech Questions	94	94
TuDiabetes News	285	287
Community Games, Other Topics	54	54
Blog Posts	9146	9185

facilitators. Patients use a themed game board, much like the well-known board game *The Game of Life*, to generate discussion and educate each other. The National Diabetes Education Program (NDEP) also offers the *Road to Health Toolkit Training Guide*, training material designed to help train-the-trainer workshops, specifically workshops that train people to work with patients with Hispanic/Latino or African American/African ancestry (NDEP, 2010).

Table 2. Metaphors Used in the TuDiabetes Community[a]

Metaphor	Number	Examples
War	78	"Diabetes is all out war . . . there is no such thing as winning too much."
		"For me it is anything that fits in the category of dessert! I have a really bad sweet tooth. I can usually control myself but for the most part I am a full time soldier fighting in the Sugar Wars! Ice Cream is my worst enemy. That is why I must keep it the closest! (insert evil laughter here.)"
		"I see you were diagnosed in 75. I was diagnosed in 73. Got any old war stories you want to share?"
Journey[b]	644[b]	"Welcome to tudiabetes . . . Here you will find a lot going on as I have for over two years now lots of friends and support. You have joined the right site, enjoy your journey with us."
		"Thankyou! I just started my journey on taking Humalog this month. It is definitely much easier than I thought. I feel this is a message that needs to go far."
Storm	24	"My heart goes out to your niece and all children with chronic conditions such as diabetes . . . it's 24/7 . . . 365/12. Diabetes NEVER takes a break . . . even asleep, it keeps on going and going. It looms over you like a threatening storm cloud."
		"My future feels bright enough for shades, but I think I should bring along an umbrella because a storm may be a-brewing."
Beast/Monster	136	"There is no reason for it and at times it can be frustrating. We blame it on the nature of the beast and we just try to do our best. Stay strong, and confident in yourself."
		"Good thread – makes me remember that I am in control of this beast."
		"But I think of it as a monster, always waiting to pull the rug out from under me when I am least suspecting, and then, while I'm down on the floor, kicking me in the face just to see me suffer. I am always on guard. I test 8-10 times a day [...]"

[a]All text from the TuDiabetes site is depicted as written on the site. I did not make any changes or corrections except to delete names.
[b]217 of these were sent from one person as a welcome message to new members.

Interpretation: The Root Metaphor of Control

Although these metaphors have various source domains, Table 3 shows that the target domain of all the metaphors is the experience of living with diabetes. Interestingly, except for certain mappings of the war metaphor and the beast metaphor, all of these metaphors are also directly linked to a root metaphor entrenched in the medical community—control. Root metaphors refer to the common-sense way in which we experience and understand any life event (Pepper, 1942). In the interactions people with diabetes have with the medical world, control is an explanatory concept (or metaphor) and is generally regarded as common sense by medical researchers and practitioners (Pendry, 2003). The prevalence of the language of control in diabetes medical discourse may partially explain this perception. A search on the key words "diabetes AND control" in PubMed, for example, resulted in 95,404 hits. The concept of control is also extensive in patient education materials like the NDEP's diabetes education campaign, which is called Control Your Diabetes. For Life. Publications used in this campaign include *4 Steps to Control Your Diabetes. For Life, Be Smart About Your Heart: Control the ABCs of Diabetes*, and *The Power to Control Diabetes Is in Your Hands* (NDEP, 2008).

This root metaphor also filters into the TuDiabetes community: a search on the key word "control" results in 18,120 hits. For the members of the TuDiabetes community, the metaphor mappings imply that diabetes (the storm, the war, the beast, the journey) must be controlled. For the war metaphor, control is established through winning. Storms and floods are characterized as unpredictable and, therefore, uncontrollable. The beast is something that needs to be beaten, tamed, or caged to be controlled. The journey metaphor mappings are more subtle, relating to being in charge of the journey or having a specific path or destiny to reach. The war metaphor mapping to comrades in arms and all of the beast metaphor mappings, however, do not tie directly to the root metaphor of control. As such, they work outside the dominant discourse of the medical community and can work as empowering metaphors.

Table 3. Source and Target Domains of Metaphors

Source	Mappings	Target
War	Comrades in arms, adversaries, winning	Diabetes lived experience
Journey	Personal odyssey or pilgrimage	Diabetes lived experience
Storm	Unpredictable, impeding	Diabetes lived experience
Beast/ Monster	Wildness, animate, need for control, adversary	Diabetes lived experience

SHARING WAR STORIES

By shifting from looking at metaphors in isolation to examining metaphors in the discourse events between the members of a community, metaphors can be seen as empowering. This empowerment emerges in a new mapping for DIABETES IS WAR, but it is most apparent in the emergence of the beast as a metaphor for diabetes (discussed in the next section). Military metaphors in the media typically focus on the battle taking place between the person (and/or society in general) and the disease (Hanne & Hawken, 2007). While war and military metaphors are less often used in diabetes education, when they are, the metaphors map much the same. The New York City Department of Health and Mental Hygiene (2009), for example, consistently uses the phrase "beat diabetes" (NYCDHMH, 2009) in its educational literature. Although many of the posts on TuDiabetes echo the war metaphor in the outside community as a "call to arms," 14 of the 78 occurrences of the war metaphor specifically use the phrase "war stories." Rather than being a call to arms, this metaphor functions as a call for stories. For example, one member started a discussion thread that told the tale of a hospital experience in which the medical staff was portrayed as less than knowledgeable about the disease than the writer:

> [...]I woke, 4 nurses, (one of the pretty ones) and two doctors were scream-ing at the top of their lungs. . . . CAN YOU HEAR ME . . . COME ON . . . WAKE UP. . . . The light in my eyes hurt but I opened them anyway, groggy as hell, wondering what the heck had happened ? . . . I can hear you just fine W-H-Y are you yelling at me. . . ? ? ? "the doctor talking to the nurse at the doorway cancel the code . . . he'll be fine. . . . One of the nurses stayed [and] wiped me down with a washcloth, my arm, gown covered in blood where they had jamned the IV in hard and fast. She helped me with a fresh gown, watching my eyes . . . you back to us hon and smiled relieved. It was a stupid question, but she meant well. Yeah . . . I said pausing not wanting to be angry at her I'm ok NEXT TIME make sure you eat all your greenbeans so this won't happen again.

As the person closed this posting, the person invited other members to share similar tales: "Anyone else have a war story from their recent or ancient past?" It generated 16 similar tales in which hospital or medical care was characterized as incompetent and other more general comments like the following:

> 1. That's really scary that nowadays doctors don't know what to do with us. I understand there are so many diseases out there, but if you're coherent, can't they call your regular doctor's office to send over your prescription dosages? I mean for them to ASSUME that they know our bodies better than WE do is just absurd.
> 2. It just amazes me how stupid some of these hospitals can be.

These stories are not about conquering the disease. They are about people empowered by knowledge of their embodied disease so the battle that rages is one between the expert patient and the uninformed in the medical community. The characterization of war as story also gives people a voice by inviting them to tell their tale, and in the telling of it they gain power. As a call for stories, this particular metaphoric mapping functions much like traditional print illness narratives. Patients' personal narratives, specifically, are seen as giving voice to suffering in a way that lies outside the domain of the biomedical voice: "narratives have gained importance in the study of chronic illness as a means for understanding the attempts of patients to deal with their life situations and, above all, with the problems of identity that chronic illness brings with it" (Hyden, 1997, p. 49). To better understand different situations, Hyden (1997) provided three narrative categories: illness as narrative, narrative about illness, and narrative as illness.

In the first type of narrative, the narrator, the illness, and the story are combined into one entity. This allows the person to integrate disease into a new whole that is a new social reality. In the second type, the narrative is basically about the illness—a way to communicate knowledge about the illness. In the third type (the narrative as illness), a narrative generates the illness. Hyden (1997) offered the example of a patient with a brain injury that hinders the person's ability to use narrative as a way to connect experiences with particular events. The war stories in the current patient community fall into the first category: integrating disease into a new whole that is a new social reality. In other words, by switching the mappings of the metaphor source and target domains from adversary to comrade, the people in the community are forming a social order that can empower by the sheer force of numbers. One component of disability oppression is its psychological internalization; it "creates a (false) consciousness and alienation that divides people and isolates individuals" (Charlton, 2006, p. 220). The building of an army of comrades, therefore, works against this oppression.

THE BEAST

Unlike the war metaphor, the beast metaphor does not appear in news accounts of the diabetes experience. Furthermore, except for one video game in development (Cowen, 2009), the beast does not seem to appear in diabetes educational efforts. Within the particular community at hand, this new metaphor, which appeared 136 times in the analyzed texts, maps to three characteristics of a beast or monster: as an adversary, as a natural state, and as a living being.

Friend or Foe?

In many of the texts, the adversarial role of the beast is tied to the root metaphor of control, but this community sees control less as the traditional struggle between doctor and patient for power and more as a struggle with the disease itself. In these texts the beast may be equated to a person's blood sugar levels, which people with diabetes must control in their daily lives, and yet, as the following examples from the community show, the beast is discussed as an exterior object rather than a beast "within." The bold words in the following examples are my emphasis.

1. [I] am **in control of this beast**. I can give in if I want, but I've never wanted to.
2. [...]we all need to get into the cage with **the beast** and **take control**.
3. We felt that it was the best way of **gaining** some type of **control** over **this beast of an illness**.
4. **The beast** is a lot easier **to manage**.
5. [...]Browse my diabetes info page for more tips on **keeping the beast at bay**.
6. [...]But I've changed my ways and have **taken** almost complete control over **this beast**.
7. [...]I still can't get **this beast under** any sort of **control**.
8. [...]Sounds like you're doing a super job at getting this D-beast under control.
9. [...]You've done a fantastic job **getting** your diabetes **"beast" under great control**.
10. There are a few parents who really know how **to tame the D-beast**, though they use cgms.
11. [...]Seriously though; the pills are like eating flavored chalk, and sometimes the need to chew something other than a hardened hockey puck is what it takes **to calm the savage beast!**

Example 2 provides the most concrete example of the beast being external as the person enters the same physical space as the beast. The use of the words *this* and *the* (rather than *my*) to describe the beast in these examples also indicates a distance between the person living with the disease and the disease. While this mapping of the beast functions within the control discourse of the medical community, this distancing has the effect of moving ownership of the disease from the individual to the community. As such, this mapping functions in a similar way as the war stories mapping and is empowering by being a shared experience.

Another adversarial relationship uncovered in the community is one between the beast and children with diabetes. A total of 13 posts with the beast metaphor come from parents about their children with type 1 diabetes. In a study with children with asthma and children with type 1, or insulin-dependent, diabetes, Clark (2004) found that when children with diabetes were shown various pictures and asked to sort them according to whether or not they related to the disease, the children with diabetes repeatedly compared insulin shots to "the sting of a bee, the bite of a spider, the scary feeling of lightning, the boom of a bomb, or a mean, bad witch who does harm" (p. 177). The beast also has the potential to bite and, therefore, cause pain. While words of war might do this as well, children better understand the bite of an animal, and this may be why the beast/monster metaphor appears in forums of parents discussing their type 1 diabetic children.

This adversarial mapping is also tied to the root metaphor of control, but in this case it is the parent who feels guilt over not being able to control the disease, as the following examples illustrate.

1. When my son was a small child he sometimes worried that there might be a monster under his bed. I could easily chase those fears away for him back then . . . but now . . . the monster sleeps with him at night and there is nothing I can do because that monster is his Diabetes. As a parent it is very hard to face the guilt knowing there is nothing I can do to make that horrible monster go away!

2. Diabetes is the monster that drives with him in his car and goes to work with him every day. Diabetes is the monster that attends college classes with him during the week. Diabetes is the monster that celebrates birthdays with him every year. Diabetes is the monster that will attend his wedding one day and be with him on the day his first child is born. Diabetes is the monster he fears will make acquaintances with his children and grandchildren one day.

These posts indicate that the parents feel helpless to protect their children from the diabetes monster. Here control is defined as banishment of the beast rather than controlling blood sugar levels.

The Nature of the Beast

Along with being an adversary, the beast metaphor maps to the disease through its unpredictable nature. According to the medical community, "the only currently 'reasonable' ethical response to life with diabetes is compliance" (Martins, 2005). And while the lived experience of diabetes indicates that compliance with medical advice does not always result in good blood sugar levels, people internalize noncompliance as bad behavior, creating a spoiled identity in which they begin to morally judge themselves as bad. (Peel, Parry, Douglas, & Lawton, 2005, p. 785). In other words, to be in control denotes power and agency, while being out of control signals chaos, madness, and moral failing (Broom & Whittaker, 2004, p. 2381). As the following excerpt from a post on the TuDiabetes site illustrates, wild beasts, like blood sugar levels and unlike pets, do not always come when they are called.

[...] There is no reason for it and at times it can be frustrating. We blame it on the nature of the beast and we just try to do our best. Stay strong, and confident in yourself. Continue to fight for your future. Keep your parents involved with your care. They are your biggest cheerleaders. They want you to stay healthy and will give you the support/help you need. I know there will be some day where I will have to give more responsibility to my daughter, but I will be there for her when ever she might need me. This is a great site to join and I wish you the best.

Still, other messages indicate that a mapping to the nature of the beast also embodies a sense of something akin to acceptance. One of the more interesting markers of acceptance on the TuDiabetes site is the "pet names" for diabetes.

1. That's a fun name Diabeasty. i like that. i will use it the next time the beast comes out!
2. Thanks for the invite. Sounds like you're doing a super job at getting this D-beast under control. Fantastic.

The first excerpt shows the beast as something internal to the person that "comes out." Although this internalization might seem contradictory to the externalization of the disease, both mappings are, in fact, empowering. Internalization may suggest acceptance, and the acceptance of the beast provides empowerment in a different way than the constructions of controlling the beast. Knowing and accepting the disease as unpredictable many times empowers people to adjust as needed rather than just adhere to a simple, straight-forward treatment regime handed to them from a medical provider. Accepting the beast's changeable nature also enables people living with diabetes to transfer blame from themselves for not always being able to maintain control over their blood sugar levels, as the following examples show.

1. Then we must stay up to check the correction. There are many times when a correction does NOT correct her highs and she needs a massive temp basal. It is the nature of the beast during this time of life. There are nights with a 200 percent plus temp basal (yes, we tried changing the site) when she will not come down from said highs. So, no we don't get much sleep. I'll sleep when I'm dead, LOL.
2. I asked the diabetic educator why this would happen. She said that if it wasn't anything listed above that maybe there was a bubble in the syringe, maybe the site of the injection played a part, or sometimes there is no answer. She said Sometimes it's just the nature of the beast! Diabetes . . . IT IS A BEAST!!

Because the medical community's focus on compliance has given rise to noncompliance being associated with being a "bad person" (Peel et al., 2005), identity and social relationships are often discussed in terms of the contradictory language of control, responsibility, and morality (Broom & Whittaker, 2004).

Such language has a moral dimension that both "acknowledges and distances the speaker from the potentially discredited identity of diabetes" (Broom & Whittaker, 2004, p. 2372). In the first example above, a post from a parent with a type 1 child, the writer distances this morality by placing "blame" on normal growth process. In the statement "It is the nature of the beast during this time of life," the parent shifts blame away from both parent and child for not doing what they "should" to control high blood sugars and toward the connection between the biological changes of a child's growth pattern and the high numbers. The second example provides a less tangible explanation for high blood sugar numbers, but after going through several possible reasons, the educator notes that there is not always a one-to-one correlation between a person's actions and the resulting blood sugar numbers. As such, the educator removes blame from the patient.

Caring for the Beast

The final way DIABETES IS A BEAST metaphor is expressed relates to the beast as a living creature. As a living being, the beast requires not only taming or controlling but feeding and care. This mapping is linked to the importance of managing and balancing food as a part of treatment in diabetes. Diabetes treatment relies heavily on diet and food regimens. In fact, prior to the development of insulin in the 1920s, treatment for the disease was limited to dietary therapy that resembles many of today's low carbohydrate diets. These therapies produced a semi-starved state, which typically ended in "coma, infection or starvation" (Feudtner, 2003, p. 6). While the metaphor "starve the beast" is most typically applied to a particular political strategy that uses budget deficits to try to force reductions in government expenditure (Bartlett, 2007), it is certainly applicable in historical diabetes treatment as well.[2] Therefore, in the metaphors people with the disease use, it is logical that food would be a feature. On the TuDiabetes site, this link is often made in terms of the person being a specific type of monster related to a food they like but "shouldn't" eat (e.g., cookie monster or pizza monster).

Other uses of the beast are empowering as well. Since diabetes cannot be cured, it requires constant attention and monitoring—like a living creature or a beast. It is through this action of caring that empowerment occurs. The following post from one parent with a diabetic child to another illustrates the constant care, management, and feeding of "the beast." The bold words in the following excerpt are my emphasis.

[2] Another interesting historical connection is that earlier insulins (prior to 1976) were derived from the pancreases of animals, usually pigs or cows. (Today insulin is produced from synthetic sources.)

1. I truly don't know exactly what you are going through, but I am the mother of a four year old who has type 1 diabetes. I can give you the run down on how we manage her diabetes.

2. First, I did and still do a lot of **researching** on the subject of type 1. There are so many new medical technologies out there that I have been learning about. She was diagnosed when she was two years old and already we have gone through three different types of insulin.

3. We also **give** multiple daily injections (MDIs).—she gets between 4–6 a day, but we usually give her injections 15–20 minutes before she eats—that is supposed to really help! Of course if she is low, then we feed her right away. We also rotate the sites of injection so the insulin gets absorbed better, but the little bugger still won't let us near her tummy!!

4. We **check** her blood sugar before breakfast, before lunch, before afternoon snack, before dinner, before bedtime, at midnight, and at three o'clock in the morning. (7:30 am, 11:30 am, 2:30 pm, 5:30 pm, 9:00 pm, 12:00 am, 3:00 am) If her number is high we do an insulin correction. We also check before and after any exercise.

5. We also **count** carbs and follow an insulin to carb ratio (for example she gets 1 unit of insulin for every 20 grams of carbs). To help with this we weigh/measure out most of her food.

6. We try to **have her eat** around the same time each day (give or take a ½ hour).

7. We **try to eat** a low fat diet (but on occasion we splurge—still got to let her be a kid :)

8. We **check** her urine for ketones every day.

9. **Joined** Tudiabetes, ChildrenwithDiabetes, and Type1parents, websites to also look for support, advice, education.

10. We try to **make sure** that she does something active each day (**exercise**).

11. We **log** all of her numbers, how many carbs she eats, and also how much insulin she receives. You can really see if there are any trends (when the high and lows are occurring). We use Microsoft excel to make a simple chart.

12. We are in **constant communication** with our endocrinologist (and diabetes educator). We send her numbers (log sheet) to Pittsburgh Children's Hospital every couple of weeks. We also visit there every three months for blood work and the A1C result.

While managing food is an important part of living with diabetes, one of the reasons the beast metaphor is used is because it is a concrete embodiment of all the other care tasks—the researching, recording, checking, and communicating—that go into these daily activities of the lived experience of diabetes. Compare the tasks above with those a person might do if he or she is going to get a dog. For example, he or she might research (1) before deciding on a breed. When the dog comes home, the owner gives the dog food and baths (2). The owner checks its fur for fleas (3 and 7) and measures its daily food (4). A routine is created for the animal (5), and food is purchased that meets its calorie requirements, puppy or senior dog food, for example (6). The owner may join an obedience school (8). The owner walks the dog (9) and monitors its daily activities (10). When necessary, the owner takes the dog to the vet (11). In other words, rather than seeing the disease as something to fight against, the mapping of the beast to a living creature makes it something to care for and own.

CONCLUSION

With its use of a war metaphor and the mapping of the beast to the root metaphor of control, the TuDiabetes community seems to embody its disease in terms of metaphors the diabetes health care community has used for decades. A critical metaphor analysis of the metaphors within the discourse of this community, however, shows the metaphors are empowering. Unlike the characterization of the disease as a war with an adversary, the metaphor of comrades in arms of a war empowers members of this community through shared experience. The beast, unlike any of the metaphors used in the media or medical community, is a living thing and therefore a concrete embodiment of the experience of diabetes. Unlike the other recurring metaphors that suggest an end to the struggle—the flood can be dammed, the storm will pass, the journey will end, and the war will be won—the beast lives and continues to need care and feeding.

Although the metaphors that resonate in this specific online community may not be able to be generalized across the entire patient population, additional work into metaphors created by patient communities outside of the context of the patient-provider encounter could lead to additional opportunities to learn how such peer communities understand their diseases. Such understanding also has ramifications in the technical communication field and disability studies. Paying attention to language generated and used by a patient community can help technical communicators develop more appropriate and useful educational and instructional materials. From a disability studies perspective, patient generated metaphors illustrate the empowerment belonging to such a community can generate.

REFERENCES

Bartlett, B. (2007). "Starve the beast" origins and development of a budgetary metaphor. *Independent Review*. Retrieved from http://www.independent.org/publications/tir/article.asp?issueID=50&articleID=641

Baynton, D. (2006). "A silent exile on this earth": The metaphorical construction of deafness. In L. J. Davis (Ed.), *The disability studies reader* (pp. 33–48). New York, NY: Taylor & Francis Group.

Black, M. (1979). More about metaphor. In A. Ortony (Ed.), *Metaphor and thought* (pp. 19–43). Cambridge, MA: Cambridge University Press.

Broom, D., & Whittaker, A. (2004). Controlling diabetes, controlling diabetics: Moral language in the management of diabetes type 2. *Social Science & Medicine, 58*, 2372–2382.

Cameron, L., & Low, G. (1999). *Researching and applying metaphor*. Cambridge, MA: Cambridge University Press.

Charlton, J. I. (2006). The dimensions of disability oppression. In L. J. Davis (Ed.), *The disability studies reader* (pp. 217–227). New York, NY: Taylor & Francis Group.

Charon, R. (2006). *Narrative medicine: Honoring the stories of illness*. Oxford, UK: Oxford University Press.

Charteris-Black, J. (2004). *Corpus approaches to critical metaphor analysis*. New York, NY: Palgrave Macmillan.

Clark, C. D. (2004). Visual metaphor as method in interviews with children. *Journal of Linguistic Anthropology, 14*(2), 171–185.

Couser, T. (2010). What disability studies has to offer medical education. *Journal of Medical Humanities, 32*(1), 21–30. doi: 10.1007/s10912-010-9125-1

Cowen, D. (2009, April 21). Game Equals Life announces diabetes awareness adventure game. Game Career Guide. Retrieved from http://www.gamecareerguide.com/industry_news/23309/game_equals_life_announces_.php

Davis, M. (1992). *Aristotle's poetics: The poetry of philosophy*. Lanham, MD: Rowman & Littlefield Publishers.

Eysenbach, G., Powell, J., Englesakis, M., Rizo, C., & Stern, A. (2004). Health related virtual communities and electronic support groups: Systematic review of the effects of online peer to peer interactions. *British Medical Journal, 328*(7449), 1166.

Feudtner, C. (2003). *Bittersweet: Diabetes, insulin, and the transformation of illness*. Chapel Hill, NC: University of North Carolina Press.

Fox, S. (2007, October 8). E-patients with a disability or chronic disease. Pew Internet & American Life Project. Retrieved from http://www.pewinternet.org/Reports/2007/Epatients-With-a-Disability-or-Chronic-disease.aspx

Fox, S. (2008, August 26). The engaged e-patient population: People turn to the Internet for health information when the stakes are high and the connection fast. Pew Internet & American Life Project. Retrieved from http://www.pewinternet.org/Reports/2008/The-Engaged-Epatient-Population.aspx

Hanne, M., & Hawken, S. J. (2007). Metaphors for illness in contemporary media. *Medical Humanities, 33*(2), 93–99.

Hurwitz, B., Greenhalgh, T., & Skultans, V. (2004). *Narrative research in health and illness*. San Francisco, CA: Blackwell Publishing.

Hyden, L. (1997). Illness and narrative. *Sociology of Health & Illness, 19*(1), 48–69.

Kovecses, Z. (2008). Conceptual metaphor theory: Some criticisms and alternative proposals. *Annual Review of Cognitive Linguistics, 6*, 168–184.

Lakoff, G., & Johnson, M. (1980). *Metaphors we live by*. Chicago, IL: University of Chicago Press.

Linton, S. (2006). Reassigning meaning. In L. J. Davis (Ed.), *The disability studies reader* (pp. 161–172). New York, NY: Taylor & Francis Group.

Lupton, D. (2003). *Medicine as culture*. London, UK: Sage Publications.

Martins, D. S. (2005). Compliance rhetoric and the impoverishment of context. *Communication Theory, 15*(1), 59–77. doi: 10.1111/j.1468-2885.2005.tb00326.x

Merck. (2010). Conversation Map® Program. Retrieved from http://www.journeyfor control.com/journey_for_control/journeyforcontrol/for_educators/conversation_maps/index.jsp

Mitchell, D., & Snyder, S. (2006). Narrative prosthesis and the materiality of metaphor. In L. J. Davis (Ed.), *The disability studies reader* (pp. 205–216). New York, NY: Taylor & Francis Group.

National Diabetes Education Program (NDEP). (2008). National Diabetes Education Program. Retrieved from http://www.ndep.nih.gov

National Diabetes Education Program (NDEP). (2010). *The road to health toolkit training guide*. Retrieved from http://www.ndep.nih.gov/publications/Publication Detail.aspx?PubId=164

New York City Department of Health and Mental Hygiene. (2009). Diabetes prevention and control. Retrieved from http://www.nyc.gov/html/doh/html/diabetes/diabetes.shtml

Pearson, A. S., McTigue, M. P., & Tarpley, J. L. (2008). Narrative medicine in surgical education. *Journal of Surgical Education, 65*(2), 99–100.

Peel, E., Parry, O., Douglas, M., & Lawton, J. (2005). Taking the biscuit? A discursive approach to managing diet in type 2 diabetes. *Journal of Health Psychology, 10*, 779–791.

Pendry, D. A. (2003). Control, compliance, and common sense: Power relations in diabetes care for Mexican Americans [Unpublished doctoral dissertation]. Austin, TX: University of Texas. Retrieved from the University of Texas digital library.

Pepper, S. C. (1942). *World hypotheses: A study in evidence*. Berkeley, CA: University of California Press.

Radley, A. (1993). The role of metaphor in adjustment to chronic illness. In A. Radley (Ed.), *Worlds of illness: Biographical and cultural perspectives on health and disease* (pp. 109–123). London, UK: Routledge.

Richards, I. A. (1936). *The philosophy of rhetoric*. Oxford, UK: Oxford University Press.

Scheper-Hughes, N., & Lock, M. (1986). Speaking "truth" to illness: Metaphors, reification, and a pedagogy for patients. *Medical Anthropology Quarterly, 17*(5), 137–140.

Seale, C. (Ed.). (2003). *Social research methods: A reader*. London, UK: Routledge.

Searle, J. R. (1979). Metaphor. In A. Ortony (Ed.), *Metaphor and thought* (pp. 92–123). Cambridge, MA: Cambridge University Press.

Segal, J. Z. (1997). Public discourse and public policy: Some ways that metaphor constrains health (care). *Journal of Medical Humanities, 18*(4), 217–231.

Segal, J. Z. (2005). *Health and the rhetoric of science*. Carbondale, IL: Southern Illinois University Press.

Siebers, T. (2006). Disability in theory: From social constructivism to the new realism of the body. In L. J. Davis (Ed.), *The disability studies reader* (pp. 173–184). New York, NY: Taylor & Francis Group.

Sontag, S. (1978). *Illness as metaphor*. New York, NY: Farrar, Straus, and Giroux.

Van Dijk, T. A. (1986). *Racism in the press*. London, UK: Arnold.

Williams Camus, J. T. (2009). Metaphors of cancer in scientific popularization articles in the British press. *Discourse Studies, 11*(4), 465–495.

Zdenek, S., & Johnstone, B. (2008). Studying style and legitimation: Critical linguistics and critical discourse analysis. In B. Johnstone & C. Eisenhart (Eds.), *Rhetoric in detail: Discourse analyses of rhetorical talk and text* (pp. 25–32). Philadelphia, PA: John Benjamins.

http://dx.doi.org/10.2190/RAAC6

CHAPTER 6

Accessibility and the Web Design Student

Elizabeth Pass

Located in the Shenandoah Valley within easy driving distance to Washington, DC, James Madison University draws both graduates and undergraduates, many of whom will seek employment in the Washington, DC, and northern Virginia area. One of my primary teaching responsibilities is to teach web design courses—primarily for students who aspire to be web designers or web project managers. The majority of these students come with backgrounds in literature, communication, business, health science, and computer science; therefore, they have little training in design or in thinking about accessibility issues on the web. In order to help them overcome this deficiency, I learned some time ago that I needed to include a significant concentration on design and accessibility, especially as they relate one to another. Now I expect effective accessibility design as a part of all the projects and so I teach it throughout every project stage.

As a part of teaching students more about actual applications of accessibility design, I did a study of the Kindle 2 to see if the students themselves preferred reading and working in a print environment or an e-book environment. I wanted to find if design *and* accessibility impact students' preference for a print or electronic medium for classroom work and wanted to give the students the experience of approaching a technology with which they themselves may have some disability. Describing this exercise and my own definition of *disability*, this chapter focuses on how I teach accessibility in web design classes, how I define *disability*, and what I expect in effective accessibility design.

115

As I will explain later, where I differ from other web design teachers is in how I define *disability*. In my opinion, a disability involves any diminished capability in a person's ability to perform a given task. The research with the Kindle 2 clearly showed both me and my students that a broader definition is necessary. Students themselves showed that design *and* accessibility directly impact their capability.

DEFINITIONS

The Americans with Disabilities Act (ADA) of 1990, Section 508 of the Workforce Investment Act of 1998, and even the World Wide Web Consortium's (W3C) Web Accessibility Initiative (WAI) define a *disability* as people with auditory, cognitive, neurological, physical, speech, and visual impairments (http://www.w3.org/WAI/users/Overview.html). Accessibility is legally mandated by Section 508 of the ADA (see chapters 10 and 11 for additional information).

The "Web-based intranet and internet information and applications" of Section 508 covers what the web developer needs to do when creating or revising a website to make it Section 508 compliant (http://www.section508.gov/index. cfm?fuseAction=stdsdoc#Web). These guidelines are basic in comparison to the W3C's WAI. The difference between the Section 508 guidelines and the WAI guidelines is that the WAI guidelines are more dynamic and more detailed. The WAI works with the basic web as well as the more advanced web technologies.

The ADA, thus, would seem to go with Section 508 above. It states that new public and private business construction must be generally accessible. It goes on to say that existing private businesses are required to increase the access-ibility of their facilities when making any other renovations in proportion to the cost of the other renovations. In other words, people with disabilities must be able to have access to documents (electronic and print) and buildings, and accommodation must be made if the same access cannot be provided. For example, for websites there may be two different websites, one in Flash and one in ADA-compliant XHTML, or in the case of an historic public building with steps to the main entrance and no room for a ramp, there may be a sign to a different entrance that is accessible.

Most of the literature in the discipline of technical communication either skips over the definition of *disability*, focusing on accessibility and assuming the reader will presume the legal definition of the term by referring to W3C's WAI or Section 508 web standards. Or the literature specifies adherence to the legal definition of the term (Adam & Kreps, 2009; Clark, 2008; Johansson, 2010; Kuzma, Weiseborn, Phillippe, Gabel, & Dolechek, 2009; Roberts & Pappas, 2010). In contrast to this position, several scholars in our discipline have specifically refined the meaning of *disability* as it applies to the web. These have struck a technical definition that bears our attention.

Jonathan Lazar (2007) addresses accessibility as more than just designing for those with disabilities: "Universal accessibility (UA) is that branch of usability engineering that promotes the design of interfaces that can be used by everyone, regardless of factors such as locale, work styles, or disabilities" (p. 49). Slatin and Rush (2003) give an operational definition of accessibility: "Web sites are accessible when individuals with disabilities can access and use them as effectively as people who don't have disabilities" (p. 3). Going a step farther, I teach that *disability* is more than a legal definition; it must also involve a diminished ability to perform. I believe my broader definition of *disability* is more useful to students in the design process and more useful to web designers in the project cycle.

If approximately 20% of the U.S. population is disabled under the legal definition, that number significantly increases when you broaden the definition (http://www.disabledinaction.org/census_stats.html). Think about all the people who are approaching the web with a diminished ability to perform everyday activities because of distractions in their personal lives. Think about a student that has stayed up all night studying. Cognitively, when that student sits down at a computer, his or her ability is severely diminished. We have all seen this behavior when students cram for exams or write a major paper at the last minute. Think about the many people on medication such as cold or pain medicine, which may temporarily affect mental capacity. What about when a student hurts a hand, a leg, or a back? Or has a bad break-up or a family issue back home? What about older students who can no longer read the standard fine text on monitors because their eyes have grown weak or cannot sit for long periods in the lab because their joints ache? All these conditions are examples of the many outside forces that can potentially affect the ability to concentrate, which in turn affects the ability to perform the functions or navigate through a website effectively.

To confront these questions, my expanded definition includes the following:

- Cognitive issues
- Physical issues
- Emotional issues
- Age

Whether permanent or temporary, disabilities related to cognitive issues are the same as far as I am concerned. For example, if a student is taking certain medications, he may have a temporary cognitive disability. It doesn't matter if the disability is temporary or permanent for the few seconds that student is on the website trying to accomplish a particular function or task. For those few seconds or minutes, the cognitive disability is keeping the student from performing, and it doesn't matter to the student or the website developer if the disability is permanent or temporary because the outcome is the same—the task or function is not accomplished.

Similarly, a student may have temporary physical issues that don't legally constitute a disability; however, when he or she tries to access or develop a website, the permanence of the disability isn't the issue. If a student has sprained or broken a hand or finger or has an eye infection, the physical disability is temporary. But the student's capability to access the website, navigate buttons, write content and code, or create graphics is as impeded *at the moment* of the attempt as if the disability were permanent.

Emotional issues come in a wide variety for students who are newly independent and under pressures they have not previously experienced. Many students have to face the stresses of financial pressures, the critical illness or death of a family member, or the serious interpersonal relationship issues that all young people experience. For many students, this is the first time they are facing serious emotional issues, and many haven't learned how to compartmentalize the issue in order to cope with everyday duties. These emotional issues interfere with their ability to focus on a website to accomplish what they intend.

Although age itself is not a disability, we are affected by age-related diseases and issues as we grow older. As web designers, we need to be aware of this and design with the awareness that baby boomers form the largest generation and are one of the fastest populations getting on the web. When we age, we have problems with physical mobility, so buttons are harder to navigate to and click. Also, our vision gets worse, so text is harder to read. Cognitively, it becomes harder to retain information, so text-heavy screens and complicated navigation can become more difficult.

Again, my expanded definition of *disability* includes all of these issues—cognitive, physical, emotional, and age. Effective accessible design doesn't just help those with permanent disabilities—it helps everyone. And that's why I use as broad a definition as possible. Whether the disability is permanent or temporary is not the issue. It matters that there is an issue keeping the user from fully understanding and navigating a website. And all it takes is a moment of difficulty on a website and a user will leave to go on to another website that may be easier to use.

HOW I TEACH ACCESSIBILITY

In many courses across the curriculum, students are either being taught to design websites or being expected to use websites for course projects or for research. Few are taught to incorporate accessibility principles into such websites or even into other documents like PDFs that they post to the web. Even fewer are taught the importance of designing accessibility as part of the foundation of effective web design.

In my web classes, students create their own course projects in conjunction with my class syllabus (the criteria for the projects are negotiated with me). We also decide on and develop a class website according to my class structure. That is, I use common books and online articles that the students read and discuss and assign exercises that we do in class. But at the beginning of the semester each student must determine his or her own strengths and weaknesses and then construct the projects for the semester based on what needs to be strengthened. For example, a student may be interested in being a web designer but feels weak in Illustrator; therefore, most of that student's projects will be Illustrator graphic design projects. Another student may want to focus on programming but feels weak in XML; many of that student's projects will be XML-designed websites.

As a result, my students' projects are varied, from websites to graphic design pieces to gaming designs to PHP database websites to websites for mobile devices. Together, we develop each project's criteria, and each project must meet accessibility standards for its particular audiences and purpose. Also, as part of the projects, students have to write memos defending their design decisions, how they created the websites, and how they made them accessible. In my classes, I follow several steps in incorporating accessibility issues.

Step 1: Discuss the Legal and Technical Definitions of Disability

I teach ADA of 1990 and Section 508 of the Workforce Investment Act of 1998; I also teach the world's acknowledged technical definition of accessibility standards, the W3C's WAI. They read articles I provide, look at the government and WAI websites, and discuss the differences.

I sometimes begin the discussion by separating the students into small groups of three or four, and ask each group to look at the three sets of definitions and compare them, coming up with differences. I give them only 15 minutes, and then each group reports what it found. Usually, each group has different findings; therefore, as a collective, the class comes up with a good collection of differences among the definitions.

Step 2: Evaluate Whether Example Websites Follow the Legal and Technical Definitions

After we discuss the differences between the legal and technical definitions of *disability*, we look at website examples. First, we look at examples of websites to evaluate whether they follow the ADA of 1990. Second, we look at examples of websites to evaluate whether they follow Section 508. Third, we look at examples of websites to evaluate whether they follow the WAI. With each of these evaluations, the students identify what the websites did effectively and what the websites did ineffectively with regards to compliance.

Step 3: Find Places Where the Legal and Technical Definitions May Fall Short

In another exercise, the students evaluate the websites to see whether the legal and technical definitions are adequate for their purposes and audiences or whether they fall short in places. For examples, websites complying with Section 508 may meet the legal definition for accessibility compliance; however, people who are having problems with temporary cognitive issues or physical issues may have problems with these websites.

For one exercise in this area, I ask the students to choose a genre they enjoy (e.g., shopping, music, sports) and then choose a specific area within the genre (e.g., minor league baseball). Next, they select several websites from this specific area and analyze the websites in the light of the legal and technical definitions. The purpose of this exercise is to have the students find specific places where websites fail to adhere to those definitions or where those definitions don't matter.

Step 4: Discuss My Broadened Definition of Disability

After we discuss the legal and technical definitions of *disability* and evaluate websites, I present my broadened definition of *disability*. I ask the students how many of them have ever had to research information for a project while they were sick or sleep deprived. I ask them if they felt they were operating at 100%. Most have experienced researching, studying, or developing a project in these conditions. I explain that while most of them may not consider themselves permanently disabled, chances are they have operated at a diminished ability. Then we discuss the importance of designing websites that are accessible not just for users with disabilities but for all users, taking into account the likelihood of people accessing a website when not at 100% capacity.

Step 5: Evaluate Whether Examples Follow the Broader Definition and Discuss How They Could Be Revised

As the students look at examples of websites with the broader definition of *disability* in mind, they evaluate whether any fall short and, if so, how they do so. At this point, it's important to discuss the role of designing with accessibility at the beginning of the project cycle. We go around the class, and as they present the websites they are analyzing, the students explain how the web designers could revise their websites to be more effective in light of the broader definition of *disability*. In order to do this, the student must explain the website's purpose and its primary and secondary audiences. This is necessary so that the other students will be able to judge whether the design is effective or ineffective. For example, a cutting-edge website with a narrowly targeted audience may be designed entirely in Flash and, therefore, not be accessible according to the definitions we have examined. However, if we take the purpose and audiences of this Flash-designed website into consideration, it may be possible that the Flash presentation is acceptable even though its audiences are restricted.

Step 6: Apply the Broadened Definition to a Class Semester Website

Throughout the semester, we continually analyze websites for accessibility effectiveness. We look at websites for audience, purpose, structure, content, graphic design, layout, navigation—all while we try to identify their audiences and check for accessibility.

As a class, we compare Section 508 and WAI, and I explain that while Section 508 is not enough, WAI is impossible to achieve. Section 508 gives only the most basic guidelines, and if followed, a screen reader most likely would still run into problems. For example, Section 508 does not address creating accessible interactive forms. However, WAI covers so many possible technologies that to meet every guideline the web designer would never be finished with the website. The web designer must choose the WAI guidelines based on the audiences and purpose specific to his or her website.

Step 7: Apply the Broadened Definition to the Students' Own Projects

During this phase, students continually check their work to ensure that what they are creating is accessible. We continue to discuss the broad definition of *disability* and how accessibility is for everyone and must be built into the beginning stages of each project. It is in this process—my one-on-one interactions with individual students and their projects in their various stages—that they more fully recognize the implications of the broader definitions of *disability* and how they are applicable to accessibility. Early in the process they may need to get feedback on their storyboards of their future websites for design and accessibility effectiveness. For example, a student's choice of colors may not have enough contrast, and in this early stage it can be easily corrected. Later, after much more time has been invested in the development of the website, it is more difficult to make the correction.

Suppose a student is creating a website for a company releasing a new product for *plantar fasciitis* (pain and inflammation of a thick band of tissue, called the plantar fascia, that runs across the bottom of your foot and connects your heel bone to your toes), a condition more common among people who are middle-aged and older. She has identified her primary audience as the people who would be most affected by this condition. But she wants to use a Flash homepage to introduce her new product. She agrees to create an HTML alternate website but wants to provide the Flash because such presentations are acceptable, even professional, within this specific genre.

Through this process, she discovers on her own what the broader definition implies, and she comes to understand the tenuous position of using the Flash presentation. At this point, she must choose and defend her design decisions.

Step 8: Review Each Project for Adherence to the Broadened Definition

Obviously, this process of creating a website, applying the definitions, and seeking feedback and validation requires many iterations. I teach the students that they should repeatedly seek feedback on their websites throughout the development process. At each iteration, they seek feedback for different focuses. Throughout each feedback stage, however, accessibility is also one of the focuses, whether the students are in the storyboarding phase or beta testing phase.

After a website is developed, an important feedback process is validation. Validation services are a set of tests used to check, among other things, a website's conformity to ADA standards. There are many validation services, but two that are credible are W3C's HTML Validation Service and WebSavvy. Once a website is put through a validator, it is up to the web designer to decide what to correct and what to ignore because some of the errors identified in a validator may not apply to the particular website. For example, a validator may check for XHTML strictness, but the website may be coded in HTML 4.0, which allows for such practices as leaving elements open.

I demonstrate that, since none of the guidelines work for all websites, each web designer must choose the appropriate ADA compliance level for his or her audiences. Since each website has a primary and usually several secondary audiences, the web designer has to match ADA guidelines to these audiences.

Step 9: Write an Accompanying Memo

When the students have completed their individual websites and are ready to turn them in, they must write a detailed narrative describing how they created their websites. This narrative must include a detailed account of their design decisions, and they must support those decisions with sources such as class textbooks, articles, and outside research. Also, they must describe in detail how they step-by-step developed the website, including screen shots of the iterations. They must describe how they made the site accessible for their purpose and audiences. Finally, they must discuss their problems, if any, in developing an accessible website to client constraints, how they overcame the problems, and what lessons and skills they learned from the project.

For example, a student may have found it difficult to see the importance of the legal or technical definition or the broadened definition of *disability* and how to apply changes that address these issues. Many students seem to have a hard time at first understanding why a website should work on multiple browser versions or platforms. They argue that if it works on their computers, the website is sufficient for any. In accessibility terms, they sometimes find it difficult to understand why they need to apply the extra step that accessibility demands. That is, until they realize that the broadened definition can apply directly to them and their friends, some students are reluctant to take the necessary steps to make their websites fully effective. For these students, overcoming self-centrism is probably their greatest challenge. One way that I have countered this self-centrism is through the Kindle 2 research. Students tend to listen to their peers more than they listen to their instructors; therefore, the lessons learned from the Kindle 2 research on accessibility help the students empathize with people with disabilities. This research makes them more conscious of the need to bring in accessibility design at the beginning of the website design process.

KINDLE 2 RESEARCH AND ACCESSABILITY

My Kindle 2 research acts as a case study to support my expanded definition of *disability* by bringing an actual experience into the classroom. Placing the student in a position where he or she may be uncomfortable using a technology teaches the student what it is like to be disabled, according to my definition. Though students today use mobile and handheld electronic devices usually without much thought, they are not familiar with using an e-book version of a textbook, especially in the case of a technical textbook. My Kindle 2 research serves as a case study to support why I use the expanded definition of *disability* in the classroom. The qualitative results, presented below, are evidence that my teaching approach and expanded definition are effective. (See Appendix A for complete research data.)

Many universities are starting to use electronic books and electronic book readers (e-readers) instead of print textbooks. Some, like the Kindle, were designed to deliver books in the more traditional way. Others, like the iPad, are also designed to deliver books, but with the added affordance of websites and streaming video. More important recently, there have been lawsuits against some universities, the most noted being the one against Arizona State University, because they were using e-readers in class in place of printed textbooks and were not fully ADA compliant (Oswalt, 2010).

With my broader definition of *disability*, issues of accessibility are ever more important. Again, anything that improves comprehension and accessibility for those with disabilities improves it for all people.

In my research on the Kindle 2, I was interested in how it may be changing reading, specifically for students, and possibly impacting disability issues. I assumed that the experience with the Kindle 2 was the same as with a handheld or mobile device. Therefore, preparing students for developing mobile environments such as the Blackberry, iPhone, Palm, or iPad should include the Kindle.

Many are touting the Kindle as the future for print books because it answers the problem of having to carry around the weight of books when traveling. Also, the Kindle allows the reader to buy books cheaper, keep entire personal libraries organized on the Kindle or a hard drive, read multiple books at the same time, look up words on the spot, and download wirelessly (http://www.amazon.com/dp/B0051QVESA/ref=sa_menu_kdptqso3).

Some, however, are concerned that marrying print and electronic channels and mediums have flattened the full-print experience. Reading print books through an electronic page denies the reader the tactile experiences of feeling the different hard or soft covers or the variety of papers and even the edges of the book. Also gone is the conceptual understanding of the reader's place in a novel; for example, the suspense when nearing the end of a mystery or the sadness when nearing the end of a great book may be lost.

Others have criticized e-readers for how they constrain the reader. Nielsen (2009), a human factors and interaction design expert, usability tested the Kindle 2 and found that it reads fine when using it for linear print; however, using the Kindle 2 for interactive reading is slow, awkward, and unintuitive. Overall, Nielsen's (2009) main complaint was that the Kindle was dominated by the book metaphor and took reading electronically and interactively back several decades.

Specifically in the case of students' using such an electronic medium, I was concerned that accessing texts will be more difficult. My research was to determine, with a limited number of respondees, whether students prefer to use the Kindle 2 or traditional print documents to complete assignments that include reading documents with text, figures, and graphics. Because college students are potentially encountering the electronic reader in the classroom and are already the customer base for publishing houses, college-aged students were my target audience. My specific target audience for this research project included selected students in the Writing, Rhetoric and Technical Communication program at James Madison University. I started with the following hypothesis:

> Students do not have a preference of learning using the Kindle 2 versus using traditional print documents.

The results were inconclusive; half the students preferred to complete their assignment using the Kindle 2 and half preferred to use a traditional print document to complete their assignment. However, in the written comments, some interesting patterns did emerge. I have included the full research of the Kindle 2 case study as an appendix and here discuss only the portion that directly applies to the pedagogy of accessibility.

METHODOLOGY, PARTICIPANTS, AND DESIGN

I chose to use a survey to collect both qualitative and quantitative information. I wanted certain quantitative information (such as closed-ended, previous-use questions or Likert-based preferences) as well as rich qualitative information (such as open-ended questions for preferences of particular methods, specific problems, and additional comments).

After I identified my target audience and knew that a random sample was impossible, I requested volunteers in two different classes. I looked at how students read textbooks in an electronic (Kindle 2) environment versus a print environment. Also, I wanted the content of the text to vary: I wanted students to read a linear text as well as a text where they had to work on an exercise and flip back and forth within the text. I created two groups to accomplish this: volunteers from a graduate research methods class and an advanced web design class (Group A) and volunteers from an advanced web coding class (Group B).

I had a very small sample size, and I consider this a pilot study. My sample consisted of 16 volunteer students. Before any of the volunteers began their study, my graduate assistant, Lindsay Deliman, trained the students on the use of the Kindle 2. Each student was scheduled to take the Kindle home to use for two to three days. Before taking the Kindle home, each student signed a permission form stating that he or she was responsible for replacing the Kindle if it was in any way damaged.

Each group was presented a sample text in print and in electronic form. The students in Group A read a technical communication article from a printed textbook and then another article from the same textbook on the Kindle 2. Then they completed an online survey in Qualtrics.

The students in Group B read from a coding book in print and completed an exercise. Then the Group B students read from another part of their coding book on the Kindle 2 and completed an exercise. The exercise required the students to flip back and forth throughout the book. Then they received an email with a URL link to complete the Qualtrics survey.

DISCUSSION

With regards to accessibility, what was interesting was the responses to the open-ended questions. One question asked what they thought of flipping through the Kindle 2 to find a specific passage, locating the document in the Kindle 2, reading the document on the Kindle 2, and reading the graphics on the Kindle 2. There was a significant difference between the students' responses regarding reading the document and reading graphics. In other words, students found reading linear text easy and enjoyable but found reading the graphics difficult if not impossible to do because of the technology (see Table 1).

The positive comments highlighted how fast the Kindle 2 allowed linear reading. One participant commented that the quick linear read lends itself to novels and less academic readings. The negative comments highlighted those frustrations addressed by accessibility issues: the inability to navigate quickly, to see the difference between types of text, to manipulate text and graphics to the user's comfort, to read tables, and to scan information quickly. I use these results to show the students in discussions that according to my broadened definition they themselves are reporting disabilities.

One of the issues, having a problem distinguishing between headings and block text with the voiceover, is a disability issue according to the legal definition.

Table 1. Positive and Negative Comments for Kindle 2

Positive comments for Kindle 2	Negative comments for Kindle 2
The Kindle was easier to read and faster to read. It allowed for user interaction and easier navigation.	The kindle was not in color. Colored examples in the printed book helped to understand how to do certain things. Also, If I needed to flip back to another page, I could do this quicker in the printed book rather than the Kindle.
T1) The typeface was clear 2) Tables were more legible	I found it hard to view the page on the kindle how I wanted to and the paper method I can see the article as a whole and read it more smoothly.
I liked how the Kindle has a built in function to define unknown vocabulary.	Some of the images were too large to display on the kindle and were cut in half. Also, during certain parts of the chapter words were cut off on the right side of the page. This made it difficult to read the chapter. There was no color to illustrate colored examples. In the book, words when bolded had more emphasis. I had a hard time seeing the difference in bolded words on the Kindle.
I feel that Kindle is a very useful tool when it comes to reading of a less academic nature. For example, the formatting of a novel is far more natural than that of the organized, bulleted text.	The kindle may be hard to use for certain text books that have a lot of tables, graphics, diagrams because the font is small and difficult to read. Plus it is hard to highlight the text in order to take notes.
The lines were shorter, so reading seemed to go faster.	I wish it would have distinguished more between headings and normal text when using the voiceover option.
	Because there was no way to enlarge images, the diagrams were sometimes difficult to read.
	The formatting of the print document made it easier to scan the material and relate the sections to one another.
	The document was not text-heavy, so the action of clicking the button on the Kindle to go to the next view was too frequent.

But all these issues can quickly become issues of accessibility when using my broader definition of *disability*. Whether permanent or temporary, cognitive, physical, emotional, or age-related issues can also affect how a person is able to use the Kindle or any e-reader. A student who is exhausted from an all-night study session, has a broken hand, or is stressed over the impending death of a family member will have disability-related issues at the particular moment the student is attempting to access the text.

Although this is a pilot study with inconclusive results, the qualitative data does point to some interesting information. When breaking the experience down specifically to navigation, print, and graphics, most students seemed to find the Kindle 2 fairly easy to navigate. However, when it came to graphics, a noticeable number of participants experienced difficulty. This is important for students, especially for our field and for a culture that is highly visual, because it gives me a way to sensitize students directly without having to be pedantic. Students reach their own conclusions, and when they see their peers reporting difficulties or problems with disability accessibility, they tend to listen to their peers.

CONCLUSION

Both the Kindle 2 research and my experience in the classroom point to the need to define *disability* broadly. My broadened definition involves any diminished capability in a person's ability to perform a given task. One should integrate accessibility as a vital core component of design when developing websites, graphics, and mobile devices. My teaching approach can benefit the entire field of technical communication because it allows the student to develop on an individual basis while still adhering to important constraints. Additionally, students learn to construct professional websites that reach wider audiences because they incorporate the broadened definition of *disability*.

APPENDIX A:
Kindle 2 Research

Half the students preferred the Kindle 2, and half preferred the printed textbook. As I said before, this was a small sample size, and the fact that almost all the students are advanced web/electronic users may have impacted the results.

Note: The survey starts with Question 2. Also, although Qualtrics automatically calculates percentages and I am using the Qualtrics statistic table reports, at this small sample size, percentages are not significant and therefore irrelevant to discuss. I will not be addressing percentages, only raw numbers.

Question 2: Is this your first time using a Kindle?

Of the 16 participants, 15 said this experience is the first time they used a Kindle (see Table 2).

Table 2. Number of Participants Who Have Used the Kindle Previously

#	Answer		Response	%
	Yes		15	94%
	No		1	6%
	Total		16	100%

Question 3: Which method of completing the assignment did you prefer more, using a print document or using the Kindle?

Of the 16 participants, eight preferred using the Kindle 2 to complete their assignments and eight preferred using a traditional print document (see Table 3).

Question 4: Why did you prefer that method?

Participants were able to include their personal thoughts on why they preferred either choice. Some participants preferred the Kindle 2 because it was an innovative learning method that was interesting to them. Some also felt that the overall reading experience made the Kindle 2 more pleasurable to use (see Table 4).

Some participants preferred text documents because they were more familiar with them and thus felt more comfortable with a familiar learning method. In addition, participants noted that the graphics and tables were not as clear on the Kindle 2 as they were in print documents (see Table 5). The formatting of the print document made it easier to scan the material and relate the sections to one another.

Table 3. Students' Preference Between the Amazon Kindle2 and Print Documents

#	Answer		Response	%
	The Amazon Kindle 2		8	50%
	The Print Document		8	50%
	Total		16	100%

Table 4. Students' Specifications for Why They Preferred
the Amazon Kindle 2

Text Response
It was a new concept that made the reading seem to go a little faster.
The Kindle provided a new experience for learning, and an effective one at that. I don't know if I would prefer it over print indefinitely, but it was a refreshing experience for sure.
The lines were shorter, so reading seemed to go faster.
I liked that it was light and easy to carry around and it can hold all of my textbooks in it.
I could double task using the "text voiceover."
If the reading involves text that I might want to flip back or forward or mark, I would prefer print. If I was just scanning through, the Kindle would be fine.
The Kindle was easier to read and faster to read. It allowed for user interaction and easier navigation.

Question 5: Please rate the Kindle on the following items:

Participants were asked to rate the Kindle 2 on five aspects: flipping to find specific pages, locating the document they were asked to read, reading the document, reading the graphics, and their overall experience. The participants were asked to rate each aspect as very difficult, somewhat difficult, somewhat easy, or very easy (see Table 6).

Question 6: Did you have problems using any of the functions on the Kindle?

Of the 16 participants, 11 did not have problems using the functions on the Kindle 2 but five reported having problems (see Table 7).

Question 7: What specific problems did you have?

The participants who had problems were asked to specify which functions they had trouble using. These were their responses: One participant had trouble underlining text and making notes, one could not enlarge the tables, and one had trouble flipping through the pages (see Table 8).

Table 5. Students' Specifications for Why They Preferred
the Amazon Kindle 2

Text Response

Primarily, because I am familiar with that medium, I can make notes easily and underline, and other tasks requiring the texts are available (photocopying, allowing someone to borrow the text, not worrying about breaking).

It was easier to hold and had a better way of navigating from page to page.

The kindle was not in color. Colored examples in the printed book helped to understand how to do certain things. Also, if I needed to flip back to another page, I could do this quicker in the printed book rather than the Kindle.

I felt more attached to a book, since I can physically hold it and flip the pages, unlike the kindle where it is just a computer screen, no attachment.

1) The typeface was clear 2) Tables were more legible 3) The document was not text-heavy, so the action of clicking the button on the Kindle to go to the next view was too frequent.

I found it hard to view the page on the kindle how I wanted to and the paper method I can see the article as a whole and read it more smoothly.

It was distracting to press the next page button on the Kindle. Each page did not hold much text and only took a few seconds to read.

The formatting of the print document made it easier to scan the material and relate the sections to one another.

Question 8: If you have any additional comments about your experience with the Kindle, please provide your comments below.

Participants included thoughts and opinions regarding the use of the Kindle 2 compared to the use of print documents. In particular, one participant believed that the Kindle 2 would be surpassed by other technologies that provided similar features, such as the netbook. Another participant specified that they would enjoy using the Kindle2 for reading novels or magazines but not for assignments (see Table 9).

Table 6. Kindle 2 Ratings

Question	Very Difficult	Somewhat Difficult	Somewhat Easy	Very Easy	Mean*
How did you find flipping through the Kindle to find specific passages?	1	4	7	4	2.88
How did you find locating the document you read in the Kindle?	0	4	7	5	3.06
How did you find reading the document on the Kindle?	0	2	6	8	3.38
How did you find reading graphics on the Kindle?	1	5	6	4	2.81
Overall, how would you rate your experience with the Kindle?	0	2	9	5	3.19

*I assigned values to the levels of difficulty (very difficult = 1, somewhat difficult = 2, somewhat easy = 3, and very easy = 4) and then calculated the mean based on the number of responses for each level of difficulty. A lower mean indicates that the students rated that task as being more difficult.

Table 7. Number of Participants Who Have Used the Kindle Previously

#	Answer		Response	%
	Yes		5	31%
	No		11	69%
	Total		16	100%

Table 8. Specific Problems Encountered by the Students

Text Response

Making notes and underlining.

I could not enlarge the tables and later found that it was a functionality that did not exist for PDF documents.

trying to highlight specific passages in order to take notes and reading the tables; they were too small.

I couldn't find the article and zoom out of the page because the words were so big.

trying to flip through the pages, I hit the wrong buttons a couple times, and trying to find which books I needed to read was difficult.

Table 9.

Text Response

I feel that the layout of the reading in this case could greatly affect opinion. The text was divided into portions, which reads differently than straight text.

It's a neat technology, but I feel like others will and can surpass the Kindle. I can access much more with my smartphone or laptop. If I had three hundred dollars for the purposes of purchasing a reading technology, I would buy a netbook.

I would enjoy this for pleasure reading—novels or magazine articles. For assignments, the screen would need to be bigger and buttons for high-lighting would need to be larger. I did like the screen better than a computer screen.

I liked how the Kindle has a built in function to define unknown vocabulary. Some of the images were too large to display on the Kindle and were cut in half. Also, during certain parts of the chapter words were cut off on the right side of the page. This made it difficult to read the chapter. There was no color to illustrate colored examples. In the book, words when bolded had more emphasis. I had a hard time seeing the difference in bolded words on the Kindle.

I want one for Christmas.

Sometimes the words were cut off from the screen.

In the previous question of very difficult to very easy, using the Kindle was easy, but annoying. So I chose difficult for some answers.

If all text books were available, I'd buy [a Kindle].

The Kindle may be hard to use for certain text books that have a lot of tables, graphics, [and] diagrams because the font is small and difficult to read. Plus it is hard to highlight the text in order to take notes.

I wish it would have distinguished more between headings and normal text when using the voiceover option.

I feel that the Kindle is a very useful tool when it comes to reading of a less academic nature. For example, the formatting of a novel is far more natural than that of the organized, bulleted text. Also, because there was no way to enlarge images, the diagrams were sometimes difficult to read.

I like the idea of the Kindle, but I think because it's so much smaller than most books, I preferred actual paper.

The Kindle was fun and easy to use. The only comment I have would be to make the Kindle available in color instead of black and white. Overall, I had a pleasant experience using the Kindle.

My time with the Kindle was enjoyable. The device was effective, refreshing, and easy to use. I don't know if I prefer the Kindle over print, but I was convinced of its strong potential.

REFERENCES

Adam, A., & Kreps, D. (2009). Disability and discourses of web accessibility. *Information, Communication & Society, 12*(7), 1041–1058.

Americans with Disability Act (ADA) of 1990, as Amended. (1990). Sec. 12102. Retrieved from http://www.ada.gov/pubs/adastatute08.htm#12102

Clark, D. (2008). Content management and the separation of presentation and content. *Technical Communication Quarterly, 17*(1), 35–60.

Johansson, R. (2010, May 31). Accessibility does not prevent you from using JavaScript or Flash. 456 Bearea Street. Retrieved from http://www.456bereastreet.com/archive/201005/accessibility_does_not_prevent_you_from_using_javascript_or_flash/

Kuzma, J., Weiseborn, G., Phillippe, T., Gabel, A., & Dolechek, R. (2009). Analysis of U.S. Senate web sites for disability accessibility. *International Journal of Business Research, 9*(6), 174–181.

Lazar, J. (Ed.). (2007). *Universal usability*. West Sussex, UK: John Wiley & Sons.

Nielsen, J. (2009, March 9). Kindle 2 usability review. Useit.com. Retrieved from http://www.useit.com/alertbox/kindle-usability-review.html

Oswalt, A. (2010, January 19). ASU settles lawsuit; Kindle program to end in May. *The State Press*. Arizona State University. Retrieved from http://www.statepress.com/archive/node/9935

Roberts, L., & Pappas, L. (2010). Accessibility on the go. *Intercom*. Retrieved from http://tc.eserver.org/36567.html

Section 508. (n.d.). Standards. Retrieved from http://www.section508.gov/index.cfm?fuseAction=stds

Slatin, J., & Rush, S. (2003). *Maximum accessibility*. Boston, MA: Addison-Wesley.

World Wide Web Consortium (W3C). (n.d.b). Web accessibility initiative (WAI). http://www.w3.org/WAI/

http://dx.doi.org/10.2190/RAAC7

CHAPTER 7

Accessibility Challenges for Visually Impaired Students and Their Online Writing Instructors

Sushil K. Oswal and Beth L. Hewett

Accessibility in online instruction often is interpreted as reaching out to students located in far-flung places or marooned in areas consumed by wars and floods. In such cases, accessibility becomes a matter of whether technology can breach the geographical or material divide. Online instruction in such contexts automatically becomes a technological boon or a badge of merit without any additional pedagogic effort from the instructor. Simply because it carries the potential to reach students, online instruction often is lauded for its accessibility. On the other hand, issues pertaining to the specific accessibility of online courses to disabled students remains, at best, on the margins.

In the more focused context of online writing instruction (OWI), advice for teaching writing online to disabled students often involves merely asking disabled students to contact the professor during the first week of classes or referring them to the disability services office on campus. In such cases, the responsibility for accessing the online course is almost entirely on the student, who must initiate such requests. For instance, one recent book about online writing courses has this single piece of advice for online writing instructors: "Students with disabilities might have a different set of rights in online courses. You'll want to provide a clear way for them to contact your local office of disability services. Remember, some of these students will not be on campus" (Warnock, 2009, p. 43).

135

Similarly, a national survey on the state of online writing instruction distributed to the Conference on College Composition and Communication (2010) community asked for, but failed to elicit, any substantive information on what college teachers were doing to accommodate the special needs of disabled students in their classes—most likely, we think, because not much is being done. For example, in written responses to the survey's open-ended questions regarding disabilities and OWI, some instructors indicated that they needed to know nothing more than what particular accommodations they must supply for disabled students; others, however, disclosed their complete lack of knowledge about the topic:

- "I've never thought about it before, so I have no idea."
- "I hadn't thought about it. To me, everyone on-line is equal. Unless they inform me of a disability, I presume they have none (except maybe technical know-how!)."
- "I'm not sure. To quote Wittgenstein, "I do not know what I do not know."

Some expressed a bland lack of interest in the issue:

- "I only need to know if it affects how I need to deliver material."
- "Has not been a problem; thus, I have no interest."

In other responses to the open-ended questions on the survey, some instructors indicated greater awareness of the vagaries of addressing disabilities in OWI, yet they wrote somewhat dismissively and indicated a surprising willingness to bar students needing accommodation:

- "How different disabilities react to online environments—are certain disabilities necessarily prohibitive to being successful online, or can any environment be adapted?"
- "What's a reasonable accommodation in the online environment and when should you just refuse and declare that the student must take the class in the face-to-face setting? (I have a dyslexic student this term and have been required to post audio files of every single text file or website that is required reading in the course, as well as audio versions of the textbooks and essays.)"
- "If they have a disability it is good to know, but, really, legally I don't think we are to make accommodations."

Some of the above comments certainly raise red flags since federal laws, particularly Section 504 of the Rehabilitation Act of 1973 and the Americans with Disabilities Act (ADA) of 1990, require that postsecondary institutions provide reasonable accommodations to ensure equal access to program offerings for qualified students who request accommodations after disclosing disabilities and presenting appropriate documentation of their disability (Burgstahler & Moore, 2009; Frank & Wade, 1993; West, Kregel, Getzel, Zhu, Ipsen, & Martin, 1993). At the same time, the above cited 2010 Conference on College Composition and Communication survey data appeared to be in line with the results of other studies where researchers found that some instructors were ignorant about the rights of their disabled students and about accommodations (Frank & Wade, 1993; Hill, 1996; Lehmann, Davies, & Laurin, 2000; National Center for the Study of Postsecondary Educational Supports, 2000).

This chapter questions the willingness of online writing instructors to remain uneducated and underprepared to assist disabled students. To do so, it looks to the particular case of blind students and their special needs because visually impaired students are doubly blind in the online environment, where visual presentation is prolific and varied. Therefore, this discussion primarily addresses the special needs of the visually impaired students as a way to understand how alternative practices may assist them, their instructors, and other students who may share some learning characteristics with blind students in the OWI setting. Overall, we hope that readers will see ways to extrapolate to other students with disabilities from the intricacies of addressing the visually disabled in OWI settings.

According to the Education Department, only about 75,000 visually impaired students attend college or trade schools at this time (Parry, 2010). This number appears to be disproportionately small even within the disabled student population attending American institutions of higher education. Having reviewed a flurry of articles about accessibility issues for the blind this year in the U.S. press, we surmise that this underrepresentation might have something to do with the peculiar obstacles this disability group might face in college environments (Waddell, 1999).

Without being technical, this chapter attempts to unpack the processes and technologies of making OWI accessible. It focuses on key accessibility issues that should concern every online writing instructor interested in meeting the obligation to make online writing courses fully accessible to the visually impaired population. In the context of this chapter, by *accessibility* we mean that the online course contents and tools can be effectively read, interacted with, and used by students who are totally blind or have severe visual impairments. We assume that these students have little or no useful vision and are what specialists call "print disabled." We also assume that not all the instructors have technical expertise in software design or programming, but we believe they can seek assistance in making a course accessible from their campus information technology department.

We address first the general needs of blind students where online technology for any course delivery is involved. Then we consider the specific needs of visually impaired students in online writing classes. Our final goal is to provide some practical guidelines that may help online writing instructors make informed technological and pedagogical choices for their blind students—and other challenged students—in online writing courses. To these ends, we begin with a discussion of the accessibility barriers that visually impaired students face. Then we describe a set of adaptive technologies that blind users employ for overcoming these barriers. Finally, we propose a number of solutions to create an OWI learning environment essential for the effective functioning of these adaptive technologies.

ACCESSIBILITY BARRIERS FOR THE BLIND

Although specialized studies about blind students in higher education and their teachers of online writing do not yet exist, general studies of institutional attitudes and student perceptions indicate that students with disabilities view administrators, faculty, and staff as lacking knowledge about disabilities and possessing a negative attitude toward their accommodation needs (Dowrick, Anderson, Heyer, & Acosta, 2005; Farone, Hall, & Costello, 1998). Some of the comments cited above from the 2010 Conference on College Composition and Communication survey qualitatively support this finding. Although students' experiences may not reflect faculty awareness regarding their needs, studies suggest that faculty often receive training about the needs of students with disabilities. For example, published literature on evaluations and interviews conducted after such faculty development workshops indicated that the faculty perceived these training sessions as helpful (Burgstahler & Doe, 2006; Cook, Rumrill, Camarata, Mitchell, Newman, Sebaly, et al., 2006; Krampe & Berdine, 2003; Rohland, Erickson, Mattews, Roush, Quinlan, & Smith, 2003; Sowers & Smith, 2004). There can be no doubt that faculty awareness training is crucial. Murray, Wren, Stevens, and Keys (2009) concluded from their learning disabilities training project that "university faculty and staff are the primary conduits through which such accessibility and support will be realized and providing these individuals with the knowledge, attitudes, and skills to create such environments is critically important" (p. 127). Despite the importance of providing accessibility and support, faculty can be remarkably unaware about the need for making their courses accessible to disabled students, even during these past two decades since the enactment of the ADA.

Definitions about the accessibility of online information to the blind abound since the passage of the ADA, yet only a small percentage of them talk about genuine equality of access. According to Gemmell (2010), "Accessibility isn't about providing simplified or alternative content; it's about ensuring everyone has equal access to your existing content." Elsewhere, he continued:

> Accessibility isn't about providing a cut-down experience, but neither is it about making your app's sighted experience available as-is. Always consider the implicit capabilities of the unimpaired user, and take steps to

even the playing field. That's what accessibility means. Not special treatment, but tailored access to the same treatment. Put another way, don't just give special treatment to fully-sighted users. (Gemmell, 2010)

To this end, we suggest that the current state of inaccessibility is related to how one defines accessibility in terms of evening the playing field. In a university setting, the fault lies not only with indifferent and ignorant designers and purveyors of technology, but also with the university buyers of these environments who fail to test them for accessibility. When one defines *accessibility* as "special treatment," this exclusionary worldview about the disabled leads inevitably to a failure to address accessibility issues in practical and workable ways.

From a legal perspective, delivering an accessible online course to disabled students involves technological as well as pedagogical and procedural considerations:

The "prime directive" of Web accessibility—the number-one item in both WCAG 1.0 and the Section 508 federal accessibility standards that took effect in June 2001—is the requirement to provide "equivalent alternatives" for visual and auditory elements of the Web site. (Slatin & Rush, 2003, p. 243)

Indeed, in the fall of 2010, a wide-ranging complaint about the inaccessibility of classroom technology to both blind faculty and blind students at the University of Pennsylvania suggested that accessibility issues in higher education are not limited to the choice of emerging technologies. For example, in 2010, orders from the U.S. Justice Department prohibited American universities from the use of Kindles and any other e-book devices until they become fully accessible to the blind and other disabled groups. This prohibition indicates that American colleges are legally responsible for making accessible choices for delivering their curriculum to their disabled students. Such changes, however, do little good to the visually impaired unless the software is designed to work with screen readers and other accessible software solutions.

Typically, students are responsible for formally requesting accommodations, but once they have been registered as disabled students with their college, the institution is legally responsible for arranging the required course materials in the format of the student's choice and ability in a timely manner. Not all students are familiar with the resources available for accommodating their special needs, and the availability or lack of careful counseling by a well-trained disability services coordinator during the first year of college can determine the student's future in higher education. While instructors might learn about the presence of a blind student in a course only on the first day of classes, it is the disability services office's responsibility to contact the instructor ahead of time to make appropriate arrangements if the student has requested accommodations at the time of admission or course registration. Instructors can advocate on behalf of the student since the missing accommodations can have a negative impact not only on the student's performance but also on the entire class. Of course, in online environments, even in the case of such an obvious disability as total blindness, instructors have no way to find out about the need for accommodations unless the student informs them about the disability and provides official documentation about it from the appropriate office on campus.

While all students are affected when their particular needs are not met, students with visual impairments confront special technological and procedural barriers in obtaining equal access to online instruction because of the primarily visual nature of the delivery tools at this time (Parry, 2010). For instance, while a student unable to use a traditional point-and-click device can be accommodated by the use of an alternate device, a blind student simply cannot point to any object on the computer screen and thus must have access to online materials that can be processed meaningfully by a screen reader or can be displayed by a Braille display system. Likewise, e-books appear to be a step above print books if they provide a speech interface; however, the poor quality of their synthesized speech and highly visual interface for accessing the various links on the e-book pages often render them useless for blind readers. In an interview about the Alliance for Rhetoric Societies, Leff voiced a concern applicable to this situation: "I fear that we are letting technology dominate education rather than putting it to effective human use" (Hewett, 2003, Online "chat" interview). From the perspective of the disabled, online technologies often have been put to use without regard for the human with different abilities or visual challenges.

Speaking from the perspective of technical communication and design theory, Johnson (2010) stated that "User-centered design (UCD) was developed from a well-balanced theory-practice integration of practical empirical evidence that was formed into theoretical understandings of how humans interact with technologies" (p. 336). But as the user-centered design theory permeated various fields of practice, it got separated from its other half of the binary and was "subsumed under [the sole category of] practice and, especially, toward application of the theories for the purpose of solving short-term user problems in the service of products that had to be validated before they went out the door" (Johnson, 2010, p. 336). Johnson (2010) asked: "How can we theorize the concept of use? Would having a deeper philosophical and rhetorical understanding of use be fruitful for furthering our understanding of user centeredness?" (p. 339). He answered this question by discussing how the "concept of use" in itself creates "complexity" (Johnson, 2010, p. 339). Going back to the classical Greek meaning of *techne*, Johnson (2010) extrapolated that "the product's maker contemplated problems associated with the product's use from the outset of the making process, thus bringing the contexts of use and the ramifications of use to the forefront" (p. 343). We argue that true user-centeredness can help us not only to move toward what Johnson (2010) called a "deeper philosophical and rhetorical understanding of use" (p. 339) but also to encourage us to perceive human-centeredness in an inclusionary context—indeed, it can help us move toward the ideal of universal.

ADAPTIVE TECHNOLOGIES

Contemporary blind students can be categorized into three groups regarding Braille:

- Those who know Braille and use a combination of Braille and audio devices for accomplishing reading and writing tasks.
- Those who know little or no Braille but are adept at using computers and depend on them for everything.
- Those who do not know Braille and are not yet fully comfortable with computer technology.

While students in all the three categories rely on audio books, the format of these books can range from online text files or web texts read by a screen reader (e.g., JAWS for Windows, Window-Eyes, or Mac VoiceOver) to pre-recorded books on cassette or available as downloadable files for especially designed digital players (e.g., from the National Library System of the Library of Congress or Learning Ally).

Only a small percentage of college textbooks are available as recordings, and even fewer titles are produced in Braille. Therefore, most blind students today use scanned books. Optical character reading (OCR) software programs (e.g., Kurzweil 1000 and OpenBook) can interpret text from scanned images of the print source and convert it to speech. Easy-to-use text-to-Braille translation software packages (e.g., Duxbury) and the availability of a range of medium-price Braille printers have placed the printing of Braille documents and books within the reach of any university computer lab or disability services office. Computer downloadable electronic Braille text files can also be used on a variety of Braille display devices without requiring the transportation of cumbersome Braille books. For strictly online course delivery environments, Duxbury Braille translation software also can produce electronic Braille files that can be emailed or saved on a CD for student use.

Most blind students are touch typists, although some are beginning to use voice recognition software for computer input. Anecdotal evidence suggests that only a very small percentage compose and revise in Braille using the traditional Braille writers. Students more comfortable with Braille keyboards (which have only seven keys) can enter text directly into a word processor through hand-held note takers (e.g., PAC Mate, Braille 'n Speak, and Pocket Braille). Whereas some of these note takers can read aloud the text entered through a speech synthesizer, others can display it in Braille. Like some sighted writers, blind students also compose their rough drafts on voice recorders or computers and later transcribe them into word processor files. Like other students, many blind writers are presently experimenting with iPods and iPhones for obtaining the same results.

Screen readers vary in speech quality from one another, but none of them offer the quality of speech found at automatic checkout kiosks and in public transportation systems. For this reason, blind students need to pay close attention to the synthesized speech while reading texts for revising and editing. On the other hand, the screen readers on the upper end of the price spectrum—JAWS for Windows and Window-Eyes—literally have hundreds of keyboard-controlled functions that can help the blind user read office documents; use email; browse online information; and perform database, spreadsheet, and PowerPoint functions, provided that all of these have been prepared as "accessible documents" or "accessible environments." One of the major limitations of screen readers is that they can read only the text elements on the screen, although accessibility features built in during the design and coding of the webpages, such as ALT tags and pre-recorded descriptions of visual elements, can make these nontextual elements accessible to the blind.

While students can take the initiative of ordering textbooks in accessible formats on their own, the ultimate responsibility for accommodative materials resides with the institution. When a print text is not available from any of the libraries in the desired format for a blind student, most college disability services offices provide students with an electronic copy of the text. In such situations, however, precautions are necessary to ensure that the scanned text is not saved as an Adobe PDF file since such files are particularly difficult to read with screen readers unless they have been formatted perfectly with all the screen reader accessibility settings in place. Because work study students and other temporary workers often perform such tasks, it is better to request Microsoft Office Word files for these purposes. In situations where the textual materials might not scan well because of the mixed graphic and text contents, the disability services office should urge the student to use a recorded version, where a human reader reads the text and describes the nontextual content. If educators want blind students to succeed in higher education, faculty will have to take a leadership role in shaping academic and procedural policies governing the disability support services for these students. So far, a great deal of such work has been solely left in the hands of disability service offices, whose employees who may or may not have a procedural and academic understanding of the course curriculum and its goals.

USING ADAPTIVE TECHNOLOGIES FOR OWI

Textbook Choices

Beginning with their textbook choices, OWI teachers must keep in mind blind students' needs. OWI is the teaching of writing in online settings—both fully online and in "blended" or "hybrid" settings that include some traditional face-to-face instruction. Teaching writing is a primarily text-based activity that is complicated for the visually impaired because the written text must be made available to the student not only at the level of computer technology but also at the most basic level of the textbook. Therefore, in choosing textbooks, instructors must reconsider their criteria for selecting the latest and the best.

At the very least, instructors should consider that a glitzy textbook's colorful pages are most likely going to be a problem for blind students' reading machines. One way to test the text for accessibility is simply to go to the nearest computer lab with adaptive technology and check the text for how its pages can be accessed when put through an OCR program. Such small-scale experimentation with adaptive technology is equally beneficial for disabled students and for instructors. Coombs (2010) claimed: "I believe that creating accessible online learning experiences for students with disabilities can do even more than give them a quality education—it can empower them to become stronger, more self-reliant people" (p. xiii). Similarly, the process of creating those empowering experiences improves the OWI instructor's qualities as a responsible and thoughtful educator.

Speaking to teachers about the Universal Design for Learning (UDL), Bowe (2000) asked:

> Is it really necessary for teachers to present the great bulk of our instruction via speech? Isn't there a way, or aren't there several ways, for us to offer much of the same material visually (in print, on disk, etc.)? Of course, the obverse obtains as well: Must we assign only printed materials for student reading? Can't we find audible (spoken) versions, too, and make those available for people who need or prefer them? (p. 2)

The challenge for OWI teachers is to find the resources, skills, and authority to make all these options a material reality in the online writing classroom, whether or not a visually impaired student is present.

In typical online course planning, instructors try to learn whether or not the students commonly use photo scanners, digital cameras, or cell phones before designing class assignments. Similarly, advance knowledge about the assistive and adaptive devices the enrolled blind students use should shape course design choices so as to not create unnecessary hindrances in the path of their learning. For example, if a blind student has no way to access the graphics and visuals in the planned textbook, instructors might decide to reserve time for describing these graphics to the whole class before discussing the data or concepts involved in designing these visual devices. In fact, they might ask other students to post podcasts describing these graphics ahead of time to include them in the accessibility planning, as well as to have the time needed to fill in any missing details in students' podcasts prior to discussing the concepts.

Knowing what tools are available to one's blind students might also assist in planning alternative or modified assignments. For instance, if the institution has no tactile drawing tools available, instructors cannot expect the blind student to develop a graph. However, some thinking ahead of time might result in another way to communicate and teach that graphic knowledge. These issues may not be as prevalent in writing courses, but even in writing courses, interpreting or developing drawings of brainstorming circles, charts, and other heuristics might be required of students.

We strongly recommend that instructors connect with the online blind student by telephone to talk with the student as soon as enrollment is announced in order to learn about the student's technology use and reading, note taking, composing, revising, and editing techniques. This opportunity also enables the instructor to learn about what special course adjustments and accommodations the student requires of them and the disability services office. Blind students are like other students in their needs to communicate with instructors, particularly in online settings (Hewett, 2010). Hence, instructors may do a favor both for the students and themselves by picking up the phone and asking whether they know what special assistance is required for getting the class work done. Such an action is akin to taking a student to the writing center or facilitating an appointment with a specialist.

Technological Choices

Modality

Modality is a time-related concept that has significant impact on the blind writing student. Synchronous environments promise an almost instantaneous interaction, which holds true when accomplished by voice technologies like voice over Internet (VOI). However, synchronous written chat can complicate matters since the need for a voice translation of the interlocutor's message must be accomplished in concert with the blind student's own typed interaction. Synchronous chat can occur quickly and in a non-turn-taking, non-threaded, and rapid-fire manner (Hewett & Hewett, 2008) that does not lend itself to adaptive technologies. To this end, we recommend asynchronous technology for most OWI in which blind students will participate.

Generally speaking, asynchronous text discussions in online courses are beneficial to blind students because they enable the use of text-to-voice adaptive technologies, pose less stringent time constraints on class participation, give the blind student a chance to review any relevant reading materials at his or her pace, and permit opportunities for revising a response before revealing it to the whole class. Sighted students with varying speeds for composing texts also appreciate asynchronous discussions for these reasons. In addition, asynchronous environments allow time for troubleshooting in case the blind student's assistive technology fails to perform as expected.

Within both synchronous and asynchronous environments, particular care is required in choosing accessible presentation tools. While streaming video and broadcast of recorded videos are familiar to most college students, the information offered through these media also must be accessible to visually impaired students. The media and their tools must be compatible with computers especially equipped with a screen reader or a Braille display. "Dynamic" e-learning content—for instance, graphics that change as a user rolls over the mouse or clicks on different parts of the image—remains beyond access to blind students since screen readers and Braille devices have to refresh the page to display any new online information. Quite often, blind students lose access at this point. Additionally, whereas advice about the use of video abounds, the concern invariably is about students not always having the pertinent technology for video playback, not on the accessibility of the information to the visually disabled. Mace (n.d.), of the Center for Universal Design, indicated that the concept of universal design would help students with special needs: "Universal design is the design of products and environments to be usable by all people, to the greatest extent possible, without the need for adaptation or specialized design" (para. 1). We support this concept primarily because it looks to accessible technology at its inception rather than as an adaptation to a completed product.

OWI teachers should consider additional questions regarding modality such as the following:

- What pacing issues are important to consider when planning course delivery in a synchronous environment with such multimedia tools?
- Besides temporal flexibility, what other advantages are there in an asynchronous environment for visually disabled students?
- How can the synchronous or asynchronous environment assist the instructor in providing supportive materials or interactions to (visually) disabled students?
- How does either the synchronous or asynchronous environment assist disabled students other than those with visual disabilities?

Course Management Systems

Whenever choice is allowed by the home institution, instructors of online writing courses also need to pay attention to accessibility in choosing a course management system (CMS). Whether the instructor has the choice or needs to play the role of accessibility informant to the institution's technology decision makers, the questions remain the same:

- Which delivery systems are compatible with screen readers and Braille displays?
- Do they meet the basic accessibility criteria for delivering writing course contents?
- What alternatives exist to deliver those components of a course that cannot be delivered in an accessible format through the campus's primary CMS?

- Is there an option to approach the technical support of such technology as Blackboard, Catalyst, or Writing Studio to get these accessibility questions addressed prior to the beginning of the course?
- What is the institution's legal responsibility regarding the accessibility of these third-party delivery systems?

Although we are not aware of any complaint regarding the inaccessibility of these online course delivery tools against universities, the U.S. Justice Department's intervention in the University of Arizona case about required Kindle use suggests that such complaints will receive sympathetic consideration. Colleges are, by law, responsible for the accessibility of the online instruction delivery tools since they make a conscious choice in adopting one certain CMS over another. Historically speaking, all major CMSs have had accessibility issues, but early in 2010, the National Federation of the Blind certified Blackboard 9.1 as a screen-reader accessible CMS. As of the end of 2011, no academic reviews about the accessibility of this version have been published.

We can mention some easy outliers, however, which might assist instructors in selecting a more accessible CMS. The CMS tools with frames are cumbersome and unwieldy to use with screen readers and Braille displays, regardless of how accessible their contents might be. Blind students tend to fare better with text-based systems with simple page designs. CMS tools that invariably obstruct accessibility include drop boxes for submitting assignments, internal grade books, discussion boards with crowded and confusing layouts or without clear text boundaries and intuitive labels, file storage areas that cannot be opened without a mouse, difficult-to-discriminate links and buttons, and unlabeled visual elements. Any pages with Java script can cause trouble for most screen readers unless a special script has been written for dealing with the page.

Multimodal Text Accessibility

This section addresses major accessibility issues currently facing visually impaired users of multimodal texts and asks readers to interrogate their assumptions about how the blind access online information. These multimodal constructs are often defined as means of communication "in which written-linguistic modes of meaning are part and parcel of visual, audio, and spatial patterns of meaning" (Cope & Kalantzis, 2000, p. 5). Whatever might be the lure of multimodal composition, writing instructors are bound both by law and by social ethics to make their courses accessible to all enrollees. The instructor's multimodality preferences easily may become someone else's multilevel headache. That handy YouTube film likely does not pass the basic accessibility standards. Just as one must ask whether a film has captions for deaf users, it is necessary to consider whether visual content is accompanied by text descriptions for screen-reader users.

Consider the complex act of reading a multimodal text in an OWI—or any other—class. The thought that blind individuals listen to all the on-screen text is just as silly as thinking all blind individuals sleep with their eyes open. Like any user, blind users listen (read) enough to orient themselves on the page and reach a decision to continue or to move on to another element. In other words, blind readers also construct their own reading experience, but this experience is rendered more meaningful when accessible to their reading abilities. For this reason, providing elaborate descriptions of every element is meaningless, but labeling every link, icon, or other pictorial element with text tags is important. Such labeling provides blind students with the same choices in how they read and integrate materials as other students have.

Misconceptions about how blind users read webpages also are common among professional and amateur web designers. Blind users, programmers, and web designers often contend that they do not access information sequentially and that "blind and partially-sighted users make every bit as much use of their memory of spatial location as sighted users do because it speeds up the process of obtaining target information" (Gemmell, 2010). However, this user experience knowledge should not give the online designers carte blanche to sprinkle various information elements around the webpage arbitrarily. Gemmell's (2010) example about a sighted person's use of the tacit knowledge for creating a new email message is insightful:

> How laborious life would be if this were true. In reality, blind and partially-sighted users make every bit as much use of their memory of spatial location as sighted users do, because it accelerates target acquisition. When you decide to create a new email message, you don't scan the whole screen to find the 'New Message' button; your hand pushes the mouse in that direction automatically.
>
> Similarly, visually impaired users will quickly learn the location of interface elements, and can access them directly. Don't take steps to artificially linearise your content for such users, and equally don't assume that you can arbitrarily move elements around either. ("Myths about Visually Impaired Users," myth 2)

The blind student will learn where the interface elements are for a particular website or webtext, but he or she will need to adapt that process in myriad ways for all subsequent webtexts as few are designed alike. Indeed, creative design often combines with rhetorical readability for websites, and instructors may choose them for these elements as much as for the textual message they convey. The OWI teacher must consider the potential losses against gains for visually impaired students when learning to write—not how to navigate webtexts—is the point of the course.

It is important to realize that photographs, pictures, and graphics are useless for blind readers unless they are accompanied by meaningful text descriptions.

Since these visually impaired readers access webpages with screen readers and electronic Braille displays, listening to long lists of items, navigational menus, ASCII art (pictures pieced together from text), and other visual objects can result in cognitive dissonance and can appear utterly purposeless because human ears cannot meaningfully process information specifically designed for visual comprehension. In these situations (and if the material really is necessary to the course), teachers should create links that will allow screen reader users to jump over such areas of the page after they have become familiar with the contents of these areas. Likewise, repetition of the same navigational menus at the top and bottom of webpages is not only fatiguing to the ear but also can be confusing in terms of the user's spatial orientation. These menus need to be addressed at the point of their creation for greatest accessibility and efficiency for all involved.

Writing instructors must further attend to the accessibility of virtual spaces as they plan the networking and peer group activities in their courses. While cell phones, chat clients, text messengers, and various commercial websites such as Twitter, Facebook, and Second Life appear to offer attractive options for engaging students in course activities, these virtual tools also can bar visually disabled students from participating in the academic activities. These technologies simply are not adaptive to blind students in any reasonable manner, and they lock out such students from the intended learning experience.

Similarly, as evidenced by published literature and professional e-list conversations, many contemporary writing instructors promote the popularity of video games and simulation programs to entice students to their courses and to teach difficult to communicate concepts. Again, in selecting such multimedia tools, writing instructors must adhere to the accessibility criteria whether or not the manufacturers of such media gave thought to the accessibility of their products. It is critical, therefore, to consider whether and how instructors can provide alternate means for obtaining information to screen-reader users when accessibility is not achievable through regular means. For example, if a photograph is central to the learning unit, a textual description may be necessary for screen reader users. For another example, popularly used single character emoticons, verticons, and other popular icons without text tags are read by screen readers either as stray punctuation marks or simply ignored if the user has set the punctuation reading level at "some" or "none." If instructors deem emoticons to be essential to communicating feelings and personality, adding a brief parenthetical description of the emoticons (e.g., "smiley face") will make them meaningful to the blind reader.

Even the minutia of creating and storing files requires consideration. For example, instructors need to learn whether the chosen organization tool is accessible to screen readers in terms of selecting means for organizing and storing files, links, and other objects. File creation and sharing are important to the contemporary OWI peer workshop approach of reading, responding in writing to, and then discussing the peer draft through text. Files need to be accessible without optical devices such as mice, track balls, and touchpads. Yet they also must meet the web standards for general accessibility. Instructors need to take further steps to understand whether organization tools such as Delicious, Google Desktop, and Microsoft OneNote are accessible to the users of screen readers and Braille display systems.

Visual Aspects of Formatting

According to Hewett (2010), text formatting (e.g., color and line spacing) helps to convey meaning to instructional response in online settings. Thus, it is useful to consider various questions that writing instructors should ask before designing the procedures for providing feedback to student work, requiring color and fancy fonts in assignments, and asking blind students to draw upon the visual aspects of the contemporary textbooks. While it is true that the availability of desktop publishing has placed the production of glitzy pages within the reach of an average computer user, screen readers and OCR devices fail to make sense of eye-catching graphics, strange fonts, varying point sizes in type, and Byzantine layouts. The proliferation of such colorful, artsy formatting can make even simple text inaccessible to readers using optical scanners and OCR devices. While OCR programs are capable of recognizing color fonts, the accuracy level of character recognition varies from color to color and shade to shade. The quality of the scanned image can further contribute to the character recognition errors.

For example, in an online setting, color can help sighted students distinguish their writing from the instructor's response. Changes in font color and the use of highlighting, for instance, can convey meaning to the student about writing and revision options. However, blind students have no reliable means of distinguishing these color changes, potentially making all text appear to be that of one writer. Even the track changes tool can prove difficult for some text readers. For non-sighted students, an obvious alternative to colored, bolded, or highlighted formatting is the simple use of parentheses and brackets to differentiate between student text and teacher response and instruction.

Indeed, regarding color, text printed on anything other than white paper can result in multiple recognition errors by the OCR engine, and paper of certain bright colors can make it impossible for a scanner camera to distinguish printed material from the background. Hence, instructors must err on the side of simplicity while preparing hard copy documents for their classes. It is important to remember that blind students have no quick means to distinguish printed color pages from white pages. Instructors, in general, make additional work for them by color-coding pages for the convenience of sighted students.

Resources Beyond the OWI Classroom

Teaching OWI courses that blind students can access carries certain elements of sheer practicality, as we have shown in this chapter. There are, however, critical elements of social justice that must be considered. Although educators may not be responsible for screen reader accessibility of article databases available through the institution's library, by assigning readings from such full-text databases, instructors must ask whether that choice is socially just for the visually disabled student. It is important to ensure that adequate arrangements exist at the library for equal access. Blind students should have the same ease of accessing these articles as other students do; they should not be expending more time on this research task than sighted students do. Indeed, it is important to consider whether such research and reading will affect blind students' performance in other areas of the course and in other courses they are taking simultaneously. Before assigning the reading, it is only right to learn whether the institution's disability services office will be able to provide these materials at the same time when other students would be reading them. It is exactly in such situations that educators need to contemplate the much-touted imperative of evaluating disabled students at par with other students.

Online Conferencing

The place of online writing centers as a point of conferencing about writing also needs to be considered, as well as online conferencing between teacher and student or among blind students and peers in OWI settings.

Anecdotal information indicates that instructors seldom call upon blind students in traditional classrooms. As the open-university pedagogy of the last four decades urges that instructors call on both male and female students to increase class interaction, disabled students also benefit from teacher encouragement through questions and comments. Since students must disclose their disability status if they want to receive accommodations, instructors should be aware of transferring pedagogical biases of face-to-face teaching to the distance learning environment.

Although Hewett (2010) suggested ways to accomplish online conferencing in a variety of online settings for students with some learning challenges, she did not consider the needs of visually disabled students. As suggested earlier, the asynchronous modality may provide visually impaired students with the greatest opportunity for equity with sighted peers (outside the use of a simple telephone call). Sometimes this process is equally necessary for sighted students. Similarly, thoughtful uses of parentheses and brackets can help make a teacher or tutor's asynchronous conferences more comprehensible.

It would be wrong, however, to imply that these two recommendations are the limit of what can be done for successful online conferencing with blind students. The sad fact is that so much research is left to be done in that area that our words here amount to little more than educated guesses for how to provide successful online writing and other conferencing assistance. All teachers and tutors must consider themselves responsible for prying open this closed box of online conferencing for blind students and to bring them to parity in this crucial resource for writing development.

Evaluation

Last, but far from least, how to evaluate blind students in the OWI setting should be considered. In "Questions to Consider in Policy Development for Postsecondary Students with Disabilities," Cox and Walsh (1997) took a middle ground while discussing the Memorial University of Newfoundland's handbook on disability awareness for students, faculty, and service providers, which stated that:

> It is commonly felt that unless all students are evaluated in exactly the same manner, an element of unfairness exists. Students with disabilities, however, may require modifications in the evaluation process in order to accurately demonstrate their achievement of course objectives. (Memorial University of Newfoundland, 1997, p. 116)

We agree with Cox and Walsh's (1997) conclusion that "The tension point commonly identified is achieving a balance between minimizing the impact of the disability on the student's performance and assuring equal opportunity to demonstrate content mastery without compromising academic standards" (pp. 9–10).

Both from a legal and an ethical viewpoint, the ultimate burden of assuring equal opportunity for blind students falls on instructors since neither university administrations nor disability services offices assigns grades to these students. We would further urge writing program administrators to develop a set of well-informed and well-considered standards for evaluating disabled students when known discrepancies exist between the academic resources available to able-bodied and disabled writing students. Of course, for these standards to have any meaningful effect, the inclusion of disabled students in discussions about assessment and instructor training workshops is just as important.

CONCLUSION

While the focus of this chapter is primarily on the special needs of the visually impaired students, the recommended alternatives and practices will help instructors improve their courses for all other students as well. Similarly, additional research and pedagogy developed for the sake of benefiting visually impaired students might one day be helpful for all students, sighted or disabled. Accessible design thinking is not a one-way street. It helps the disabled, but it can also help the general population. For example, digital designers are looking at using Braille-style passwords for ATM machines to provide additional password protection to users. Presented underneath the fingertips, Braille passwords cannot be viewed by prowling observers and can be retained in memory by both blind and sighted users (Kuber & Yu, 2010).

Warnock (2009) wrote that providing information to students through multiple means is pertinent to the OWI context: "Redundancy and repetition will help students stay on track so we can focus on the more challenging and complex task of helping them improve their writing" (p. 56). Many of the steps taken for accommodating the blind students' special needs are just the kind of redundancies he advised educators to build in the design of the courses overall. To accommodate a range of learners, it is only reasonable to provide a range and redundancy of information processing solutions.

Becoming familiar with tools and techniques essential for delivering accessible online writing courses can assist educators not only in meeting their legal obligations as teachers but also engendering confidence for developing a more inclusive pedagogy based on equality and social justice. It will help OWI instructors, particularly, to understand the writing processes that this group of students employs for accomplishing the assigned academic tasks and will bring everyone closer to recognizing visually impaired students as members of our learning communities.

In sum, this chapter asks many necessary questions and attempts to provide provisional responses to some of them. At the very least, our intention has been to act as gadflies of parity for the OWI community and the students it serves.

APPENDIX:
Tools for Improving Accessibility of Electronic
Materials for the Blind

The Inclusive Design Research Centre (in partnership with the Government of Ontario and the United Nations Educational, Scientific, and Cultural Organization [UNESCO]) has published the "Authoring Techniques for Accessible Office Documents" (http://adod.idrc.ocad.ca/). This print and online publication consists of several desktop reference guides for producing word processing, presentation, and spreadsheet documents.

These guidelines may serve as a starting point for the online writing instructors of the blind as these are meant for accessibility specialists, disabled users, and professionals working with the disabled. These publications comply with the new accessibility standard, the W3C's WAI process, since these are based on WCAG 2.0 and ATAG 1.0 standards. None of these documents promise full accessibility for the users with diverse disabilities and not all the guides are for the latest version of the software since these help guides are created as retrofits to provide accessibility. Instructors are urged to perform a quick Internet search to check the availability of the guides for the software packages and versions they plan to use.

As of 2011, the word processing guides are available for the users of OpenOffice Writer, Microsoft Word, Corel WordPerfect, Google docs, and iWork Pages.

The presentation instructions are available for these application packages, OpenOffice Impress, Microsoft PowerPoint, Corel Presentations, Google docs: Presentation, and iWork Keynote.

The spreadsheet guidelines are for OpenOffice Calc, Microsoft Excel, Corel Quattro Pro, Google docs Spreadsheet, and iWork Numbers.

For information on how to make the Adobe PDF files accessible, visit http://www.adobe.com/accessibility/index.html.

To learn about National Instructional Materials Accessibility Standard (NIMAS), a technical standard used by publishers to produce source files (in XML) that may be used to develop multiple specialized formats (such as Braille or audio books) for students with print disabilities, visit http://aim.cast.org/learn/policy/federal/what_is_nimas. According to the NIMAS website, the standard applies only to instructional materials published on or after July 19, 2006, and the textbooks for such adaptive use are available only if the publisher owns the rights to the materials. The U.S. Department of Education's NIMAS Q&A webpage offers additional information about the National Repository of such adaptable books operationalized in 2006.

A webpage for easier viewing of YouTube videos is at http://icant.co.uk/easy-youtube/.

WebAIM offers a tutorial for captioning streaming download videos (http://webaim.org/techniques/captions/hicaption/#intro).

The Apple Developer website offers an Accessibility Programming Guide to iOS, which might be a useful resource for instructors with some programming experience who are interested in offering accessible course materials to the blind on iPads and iPhones via the built-in Mac screen reader VoiceOver (http://developer.apple.com/library/ios/#documentation/UserExperience/Concep tual/iPhoneAccessibility/Introduction/Introduction.html). Although the champions of VoiceOver and all the Apple devices that can run this software are bullish about its capabilities, online instructors must remember that these are the claims from the programmers and casual users. Only after VoiceOver has undergone significant testing in the hands of blind users for educational and professional purposes will we have an understanding of its capabilities.

The Advisory Commission on Accessible Instructional Materials in Post-Secondary Education for Students with Disabilities is also a good resource for faculty interested in developing accessible curricular materials (http://aim.cast.org/collaborate/p-s_commission).

The American Foundation for the Blind has a service called AFB Consulting that will work with organizations to help them achieve accessibility of their products. Readers can visit www.afbconsulting.org to find out more.

REFERENCES

Bowe, F. G. (2000). *Universal design in education: Teaching nontraditional students.* Westport, CT: Bergin & Garvey.

Burgstahler, S., & Doe, T. (2006). Improving postsecondary outcomes for students with disabilities: Designing professional development for faculty. *Journal of Postsecondary Education and Disability, 18*(2), 135–147.

Burgstahler, S., & Moore, E. (2009). Making students welcome and accessible through accommodations in universal design. *Journal of Postsecondary Education and Disability, 21*(3), 155–174. Retrieved from http://www.ahead.org/publications/ jped#content

Conference on College Composition and Communication. (2010). Hybrid/blended courses survey results. Committee for Best Practices in Online Writing Instruction. Retrieved from http://www.ncte.org/cccc/committees/owi

Cook, B. G., Rumrill, P. D., Camarata, J., Mitchell, P. R., Newman, S., Sebaly, K. P., et al. (2006). The impact of a professional development institute on faculty members' interactions with college students with learning disabilities. *Journal of Postsecondary Education and Disability, 14*, 67–76.

Coombs, N. (2010). *Making online teaching accessible: Inclusive course design for students with disabilities.* San Francisco, CA: Jossey-Bass.

Cope, B., & Kalantzis, M. (Eds.). (2000). *Multiliteracies: Literacy learning and the design of social futures.* New York, NY: Routledge.

Cox, D., & Walsh, R. M. (1997). Questions to consider in policy development for postsecondary students with disabilities. *Journal of Postsecondary Education and Disability, 13*(2). Retrieved from www.ahead.org/uploads/docs/jped/.../13.../jped132 coxquestions.doc

Dowrick, P. W., Anderson, J., Heyer, K., & Acosta, J. (2005). Postsecondary education across the USA: Experiences of adults with disabilities. *Journal of Vocational Rehabilitation, 22*(1), 41–47.

Farone, M. C., Hall, E. W., & Costello, J. J. (1998). Postsecondary disability issues: An inclusive identification strategy. *Journal of Postsecondary Education and Disability, 13*, 35–45.

Frank, K., & Wade, P. (1993). Disabled student services in postsecondary education: Who's responsible for what? *Journal of College Student Development, 34*(1), 26–30.

Gemmell, M. L. (2010, December 19). Accessibility for iPhone and iPad apps. Retrieved from http://mattgemmell.com/2010/12/19/accessibility-for-iphone-and-ipad-apps

Hewett, B. L. (2003). Interview with Professors Andrea Lunsford and Michael Leff about the Alliance for Rhetoric Society (ARS). *Kairos, 8*(2). Retrieved from http:// english.ttu.edu/kairos/8.2/binder.html?interviews/arsinterview/index.htm

Hewett, B. L. (2010). *The online writing conference: A guide for teachers and tutors.* Portsmouth, NH: Heinemann.

Hewett, B. L., & Hewett, R. J. (2008). IM talking about workplace literacy. In K. St.Amant & P. Zemliansky (Eds.), *Handbook of research on virtual workplaces and the new nature of business practices* (pp. 455–472). New York, NY: Information Science Reference.

Hill, J. L. (1996). Speaking out: Perceptions of students with disabilities regarding adequacy of services and willingness of faculty to make accommodations. *Journal of Postsecondary Education and Disability, 12*(1), 22–43.

Johnson, R. R. (2010). The ubiquity paradox: Further thinking on the concept of user centeredness. *Technical Communication Quarterly, 19*(4), 335–351.

Krampe, K. M., & Berdine, W. H. (2003). University of Kentucky engaging differences project: Providing information about accommodations on line and just in time. *Journal of Postsecondary Education and Disability, 17*(1), 21–32.

Kuber, R., & Yu, W. (2010). Feasibility study of tactile-based authentication. *International Journal of Human-Computer Studies, 68*(3), 158–181.

Lehmann, J. P., Davies, T. G., & Laurin, K. M. (2000). Listening to student voices about postsecondary education. *Teaching Exceptional Children, 32*(5), 60–65.

Mace, R. (n.d.). About UD. The Center for Universal Design. Retrieved from http://www.ncsu.edu/www/ncsu/design/sod5/cud/about_ud/about_ud.htm

Memorial University of Newfoundland. (1997). *Partnerships to access learning: A resource book for students, faculty, and service providers*. St. John's: Author.

Murray, C., Wren, C., Stevens, E., & Keys, C. (2009) Promoting university faculty and staff awareness of students with learning disabilities: An overview of the productive learning strategies project. *Journal of Postsecondary Education and Disability, 22*(2), 117–129.

National Center for the Study of Postsecondary Educational Supports. (2000). *Postsecondary education and employment for students with disabilities*. Honolulu, HI: University of Hawaii.

Parry, M. (2010, December 12). Colleges lock out blind students online. *Chronicle of Higher Education*. Retrieved from http://chronicle.com/article/Blind-Students-Demand-Access/125695/

Rohland, P., Erickson, B., Mathews, D., Roush, S. E., Quinlan, K., & Smith, A. D. (2003). Changing the culture (CTC): A collaborative training model to create systematic change. *Journal of Postsecondary Education and Disability, 17*, 49–58.

Slatin, J., & Rush, S. (2003). *Maximum accessibility: Making your web site more usable for everyone*. Boston, MA: Addison-Wesley.

Sowers, J., & Smith, M. R. (2004). Evaluation of the effects of an inservice training program on nursing faculty members' perceptions, knowledge, and concerns about students with disabilities. *Journal of Nursing Education, 43*(6), 248–252.

U.S. Department of Justice. (2010, April 15). Letter of Resolution, D.J. No. 202-48-213 Princeton University. Retrieved from http://www.ada.gov/princeton.htm

Waddell, C. D. (1999, May). The growing digital divide in access for people with disabilities: Overcoming barriers to participation in the digital economy. *Understanding the digital economy: Data, tools, and research*. Symposium conducted at the meeting of the National Science Foundation. Washington, DC. Retrieved from http://www.icdri.org/CynthiaW/the_digital_divide.htm

Walters, S. (2010). Toward an accessible pedagogy: Dis/ability, multimodality, and universal design in the technical communication classroom. *Technical Communication Quarterly, 19*(4), 427–454.

Warnock, S. (2009). *Teaching writing online: How and why*. Urbana, IL: National Council of Teachers of English (NCTE).

West, M., Kregel, J., Getzel, E., Zhu, M., Ipsen, S., & Martin, E. (1993). Beyond Section 504: Satisfaction and empowerment of students with disabilities in higher education. *Exceptional Children, 59*(5), 456–467.

http://dx.doi.org/10.2190/RAAC8

CHAPTER 8

Disability, Web Standards, and the Majority World

Sarah Lewthwaite and Henny Swan

Web standards offer a powerful tool for achieving global web accessibility. However, the success of such standards may be limited while standards fail to account for disability as a socio-cultural product dependent on any given context. This chapter seeks to map potential problems with international web accessibility standards—with a specific focus on how such standards may implicitly export certain ways of thinking about disability from minority countries to the majority world.

Within this chapter, we make the distinction minority/majority rather than developed/developing, first world/third world or North/South. The minority/majority distinction is made after Katsui (2006) to politicize notions of development and to acknowledge that "the distinction between North and South has been blurred in disability discourse, because no country has achieved equality for disabled people" (p. 86). In disability studies, Stone (1999) makes an early reference to majority experience: "The majority world is the world that the vast majority of the world's people live in, yet they have access to a fraction of the world's wealth and power" (p. 4). In this way, minority/majority allows us to recognize that inequality can be located between continents but also within a small locale. Majority experience is not necessarily geographically specific.

Disability and impairment in the majority world are, as yet, poorly understood at the national and international level. There are clear and powerful correlations between poverty (Katsui, 2005; Yeo, 2003), war, disaster, and famine, and the levels and types of disability that a particular country will face and prioritize. Geography and global economics play a part. There are also cultural issues that

157

lead to disablism. Disablism is the "discriminatory, oppressive or abusive behavior arising from the belief that disabled people are inferior to others" (Miller, Parker, & Gillinson, 2004). Instigating factors may include stigma (Goffman, 1963); traditional perspectives informed by superstition, religion, belief systems, custom, and taboo (Coleridge, 1993); and more latent aversive disablism (Deal, 2007). Within this nexus, disability may be bound into other indices of marginalization according to age, gender, sexuality, ethnicity, class, and so forth.

Here, we argue that it may be counter-productive to assume that the primary accessibility battles being fought in minority nations are those most important in other regional and local contexts. This is a complex issue, as globally both disability and accessibility represent "blank spots" (Wagner, 1993) in research terms. We assert the importance of bringing perspectives from disability studies to bear within this landscape of technical accessibility discourse. However, we also note that such perspectives must be globalized, acknowledging the different ways in which disability is constructed and understood in the majority as well as the minority world, post-colonializing disability studies in the process. Over the course of this discussion we focus on the application of the Web Content Accessibility Guidelines (WCAG) of the World Wide Web Consortium (W3C).

WEB STANDARDS

The Web Accessibility Initiative (WAI), part of the W3C, publishes WCAG (Caldwell, Cooper, Reid, & Vanderheiden, 2008). First published in 1999, WCAG is accepted worldwide as the de facto standard for web accessibility. While other guidelines exist, for example Section 508 in the United States, the vast majority derive from WCAG and are adapted according to each country's context. Some governments worldwide reference WCAG verbatim within their disability legislation. In this way, governments seek to effect equality measures that commensurate with disability discrimination laws, for example, Spain with Law 49/2007 (European Commission, 2008). Others, such as Australia's Human Rights and Equal Opportunity Commission simply reference WCAG (Australian Human Rights Commission, 2010).

The W3C itself is an international body comprised of volunteer organizations, experts, and full-time staff who work together to develop web standards. During the development process, the public is invited to provide feedback on the guidelines before they become an official "normative" document. The process is internationally open and transparent; however, it is also lengthy and complex.

Without a doubt, WCAG has been at the core of the accessibility movement worldwide, providing a foundation on which the developer community can build accessible websites and website owners can commission accessible websites. Without WCAG, governments would not have had a globally respected source to reference in disability legislation and accessibility would have been defined by individuals and organizations in a way that was not standardized or scalable.

While legislation requiring accessible web content exists on a local level, it was not until 2006 that the first international human rights initiative enforcing accessibility came into being. Article 9 of the United Nations' Convention on the Rights of Persons with Disabilities (2006) compels member parties to take appropriate measures to ensure that people with disabilities have equal access to, among other things, information and communications including information and computer technology (ICT). This is significant as many member parties (including China, Ethiopia, Malta, and Lebanon) who have ratified the Convention have hitherto not had any disability legislation enforcing access to web content. As a result, WCAG has become a matter of majority world policy, with the potential to influence the lives of millions of disabled people.

The wholesale governmental adoption of WAI and WCAG has been critiqued by those who have called for a standards-based approach to be applied in a more nuanced way. Issues raised include the need for evidence base and the recognition of contextual factors such as economic stringencies, legacy technologies, and other framing issues (see Kelly, Neville, Sloan, Fanou, Ellison, & Herrod, 2009; Kelly, Sloan, Brown, Seale, Petrie, Lauke, et al., 2007; Kelly, Sloan, Phipps, Petrie, & Hamilton, 2005). Such critiques are important and point to a more holistic, contextual approach to web accessibility. Such arguments engage explicitly with the central problem of standardizing as an idealized practice, an act that reduces complex experience. However, as yet, such critiques have yet to apply critical disability studies perspectives in a more systematic deconstruction of these standards and their socio-cultural effects.

DISABILITY AND STANDARDS

The appropriation of WCAG for information and communications policy is important. In short, in these national circumstances WCAG are applied as standards, rather than guidelines. In this new context, guidelines cease to function contextually. A web standard is a formal term for technical specifications. These are fixed and unambiguous. Guidelines are a set of recommendations, or best practices, that are more open to multiple interpretations. As such, guidelines are applied and interpreted according to the context (location, culture, technology, and so on) in which they are being applied. Version 2.0 of WCAG has tried to accommodate this ambiguity by providing a set of success criteria that should be met in order to make a site accessible rather than a step-by-step guide of what to do. Standards imply a more systematic duality of compliance and non-compliance. This subtle shift is not simply semantic; it gestures to a completely different epistemology of both technology and disability. It is to this implicit issue of what standards *do* that we now turn.

Although there has been a great deal of debate about the definition of *disability* in national and international policy, as Bowker and Star (1999) and others observe, the "invisible power" of standards in information technology remains largely unreflected.

> Despite the contentiousness of some categories, . . . none of . . . [the critical] disciplines or social movements has systematically addressed the pragmatics of the invisible forces of categories and standards in the modern built world, especially the modern information technology world. (Bowker & Star, 1999, p. 5)

To answer this call, we assert that when WCAG is applied as a standard it may also induct a potentially colonial, minority perspective. In short: "Each standard . . . valorizes some point of view and silences another" (Bowker & Star, 1999, p. 5). In this respect, the act of standardization bears close consideration. Since web standards represent a minority standard for the majority world, critical engagement with this action is vital. The boundaries, language, and detail of compliance and non-compliance are heavily contested; however, the activity of applying the standards which create and enact these boundaries has not been scrutinized to the same extent.

Since the very activity of standardizing (separating the acceptable from the unacceptable) frequently results in the substitution of precision for validity (Bowker & Star, 1999), this form of technical writing bears close consideration. Bowker and Star (1999) identify six elements implicit within any act of standardization:

1. A "standard" is any set of agreed-upon rules for the production of (textual or material) objects.
2. A standard spans more than one community of practice (or site of activity). It has temporal reach as well in that it persists over time.
3. Standards are deployed in making things work together over distance and heterogeneous metrics. [...]
4. Legal bodies often enforce standards. [...]
5. There is no natural law that the best standard shall win. [...]
6. Standards have significant inertia and can be very difficult and expensive to change. (pp. 14-15)

Standards are frequently idealized and written in the abstract rather than the concrete. As a result, all too often there is a significant disjuncture between the goals embodied within standards and the reality and pragmatics of application. More importantly, standards represent a fixed point of view. In this respect, they elevate one perspective at the expense of others. This is significant as it reveals a dual function within accessibility standards; ostensibly they function to promote certain practices, however, to achieve this end, they must also 'scaffold' the standard-user into a new and fixed epistemology or perspective. In this sense, technical accessibility guidelines and associated materials are not only transmitting expertise, they are also pedagogic. WCAG-as-standard teaches the standard-user not only how to create web content to a certain criteria but also, within that, requires acquiescence to an external (standards) perspective that incorporates certain views on disability and technology. As we have previously stated, standards have clear value for advancing and scaling accessibility best practice. Within this, however, it is important to recognize that standards also function as a tool for transforming the developers' and users' perspectives. Web standards thereby represent an opportunity to refashion understandings of disability. This affordance is double-edged. On the one hand, it represents the opportunity to inherently promote disability rights; on the other, there is the potential for a form of a socio-cultural assimilation to take place. In this way, a majority world developer may take on a minority worldview that cannot account for the socially ascribed realities of disability within the developer's home culture (for example, the availability of assistive technologies, home access, literacy levels). As this assimilation takes place at the level of the developer or designer, there is a risk that colonization may propagate forms of web practice that exacerbate the exclusion of groups of disabled people outside the norms of minority accessibility practice. To explore this concern, it is useful to consider hierarchies of impairment.

HIERARCHIES OF IMPAIRMENT AND WEB STANDARDS

The term *hierarchy of impairment* denotes the ways in which physical and cognitive differences are identified and arranged within society. We know that different cultures imbue different impairments with different cultural significance. These understandings permeate everything, including technology and accessibility practice. It is therefore vital for us as researchers and practitioners to engage critically with the social forces we are caught up in and to recognize that hierarchies of impairment will change depending on the local culture we are engaging with. Such issues are explicitly recognized within the UN Convention on the Rights of Persons with Disabilities (2006), in the Preamble which actively refuses to define *disability* in universal terms without reference to local context:

> "Disability" is an evolving concept resulting from attitudinal and environmental barriers hindering the participation of persons with disabilities in society. Consequently, the notion of "disability" is not fixed and can alter, depending on the prevailing environment from society to society. (UN, 2010)

The effects of hierarchies of impairment can be traced within WCAG and associated documents. For example, WCAG has been criticized for not accommodating various disabilities in equal measure. Kelly, Lewthwaite, and Sloan (2010) draw together two sources as possible examples in which cognitive disabilities and learning difficulties are granted lower status in web accessibility discourse. They cite Clark's (2006) observation that the development of WCAG lacked adequate provision for users with learning difficulties and cognitive disabilities and Seeman's (2007) formal objection to WCAG 2.0, which requests that implicit claims that the guidelines did cover cognitive disabilities be omitted from the guidelines' abstract altogether. WCAG's perceived lack of focus on cognitive disabilities and learning difficulties reflects an extant hierarchy of impairment that has been researched since the 1970s. In Tringo's (1970) research, a group of non-disabled people who, when asked to rank 21 impairments from "would marry" to "would put to death," placed "mental retardation" as the least desirable. Thomas (2000) found this perception nearly unchanged 30 years later. More recently still, Deal (2003) found such hierarchies exist between and amongst disabled people themselves.

While such disablism appears to inform the conditions in which technical writing takes place, the nature of technology itself may also explain such disparity. WCAG is widely criticized as privileging visual impairment among impairment groups because of the visual nature of the web. In order to access a webpage, a blind user must use a screen reader that outputs code audibly just as a browser outputs code visually for sighted users. It is relatively straightforward to write guidelines that reinforce good practice in generating code for screen readers, whereas knowing how to accommodate users with cognitive impairments, intellectual impairments, and learning difficulties is more complex. Blind users share a defined set of commonalities in terms of challenges when accessing webpages: all users need to be able to access the heading structure, alternative text for images, transcripts for video, and so on. Users with cognitive disabilities and learning difficulties also have commonalities in terms of challenges but with many more variables. In this respect, the development of research and attendant standards development can be observed to be socio-technical, stemming from both culture and technology, and borne out in an iterative cycle that marginalizes a particular impairment group.

Other critical engagement with the WAI process illuminates this hierarchy further, demonstrating this hierarchy to implicitly model both the standards-user as well as a disabled end-user. Here we present a brief critique based on the language of WCAG and a cultural normativity visible in WCAG's accessibility scenarios. These examples are by no means exhaustive; however, they have particular pertinence for our expanded global focus.

THE LANGUAGE OF WCAG

A significant criticism of WCAG that has the potential to reinforce hier-archies of impairment within accessibility discourse and standards implemen-tation relates to how the document itself is presented.

Many consider WCAG, which is a large document, to be poorly organized, too heavy in its use of technical language, and not user friendly. It can be cumbersome for non-native speakers of English, Deaf users (whose first lan-guage may be, for example, Australian Sign Language), and for people with cognitive disabilities, learning difficulties, print impairments, and so on. Many advocates have discussed the need for plain language (Herrod, 2008). Others (Clark, 2006; Moss, 2006) have wryly noted that WCAG's glossary of defini-tions is, itself, teeming with complex language. For example,

Programmatically determined:
Determined by software from data provided in a user-agent-supported manner such that the user agents can extract and present this information to users in different modalities.

Web unit
A collection of information, consisting of one or more resources, intended to be rendered together, and identified by a single Uniform Resource Identifier (such as URLs). (Caldwell et al., 2008, "Appendix A")[1]

This complexity is genre specific and disadvantages non-specialist web developers. However, it also places particular burdens on specialist translation for global contexts. WAI placed a strong emphasis on collaborative and voluntary translation to make WCAG available in 51 languages. Nonetheless, the problem of translation is an important one. While language describing technical items and operations may be relatively straightforward, the notion of accessibility as accounting for disabled people may be problematic in societies where disability itself is not easily translated. For example, Lwanga-Ntale (2003, p. 4) found translating "disability" within his Ugandan research problematic, as in this context, disability is understood to refer to only physical impairments, without reference to sensory or cognitive impairments. Singal (2010) highlights further concerns, noting that "in Hindi, the word *viklang* used commonly for 'disability' does not encompass all types of disabilities but is only indicative of physical impairments" (p. 418). Singal proceeds to observe that in some countries the only language available for the discussion of disability is in itself stigmatizing.

---

[1] Readers should note that many of the Web documents cited within this chapter are dynamic and change over time. For this reason all online references are dated and quoted in full where possible at the time of writing.

"'Wasiojiweza' used in parts of Kenya to refer generally to persons in all categories of disabilities embodies the assumption that the individual is incapable of gainful employment" (Ndurumo as cited in Singal, 2010, p. 418). In such contexts, the notion of accessibility as an expression of barrier removal and the social dimensions of disability are diametrically opposed to local understandings of capability and the nature of disability.

DEPICTIONS OF DISABILITY AND
WEB ACCESS

Aside from the guidelines themselves, WAI publishes non-normative supportive documentation to enable web designers and developers to better understand the groups they are addressing. Resources such as those available for Education and Outreach[2] regarding how disabled people use the web, represent culturally normative depictions of people with disability and do not take into account scenarios in majority countries.

For example, culturally-specific scenarios include depictions of Repetitive Strain Injury, predicated on a lifetime's use of PC-based information technology, implying a minority location and life experience and, arguably, a minority impairment. Other scenarios relate to online shopping, referring to consumerism and disposable income and the case of a "retiree." Again, retirement itself is a situation predicated on a context of job security, certain working conditions, a health and social security infrastructure, life expectancy, and retirement benefits that are not majority experiences. In this respect, it is clear that such scenario documentation designed to help web developers better address their users is, in fact, only supporting minority developers to understand minority users. The addition of scenarios that recognize majority situations would be a valuable addition to these vignettes, increasing the relevance of these depictions of disability for all web developers and aligning them with majority experiences.

GLOBAL PERSPECTIVES ON HIERARCHIES
OF IMPAIRMENT

Our concerns with hierarchies of impairment and the socio-cultural construction of disability that can be traced within WCAG are thrown into sharp relief when considered against alternative, global contexts. Here we consider alternatives across two axes:

- Technological specificity: focusing on what we know about the technological reality of the majority world
- Cultural specificity: relating examples of diverse approaches to disability with relevance to accessibility and WCAG

---

[2] See the working drafts at http://www.w3.org/WAI/EO/

Technological Specificity

Current standards in web accessibility are largely driven by the developed minority world. The W3C is made up of large global organizations such as Microsoft, Adobe, IBM, Google, Mozilla, Sony, and Toshiba (to name only a few) as well as universities and disability groups. Many organizations have a vested business interest in contributing to the standards-making process, and few, if any, directly represent countries from the majority world. Equally, the developer community is largely based in North America, Europe, and Australia.

What are not so well represented are the views and requirements of disabled people in countries where disability has been affected by the cultural context such as war, poverty, limited health, education, transport, and communications infrastructure. In such contexts, access to connectivity, hardware, and software— including access to generalized and specialized assistive technologies such as screen readers and screen magnifiers—may be the exception rather than the rule.

Lack of access to the hardware and software needed to browse the Internet is beginning to be compensated in part by the rise of mobile browsing. Over the last few years it has become evident that mobile usage is catching up and exceeding desktop usage in majority countries so much so that some people's first, and only, experience of the Internet is through a mobile device rather than a desktop or laptop. In light of this, Microsoft now describes some collected majority nations as "Phone-First Economies" (Herbert, 2010). This is under-standable, given that mobile is cheaper and easier to attain since users need not have a telephone line, expensive hardware, or even a fixed address.

For disabled and older users (who may have some form of impairment but do not consider themselves disabled), this brings additional challenges since, compared to desktop browsers, mobile browsers are not as feature rich in terms of accessibility features. The accessibility of web content can also be undermined by the handset itself, which may render colors badly, lack options to change contrast, have no options to output mono audio or pinch/zoom, and so on. Accessibility features such as voice output and voice input and the ability to scale text and choose system colors are generally only available on high-end phones such as the iPhone and Blackberry, which have little penetration in majority countries. The State of the Mobile Web report (Opera Software, 2010) demonstrates that the top ten handsets used in Africa are all Nokia produced and do not feature any smartphones.

The W3C published the Mobile Web Best Practices 1.0 guidelines (Rabin & McCathieNevile, 2008), which gives guidance to developers of web content on how to make their content mobile ready. This document is not intended as a set of best practices to make mobile web content accessible to disabled users; however, there is significant crossover with WCAG. So much so, in fact, that WAI wrote a document mapping the relationship of Mobile Web Best Practices to WCAG. While useful, this mapping does not address specific issues regarding accessible mobile content, and there is no other publicly available documentation elsewhere. In short, the predominance of mobile access in the majority world highlights a WCAG limit in which mobile is secondary rather than central to web accessibility. WCAG is adaptable, but its technical focus arguably inducts a socio-technical minority outcome, representing a gap in standards to majority Internet access and a potentially significant impact on the lives of disabled people.

Cultural Specificity

Disability and impairment are diverse and heterogenic categories. They are permeable, unstable and socially contingent. Indeed, Shakespeare and Watson (2002) identified disability as the quintessential post-modern concept. It defies classification because it is "so complex, so variable, so situated" (p. 19).

An early point to make is to observe that within development discourse, the measurement of disability is fraught. Global levels of disability are "guesstimates." Disability and impairment levels are generally more highly reported within wealthier nations (Eide & Loeb, 2006). Within majority situations, it is estimated that half a billion disabled people are among the poorest of the poor (Metts as cited in Sheldon, 2010), constituting 15%–20% of the poorest in low-income countries (Elwan as cited in Sheldon, 2010). Increasingly, large-scale survey work is being undertaken to establish levels and types of impairment in majority countries; however, discrepancies in methods, definition, and so forth make this process difficult and data varies in comparability. For example, Sierra Leone is a country emerging from a conflict that has resulted in many people becoming disabled. The African Policy on Disability and Development (A-PODD, n.d.) project made the following statements:

> There is no clear data available about the prevalence of disability in Sierra Leone. The census data from 2003 indicate that 2.7% of the population have a disability. However, this percentage is highly likely to [be] underestimated as war in the country has led to much impairment, e.g. amputations. There are only a few Disabled People's Organizations in Sierra Leone, and these are all relatively new and therefore do not have much capacity. Sierra Leone Union of Disability Issues is the umbrella body responsible for matters. (para. 2)

This issue is not necessarily a quantitative one. That is, this is not simply a matter of knowing the number of disabled people in a country and working to accommodate them. This is a qualitative issue. In international development terms, the nature of Internet access among a disabled population in such situations is entirely unknown, ranking beneath international interests in the concerns of health, education, and economics. Outside international development initiatives, it bears consideration that such digital divides are among the least understood in both majority and minority contexts and that disability is frequently "the Other of the Other" (Wendell, 1996) within digital inclusion drives. This highlights a key paradox of WCAG and related standards. The lack of research base at the cutting edge of majority web development requires a standards-based model that can apply best practice from the top down. However, the impact of such standards cannot be known until a more cooperative process of multi-lateral engagement and mutual acknowledgment is achieved with disabled people and accessibility research and development globally.

In addition to such issues, there are certain disabilities that are increasingly well recognized within minority societies and may be conceived as minority impairments. For example, Barnes and Mercer (2003) assert that some impair-ments, such as dyslexia, are potentially disabling in technologically advanced societies but present fewer problems to people living in rural environments. Indeed, globally the status of dyslexia varies between and across majority *and* minority countries. As Lewis and Norwich (2005) observe:

> While dyslexia is recognized in most countries, there are still across-cultural differences in perceptions and definitions of dyslexia. These per-ceptions can be a result of policy differences or factors attributed to the language of the country. In the UK, it is estimated that there are two million severely dyslexic individuals, including 375,000 school children (Smythe, 2002). In contrast, there are no such estimates in China. Whether this reflects perceived importance or differences in incidence is as yet unknown; however, it is known that differences in awareness will lead to variations in provision. (p. 145)

Since Lewis and Norwich made this review, recognition of dyslexia has grown. The year 2010 marked the first World Forum for Dyslexia, which was held in Unesco, Paris, and attended by representatives from 150 countries. This is a reminder of the shifting nature of people's understandings of disability as a socially and culturally bound phenomenon. However, if we continue to focus on dyslexia in light of Barnes and Mercer's (2003) assertions, there is a concern that as technological advancement is inducted, so too is the experience of print impairment. WCAG has a role within this social shift. In majority contexts where educational infrastructural and literacy levels vary, print impairments such as dyslexia may be superseded by a need for information that is accessible in audio or visual formats, such as video. This creates tensions with technological constraints relating to bandwidth, mode of access, and so forth. Nonetheless, video can be accessible to majority users in ways that may be currently under-recognized by WCAG. Indeed, WCAG 1.0 (1999) made reference to supplementing text with graphic or auditory presentations in order to facilitate comprehension of the page: "14.2: Supplement text with graphic or auditory presentations where they will facilitate comprehension of the page" [Priority 3] (W3C, 1999).

However, WCAG 2.0 (Caldwell et al., 2008) does not include checkpoints, instead relegating it to a "technique" that is not part of the normative document. By not being part of the normative document (so often adopted by policy makers) this action becomes voluntary. In this way, a primary global concern— literacy—is rendered as a secondary issue within minority standards. Thus, a minority worldview, manifested through standards, may not strategically account for the most disadvantaged and digitally excluded within in any given majority context, leading to potentially counter-productive outcomes.

RECOGNIZING COMPLEXITY

As previously stated, critics of exclusive standards-based approaches such as WCAG highlight important caveats that must be employed when seeking to provide accessible websites and services. In addition, Kelly et al. (2010) demonstrate the value of using disability studies perspectives to help inform the development and application of web standards. However, even these critiques (and the present chapter) come from within an academic, minority discourse. Disability studies itself is not yet a global discipline. It is important to deconstruct such discourse and to seek to engage with the majority perspectives on disability that are currently unrepresented, while also acknowledging the limits and ambiguity of "disability" as a totalizing category. We have already gestured to gaps in research and knowledge exchange at the macro-level; it is also useful, however, to consider the challenge of local disconnection. Accessibility is an interconnected practice. Nowhere is this more apparent than within usability testing.

Implementing accessibility guidelines when building accessible websites is best achieved in conjunction with users and through usability testing with a variety of disabled users (British Standards Institution, 2006). For local developers to engage disabled people in usability testing, the lack of disabled people's organizations and such "disability" infrastructure may make this difficult (A-PPOD, n.d.).

Implementing web standards without usability testing can lead to websites that satisfy automated tests for accessibility guidelines and, in turn, access for assistive technologies. This can reinforce a hierarchy of impairment in technology since, for example, a screen reader user's needs may be met in a more satisfactory way than those with alternative access requirements. As Singal (2010) asserts, "In contexts where people with disabilities are not only marginalized but have also been systematically made invisible in policy and academic discourses the value of research which attempts to hear their voices is difficult to exaggerate" (p. 416).

In this sense, usability testing becomes deeply politicized. Moreover, there is a need for the practice of standards-making to free itself from a focus on minority developer communities and engage with the greater project of dialogue with those most oppressed and disadvantaged by current global information infrastructures and socio-economic power relations. Indeed, while this division remains unaddressed and disabled people in the majority world are under-represented in web standards, the project of accessibility may be seen as counterproductive, supporting an inequitable status quo in which disabled people in emerging economies are excluded from the knowledge capital that the Internet represents, entrenching economic and social disadvantage.

WAYS FORWARD

To refute the invisibility of disabled people in the majority world, we encourage a more nuanced approach to the understanding and application of web standards that recognizes the constraints of the standards-making exercise and disability studies as a still predominantly minority discipline. We have highlighted some of the complexities involved in technical writing across cultures. Where standards-makers have the opportunity to engage with the critical and global perspectives afforded by disability studies, it becomes clear that there are some relatively straightforward moves that can be made to augment standards. More nuanced and complex issues that gesture to the wider status of disability and its iterative relationship with poverty and globalized economics must be understood because they present a significant challenge for those engaged in the shared project of accessibility. A first step within this is a cooperative engagement with global perspectives on disability. To achieve this inter-disciplinary work is necessary bringing together technologists and those engaged with global disability studies.

Notably, the benefit of this engagement is not one-way; in developing a more sensitive understanding of the different ways that disability is constructed and impairment is created, it also becomes clear that many majority world accessibility issues incorporate minority issues that are experienced by disabled people in wealthy nations, issues that are under-represented or rendered invisible by the status quo. Both impairment and disability are linked to poverty. Discourse surrounding the ownership of assistive technologies and general access to information and computer technologies (ICTs) suggests that WAI understands disability in terms of Whyte and Ingstad's (1995) assertions, "In Europe and North America, disability is a political privilege entitling one to financial support and a series of services" (p. 9).

However, as Sheldon (2010) argues, even within minority contexts, this is not true for all. For example, Beresford (1996) stated that more than 60% of disabled people in Britain and the United States live below the poverty line. Furthermore, disability exists across indices inclusive of indigenous communities within minority countries such as Australia, homeless people (Sheldon, 2010), and those in disaster situations. In their research into the impact of Hurricane Katrina on disabled people, Fox, White, Rooney, and Cahill (2010) have shown that disabled people are disproportionately affected within minority communities devastated by natural and man-made disasters. This is by no means an exhaustive list; however, by turning a post-colonial lens on and within nation states, a sensitized deconstruction occurs, quickly identifying how normative minority conceptions of disability are, even within their own terms.

Deal (2003) argues that placing those who are most marginalized (within disability groups) at the center of the design process will reap the greatest rewards for all (a further microcosm of those arguments that accessibility as a whole also benefits non-disabled groups). This leads us to almost a point of deconstruction in every context, asking "who is missing here?" To answer this question, it is necessary to engage with the developer and population in question and promote a reflexive understanding of disability in a targeted and accessible way. This active questioning highlights the importance of global dialogue in web standards. Standards are currently reviewed and debated; however, further space for multiple perspectives and ambiguity to be incorporated into this discourse at the micro-level, the unit of instruction, is also desirable. "We need an ethics of ambiguity, still more urgently with the pressure to globalize, and the integration of systems of representation through information technologies world-wide" (Bowker & Star, 1999).

In summary, web standards development and application will benefit strongly from a close engagement with the critical perspectives of disability studies. Placing global, post-colonial concerns at the heart of this engagement will benefit web development, digital inclusion, and the disability rights project as a whole. This is a complex area. Standards act as a powerful catalyst for positive change but are, by their nature, simplifying, exploring a fixed point of view that is necessarily idealized. Forefronting the realities of majority perspectives will assist standards to cease to perpetuate that minority/majority dichotomy. Acknowledging this fact and adopting more holistic strategies that incorporate standards will allow us to better recognize ambiguity across differences in the heart of our practice. Disabled people are the "poorest of the poor" in all societies (Hurst & Albert, 2006, p. 24). To ensure that the pro-disabled project of accessibility does not itself marginalize disabled people globally by reifying, rather than deconstructing, digital divides, standards must seek to discover and engage with those most disadvantaged by technical writing.

REFERENCES

African Policy on Disability and Development (A-PODD). (n.d.). Sierra Leone. Retrieved November 14, 2010 from http://www.a-podd.org/index.php?option=com_content&view=article&id=6&Itemid=7

Australian Human Rights Commission. (2010). World Wide Web access: Disability Discrimination Act advisory notes, version 4.0. Retrieved November 10, 2010 from http://www.hreoc.gov.au/disability_rights/standards/www_3/www_3.html

Barnes, C., & Mercer, G. (2003). Exploring disability. Cambridge, MA: Polity Press.

Beresford, P. (1996). Poverty and disabled people: Challenging dominant debates and policies. Disability & Society, 11(4), 553–566.

Bowker, G. C., & Star, S. L. (1999). *Sorting things out: Classification and its consequences*. London, UK: MIT Press.

British Standards Institution (BSI). (2006). *PAS 78: Guide to good practice in commissioning accessible websites*.

Caldwell, B., Cooper, M., Reid, L. G., & Vanderheiden, G. (2008). Web content accessibility guidelines (WCAG) 2.0. World Wide Web Consortium (W3C). Retrieved November 19, 2010 from http://www.w3.org/TR/WCAG20/

Clark J. (2006, May 23). To hell with WCAG 2. *A List Apart*, no. 217. Retrieved November 19, 2010 from http://alistapart.com/articles/tohellwithwcag2

Coleridge, P. (1993). *Disability, liberation, and development*. Oxford, UK: Oxfam Publishing.

Convention on the Rights of Persons with Disabilities. (2006). Convention on the Rights of Persons with Disabilities. United Nations Enable. Retrieved October 10, 2010 from http://www.un.org/disabilities/default.asp?navid=14&pid=150

Deal, M. (2003). Disabled people's attitudes toward other impairment groups: A hierarchy of impairments. *Disability & Society, 18*(7), 897–910.

Deal, M. (2007). Aversive disablism: Subtle prejudice toward disabled people. *Disability & Society, 22*(1), 93–107.

Eide, A. H., & Loeb, M. E. (2006). Reflections on disability data and statistics in developing countries. In B. Albert (Ed.), *In or out of the mainstream? Lessons from research on disability and development cooperation*. pp. 89–103. Leeds, UK: Disability Press.

European Commission. (2008). *Spain einclusion*. Retrieved October 12, 2010 from http://www.epractice.eu/en/factsheets/

Fox, M. H., White, G. W., Rooney, C., & Cahill, A. (2010). The psychosocial impact of Hurricane Katrina on persons with disabilities and independent living center staff living on the American Gulf Coast. *Rehabilitation Psychology, 55*(3), 231–240.

Goffman, E. (1963). *Stigma: Notes on the management of spoiled identity*. New York, NY: Prentice-Hall.

Herbert, A. (2010). New technologies for the digital economy. Digital Economy All Hands Meeting, Digital Futures 2010. Nottingham, England, October 11–12, 2010.

Herrod, L. (2008). Deafness and the user experience. *A List Apart*, no. 265. Retrieved October 10, 2010 from http://www.alistapart.com/articles/deafnessandtheuser experience

Hurst, R., & Albert, B. (2006). The social model of disability: Human rights and development cooperation. In B. Albert (Ed.), *In or out of the mainstream? Lessons from research on disability and development cooperation* (pp. 24–39). Leeds, UK: Disability Press.

Katsui, H. (2005). *Towards equality: Creation of the disability movement in Central Asia*. Helsinki, Finland: Helsinki University Press. Retrieved October 10, 2010 from http://www.disability-archive.leeds.ac.uk

Katsui, H. (2006). Human rights of disabled people in the South. (Originally published in Finnish as Vammaisten Ihmisoikeuksista Etelässä.) In A. Teittinen (Ed.), *Vammaisuuden Tutkimus* (pp. 86–119). Helsinki, Finland: Helsinki University Press. Retrieved October 10, 2010 from http://www.disability-archive.leeds.ac.uk

Kelly, B., Lewthwaite, S., & Sloan, D. (2010). *Developing countries; developing experiences: Approaches to accessibility for the real world*. New York, NY: Association for Computing Machinery.

Kelly, B., Nevile, L., Sloan, D., Fanou, S., Ellison, R., & Herrod, L. (2009). From web accessibility to web adaptability. *Disability and Rehability: Assistive Technology, 4*(4), 212–226.

Kelly, B., Sloan, D., Brown, S., Seale, J., Petrie, H., Lauke, P., et al. (2007). Accessibility 2.0: People, policies and processes. W4A 2007: International Cross-Disciplinary Conference on Web Accessibility. Banff, Canada, May 7–8, 2007. Retrieved from http://www.w4a.info/2007/prog/15-kelly.pdf

Kelly, B., Sloan, D., Phipps, L., Petrie, H., & Hamilton, F. (2005). Forcing standardization or accommodating diversity? A framework for applying the WCAG in the real world. Proceedings of the 2005 International Cross-Disciplinary Workshop on Web Accessibility (W4A). Chiba, Japan, May 10–14, 2005. New York, NY: ACM Press.

Lewis, A., & Norwich, B. (2005). *Special teaching for special children?: Pedagogies for inclusion*. Cornwall, UK: Open University Press.

Lwanga-Ntale, C. (2003). Chronic poverty and disability in Uganda. Staying Poor: Chronic Poverty and Development Policy Conference. Manchester, England, April 7–9, 2003. Retrieved October 10, 2010 from http://www.chronicpoverty.org/publications/details/chronic-poverty-and-disability-in-uganda

Miller, P., Parker, S., & Gillinson, S. (2004). *Disablism. How to tackle the last prejudice*. DEMOS. Retrieved December 2, 2010 from http://www.demos.co.uk/files/disablism.pdf?1240939425

Moss, T. (2006). WCAG 2.0: The new W3C accessibility guidelines evaluated. Webcredible. Retrieved November 17, 2010 from http://www.webcredible.co.uk/user-friendly-resources/web-accessibility/wcag-guidelines-20.shtml

Opera Software. (2010). State of the Mobile Web, June 2010. Retrieved November 17, 2010 from http://www.opera.com/smw/2010/06

Rabin, J., & McCathieNevile, C. (Eds.). (2008). Mobile web best practices 1.0. World Wide Web Consortium (W3C). Retrieved October 12, 2010 from http://www.w3.org/TR/mobile-bp/

Section 508. (2007). Laws. Retrieved September 15, 2007 from http://www.section508.gov/index.cfm?fuseaction=Laws

Shakespeare, T., & Watson, N. (2002). The social model of disability: An outmoded ideology? *Research in Social Science and Disability, 69*, 9-28.

Sheldon, A. (2010). Locating disability in the majority world: Geography or poverty? Disability and the Majority World: Challenging Dominant Epistemologies Conference. Manchester Metropolitan University, Manchester, England, July 9, 2010. Retrieved from http://www.disability-archive.leeds.ac.uk/

Singal, N. (2010). Doing disability research in a southern context: Challenges and possibilities. *Disability & Society, 25*(4), 415–426.

Smythe, I. (2002). Cognitive factors underlying reading and spelling difficulties: A cross-linguistic study. Unpublished PhD thesis, University of Surrey. Cited in Lewis, A., & Norwich, B. (2005). *Special teaching for special children? Pedagogies for inclusion*. Cornwall, UK: Open University Press.

Stone, E. (1999). Disability and development in the majority world. In E. Stone (Ed.), *Disability and development: Learning from action and research on disability in the majority world* (pp. 1-18). Leeds, UK: Disability Press.

Thomas, A. (2000). Stability of Tringo's hierarchy of preference toward disability groups: 30 years later. *Psychological Reports, 86,* pp. 1155–1156.

Tringo, J. L. (1970). The hierarchy of preference toward disability groups. *Journal of Special Education, 4,* 295–306.

United Nations (n.d.). Article 1 Preamble IN *Frequently Asked Questions regarding the Convention on the Rights of Persons with Disabilities.* Retrieved November 11, 2011 http://www.un.org/disabilities/default.asp?id=151#sqc3

W3C (2006, June 20). Formal objection explained. World Wide Web Consortium (W3C) WCAG 2.0 public comments list. Retrieved March 19, 2010 from http://lists.w3.org/Archives/Public/public-comments-wcag20/2006Jun/0119

W3C (1999) *Web Content Accessibility Guidelines 1.0.* Retrieved April 9th, 2010 from http://www.w3.org/TR/WCAG10/

Wagner, J. (1993). Ignorance in educational research or, how can you not know that? *Educational Researcher, 22*(5), 15–23.

Wendell, S. (1996) *The rejected body: Feminist philosophical reflections on disability,* New York, NY: Routledge.

Whyte, S., & Ingstad, B. (1995). Disability and culture: An overview. In B. Ingstad & S. Whyte (Eds.), *Disability and culture* (pp. 1-34). Berkeley, CA: University of California Press.

Yeo, R. (2003). Including disabled people in poverty reduction work: "Nothing about us, without us." *World Development, 31*(3), 571–590.

http://dx.doi.org/10.2190/RAAC9

CHAPTER 9

Web Accessibility Statements: Connecting Professional Writing, Corporate Social Responsibility, and Burkean Rhetoric

Antoinette Larkin

Once upon a time, a disabled web user surfed his way to a web site.
On that web site was a tantalising link that simply said "Accessibility Statement."
"Oooo . . . intriguing" said The Surfer, "I will follow that link."
And lo, The Surfer did follow the link,
and he was transported to a magical new page filled to the brim
with a wealth of information.
(Griffiths, 2005)

In 2006 the United Nations (UN) drafted the Convention on the Rights of Persons with Disabilities (UN, 2006). This Convention declared that persons with disabilities (PWDs) deserve access to unbridled citizenship in the world with an emphasis on their abilities rather than their disabilities. For this reason, the UN, along with the United States, championed accessibility to the world wide web and new technologies as a right. But the work that web designers, corporations, and governments, among others, have done to date to ensure accessibility for PWDs when using the web still has much to do to achieve complete compliance with that Convention, especially with regard to assistive technologies and navigational tools. Since the pursuit of wealth is now largely the pursuit of information, the stakes for PWDs to have easy and effective access to information in electronic and other forms are high (Wriston, 1992, p. 8). However, information

175

has value only if it is usable, accessible, and relevant to its primary audience or those who will ultimately use it. Progress toward this goal has not always been voluntary, nor is it complete. The more one investigates the performance of self-proclaimed accessible websites or the compliance levels of sites attempting to abide by the standards and laws, the more one realizes that much work remains to ensure that PWDs have the tools they need to harvest information from the web seamlessly and effectively (De Andrés, Lorca, & Martinez, 2009). Often small, overlooked, and difficult to find, web accessibility statements (WACs) are nonetheless significant indicators of actual versus intended accessibility. These seemingly innocuous documents take on the role of representing an organization's stance on accessibility issues, a stance that is often conflicting and does little to advance the reputation of organizations in the eyes of PWDs.[1]

Using Burke's (1950/1969) framework for consubstantiality—shared identification between people and/or organizations that is achieved through the practice of rhetoric—this chapter analyzes 21 organizations' WACs for their navigational functionality, ease of use, declared audience and their context within a larger corporate social responsibility (CSR) perspective. By considering a WAC as an integral component of CSR and having professional writers compose the document, an organization can effect both compliance and accessibility while elevating its WAC to a level of strategic importance similar to its mission statement. On the one hand, WACs encapsulate what may appear at first glance to be a begrudging slog toward minimal letter-of-the-law compliance with regard to accessibility. On the other hand, as this study shows, some WACs can combine an enthusiastic spirit-of-the-law commitment to providing efficacious access to PWDs—one celebrating their abilities instead of focusing on their disabilities. Moreover, if written clearly, succinctly, and with the intended rhetorical audience in mind, WACs can, in fact, achieve much of what the UN Convention on the Rights of Persons with Disabilities intended, at least in terms of web accessibility. By applying Burke's (1950/1969) theory of consubstantiality, this study underscores missed opportunities by organizations to meet the accessibility needs of PWDs and build common ground between stakeholders.

WACs: DEFINITION AND HISTORY

WACs have been defined as an organization's "declarations on a website, [usually] produced by the web developer . . . about the accessibility of the website to disabled people and others with accessibility needs" (Parkinson, 2007, p. 29). To understand the history of the developments of WACs and their current makeup, it is necessary to briefly discuss what constitutes an accessible website. Essentially, the ability of people with any limitations or impairment with regard to

---

[1] I have added the modifier "web" to highlight the virtual nature of these documents and to avoid any confusion with other AC acronyms.

vision, physical disability, or cognitive and learning disabilities to successfully navigate a website constitutes accessibility. Although the final chapter of this book details the specifics of the legislative and public opinion forces—including the World Wide Web Consortium's (W3C) Web Accessibility Initiative (WAI)— that have been enacted and brought to bear to enhance accessibility on the world wide web, it is worth noting here that none of the U.S. standards and policies suggest or even require a WAC on websites.

However, the British Standards Institute's (2006) guide to good practice in commissioning accessible websites does argue for the creation of an accessibility policy for any entity's site, which should include ways in which websites are accessible to disabled people, instructions on how PWDs can use the site, and the level of technical compliance of the website. Given the global reach of companies today, U.S. standards and policies, European legislation, and UN mandates have combined to produce the growing ubiquity of WACs. Although the British Standards guide was not produced until 2006, it seems to have confirmed a trend in content in the drafting of WACs. The British government's 2005 legislation specified that a policy statement on accessibility needed to be included on websites. Web developers sought to fulfill this requirement merely by including a WAC on their site. They often based them on ones already in existence and ideas put forth by established web developers and consultants (Abrahams, 2007; Clark, 2002; Pilgrim, 2002; Quinn, 2008).

In other words, it appears that the current conventions for WACs have developed *a priori* rather than in a *prescriptive* way that consciously considers the needs of the organization and the audience—the PWDs and others concerned with accessibility. Thus, it is not terribly surprising that limited scholarly research has been done on WACs in both professional communication and disability studies. Parkinson's (2007) quantitative and qualitative study of 55 British companies and 55 local British government websites is the first to have extensively analyzed WACs. The study found "considerable differences in the presence, execution, and quality of accessibility statements between the two sectors," as well as a wide variation in the information presented (Parkinson, 2007, p. 29). Researchers (Petrie, Badani, & Bhalla, 2005) at the University of London's Centre for Human Computer Interactive Design examined WACs for the accuracy of their claims, but they did not engage in a close textual analysis from a rhetorical perspective. Figures 1 and 2 feature a typical WAC.

UBIQUITY AND THE RESEARCH CHALLENGE: CHOOSING REPRESENTATIVE WACs

Claims of the ubiquity of WACs on the web abound—including a suggestion that a Google search for the phrase "Accessibility Statement" returned over 12 million results (Krantz, 2006). These claims serve to highlight the difficulties inherent in choosing a representative sampling of WACs for analysis.

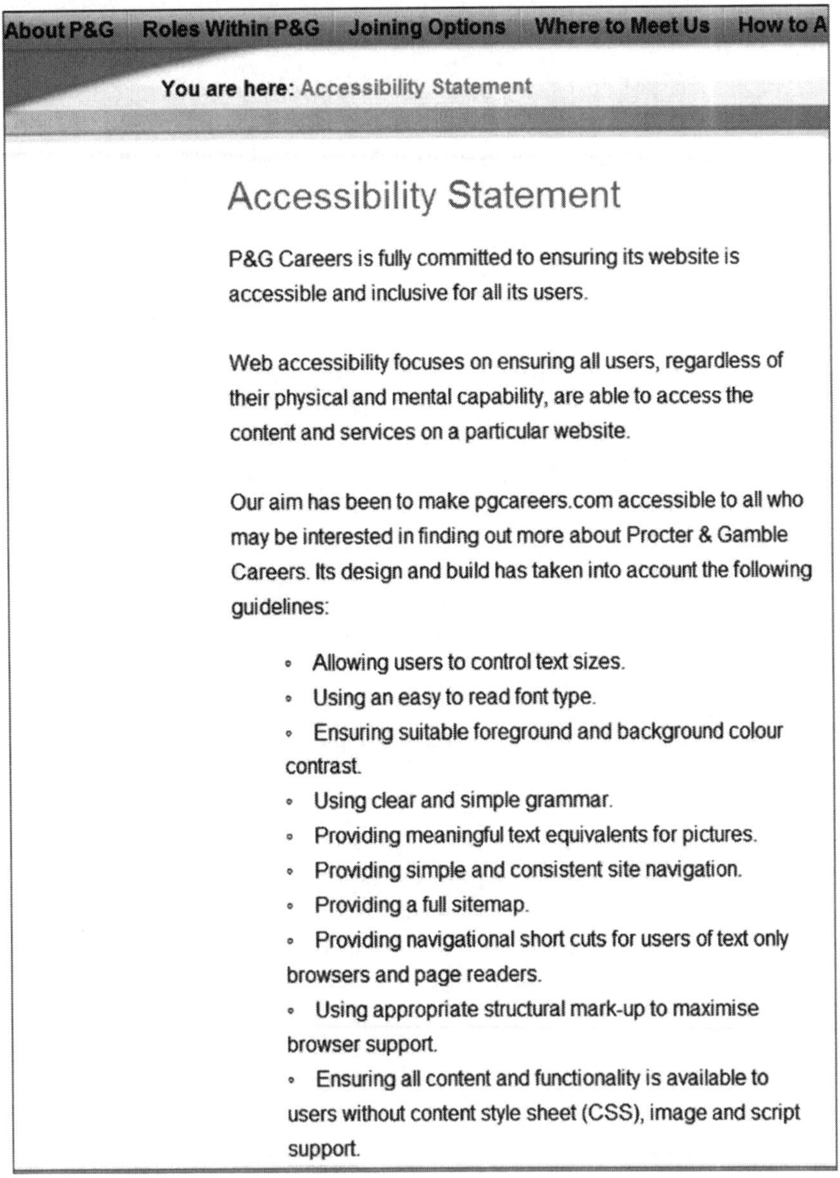

About P&G   Roles Within P&G   Joining Options   Where to Meet Us   How to A

You are here: Accessibility Statement

Accessibility Statement

P&G Careers is fully committed to ensuring its website is accessible and inclusive for all its users.

Web accessibility focuses on ensuring all users, regardless of their physical and mental capability, are able to access the content and services on a particular website.

Our aim has been to make pgcareers.com accessible to all who may be interested in finding out more about Procter & Gamble Careers. Its design and build has taken into account the following guidelines:

- Allowing users to control text sizes.
- Using an easy to read font type.
- Ensuring suitable foreground and background colour contrast.
- Using clear and simple grammar.
- Providing meaningful text equivalents for pictures.
- Providing simple and consistent site navigation.
- Providing a full sitemap.
- Providing navigational short cuts for users of text only browsers and page readers.
- Using appropriate structural mark-up to maximise browser support.
- Ensuring all content and functionality is available to users without content style sheet (CSS), image and script support.

Figure 1. Proctor & Gamble's careers in Western Europe WAC 2011.
Source: http://www.pgcareers.com/aboutpg/accessibility/page/242/default.htm

Javascript

Javascript is no longer extensively used on our site and at present is used primarily for content layout. The site is still useable and accessable with it disabled. We are currently reviewing any other areas where Javascript is used in an effort to enusre accessiblity.

Access Keys

Important navigation options have been assigned keyboard access keys for users who do not use pointing devices (such as a mouse).

The access keys we have used are as follows (Section, Access key):

Home page, 1
Main content, 2
Site map, 3
Contact us, 4
Help, 5
Accessibility statement, 0

To use an access key in Mozilla browsers press the 'Alt' key plus the access key listed below. In Internet Explorer, press the 'Alt' key plus the access key, and then press return. If you use a different Internet browser, please refer to its help documentation.

Known browser support

This website operates on a wide range of browsers.

PC operating systems:
Internet Explorer 6
Internet Explorer 7
Mozilla Firefox 1.5
Opera 8.5

Mac operating systems:
Firefox 2.0.0.1
Safari 2.0.4
Opera 9.10

Feedback

P&G Careers welcomes your feedback and suggestions for improvement to our website. Please send your comments to wecareers.im@pgcareers.com.

Figure 2. Proctor & Gamble's careers in Western Europe WAC 2011.

Nevertheless, the New York-based financial magazine *Fortune* (2010) did provide a manageable group, based on its research in producing its annual lists of America's largest companies against a series of economic benchmarks. Of particular value for this chapter's discussion are the "most admired" companies and the "industry champions"—those companies which others admire in their own industries based on broad categories ranging from investment potential to CSR. This chapter initially looked at 20 of the top companies that appeared simultaneously on both lists in 2010. In view of recent revelations about questionable business practices, Goldman Sachs Group was eliminated from consideration. Table 1 details the companies initially selected, together with their ranking and whether WACs could be located on their websites.

Of the 20 companies selected, a cursory examination found some surprising, if not disappointing, results. Only 55% had WACs, and in the case of three of those companies—Procter & Gamble, Coca-Cola, and McDonald's—their WACs appear only on company websites outside the United States.

Since the initial research methodology did not result in a sample size large enough to draw any definitive conclusions, the list of organizations was increased by 10. Some of these additions are nonprofit companies (non-government organizations [NGOs] and universities) and a small sampling of Fortune Global 500 companies for comparative purposes. Though it did not rank as an industry champion, Starbucks was also included. With a ranking of 26th among the "most admired" Fortune 50 companies, a dominant global footprint, and a reputation for CSR, Starbucks seemed likely to produce a WAC with a more strategic vision. The same rationale was applied for the inclusion of American Express and Sodexo. Sodexo is intriguing because it not only made *Fortune*'s "most admired" list but was also honored as the top company of "The Top Ten Companies for People with Disabilities" (Diversity Inc., 2010) and was named one of the "World's Most Ethical Companies" for 2010 by the Ethisphere Institute for the second consecutive year (Coster, 2010). Table 2 catalogs these additional organizations.

Not surprisingly, all 10 organizations listed in Table 2 did have WAC links on their websites. Thus the final research sample was 21. While the methodology was not scientific, the final list of 21 companies provides interesting insights into the way WACs are being written and presented worldwide.

EPIDEICTIC RHETORIC, WACS, AND PUBLIC RELATIONS

From Burke's (1950/1969) standpoint, the rhetor uses words to shape attitudes "or to induce actions in human agents" (p. 41). From a rhetorical perspective, WACs provide an interesting case of a missed opportunity for what Burke (1950/1969) calls consubstantiality (1950/1969, p. 21). Through the thoughtful construction of a rhetorically persuasive document, Burke (1950/1969) argues

Table 1. *Fortune* "Industry Champions" Explored

Company name	Industry type	*Fortune* ranking[a]	WAC located
Apple	Computers	1	Yes
Proctor & Gamble	Soaps and cosmetics	6	Yes
Toyota Motor	Motor vehicles	7	No
Wal-Mart	General merchandisers	9	No
Coca-Cola	Beverages	10	Yes
McDonald's	Food services	14	Yes
IBM	Information technology	15	Yes
General Electric	Electronics	16	Yes
Walt Disney	Entertainment	19	No
Ciscos Systems	Network and other communications equipment	20	Yes
Costco Wholesale	Specialty retailers	21	No
BMW	Motor vehicles	22	No
Nike	Apparel	24	No
Singapore Airlines	Airlines	27	No
Exxon Mobil	Petroleum refining	28	Yes
Intel	Semiconductors	31	Yes
UPS	Delivery	33	No
Nestlé	Food production	34	Yes
Caterpillar	Industrial and farm equipment	35	No
Marriott International	Hotels, casinos, and resorts	48	Yes

[a]Ranking information taken from *Fortune* (2010). Companies appear in table in ranked order.

Table 2. NGOs, Universities, Media Organizations, and
High-Profile CSR Companies

Company name	Industry type	WAC located
American Express	Financial services	Yes
British Broadcast Corporation (BBC)	Publicly funded media corporation	Yes
Comhlámh, the Irish Association of Development Workers	NGO	Yes
Diageo	Beverages alcohol	Yes
HelpAge International	NGO	Yes
Johns Hopkins University	Third-level educational institution	Yes
Olympic Games (2012)	NGO	Yes
Starbucks	Beverages	Yes
Sodexo	Food and facilities management services	Yes
University of Oxford	Third-level educational institution	Yes

that an experienced rhetor can, in fact, achieve consubstantiality, shared identification between individuals or groups. For Burke (1950/1969), identification and consubstantiality are synonymous: "To identify A with B is to make A 'consubstantial' with B" (1950/1969, p. 21). Moreover, in Burkean terms, the artifacts (in this case the WAC) produced through the practice of rhetoric become "equipment for living" if successful (1941/1973, pp. 293-304). Certainly, the relevance of this concept is particularly pertinent for PWDs who are looking for "equipment for living" on a website through a WAC (Burke, 1941/1973, p. 293). Unfortunately, as this chapter's study makes clear, the achievement of consubstantiality and the ability of a large majority of WACs to enable users to act successfully on the contents of these documents are rare. This is in part because of a failure to understand the importance of applying rhetorical theory to what should be a key online public relations document—the WAC.

For many years, the discipline of public relations and its sub-discipline, CSR, have understood that public relations can be considered "the study and practice of corporate public rhetoric" (Cheney, 1992, p. 166). Despite this acknowledgement, little attention has been focused on Aristotle's (2005) divisions of rhetorical practice into deliberative, epideictic, and forensic communication in public relations—loosely defined as political, legal, and ceremonial (or demonstrative) communication. Recent work by Edwards (2006), however, usefully categorizes public relations documents into these Aristotelian divisions as a way to enhance understanding of the audience's "role in communication relationships" (p. 837), while recognizing that rigid divisions in rhetoric have been largely abandoned in professional communication—a recognition of the multipurpose messages at work in complex communication. Even so, Edwards (2006) sees forensic public relations at work in annual reports, for example, because "the emphasis is on a past event/action for which the speaker [rhetor] offers a defense or explanation and the audience determines the acceptability or unacceptability of that action" (p. 841) and sees epideictic rhetoric at work in "an organization's strategic philanthropy activities or cause-related outreach" (p. 841). Both come under the aegis of CSR, which is primarily tasked with communicating the ways in which a corporation demonstrates responsible citizenship. Obviously, then, CSR should include accessibility, although in the study presented in this chapter, statements and issues of accessibility were not found on the CSR pages of the websites examined.

Nevertheless, this link between public relations, corporate social responsibility, WACs, and rhetoric is important in ensuring that effective WACs are available to PWDs. Unfortunately, examined as multi-message documents engaged in epideictic rhetoric, the majority of WACs analyzed in this chapter's study emerged as case studies of a failure to achieve consubstantiality. At the same time, the ongoing debate in global entities over the need for WACs among web designers and perhaps their CSR colleagues points first to a fundamental failure to comprehend the context that gives rise to the documents. It also provides an opportunity to construct a model WAC that could serve multiple functions within the organization, not the least of which could be an effective corporate document that evokes positive responses and furthers the CSR reputation of organizations, thus achieving Burke's (1950/1969) goal of consubstantiality.

DESIGN, RHETORIC, AND THE WACS OF THE FORTUNE 50 COMPANIES

Professional writing operates from the standpoint that all communication is rhetorical and that to be accessible, usable, and relevant to its audiences, and so it must be composed with the needs, expectations, and purposes of particular audiences in the forefront. Understandably, web design intersects with professional communication. Garrett (2003) points to this intersection and sees the structure of a webpage in terms of interface design, navigation design, and information design (p. 114). Of these three elements, this study is concerned with the latter two design elements as they relate to WACs and the experiences of PWDs. To evaluate the rhetorical effectiveness of WACs and the implications of Burke's (1950/1969) definition of consubstantiality, this section analyzes the WACs appearing in Table 1 in terms of audience awareness, navigation design, and relevance of content.

1. Audience Awareness

A website can be defined as a "form of communication in which the narrator will ultimately be called upon to account for the identity constructed in inter-action" with an audience (Coupland, 2005, p. 355). From Burke's (1950/1969) perspective, knowledge of one's audience is crucial in establishing consub-stantiality. This is because it is only through the act of rhetoric that any initial state of dissociation between an audience and a rhetor can be bridged. Without under-standing the audience, a rhetor is likely to induce, what Burke calls "alienation" (1941/1973, pp. 306-308)) rather than "identification" (1950/1969, pp. 21–22). Yet the contents of WACs are striking for their lack of identification with their audience. The only way to account for the lack of focus on the PWDs as the primary audience, which the content of the WACs makes clear, is an erroneous and highly ironic assumption that PWDs are not, in fact, the primary audience. This assumption is made because the authors of the WACs currently appear to be web developers or designers. Their models for writing WAC statements have come from veteran web developers, among whom Clarke seems to hold the most sway. As early as 2002, Clarke was instructing web designers to compose and post a statement regarding the standards used in writing the web pages. He stipulated that this declaration should include a brief statement of the company's accessibility policy. Clarke argued against what he saw as insincere boilerplate statements, which opened with expressions of pleasure and pride at offering accessible pages, and he, instead, exhorted his readers to keep their statements as short and simple as possible. At the same time, he also urged the inclusion of a link to the WAC in the footer of the homepage. Ironically, as the following dis-cussion on navigation will show, Clarke's recommendations for brevity were heeded in the extreme, although expressions of company pride were not.

Clarke's target audience was and is web developers, and he has succeeded in reaching them, judging by the extensive range of references to Clarke's work. However, the blog discussion that followed Krantz's (2006) blog post, "Don't Provide an Accessibility Statement," reveals ongoing confusion con-cerning audience and the WAC. One of the bloggers responding to Krantz (2006) conceded that WACs are potentially useful if they are written in plain language for everyday consumption or written in a way to "encourage and incite other developers to actually become aware that accessible practices exist." The need for clear language in all accessibility statements accepts PWDs as the primary audience. However, the consensus reached by the developers and designers responding to Krantz's (2006) argument is that the accessibility state-ment has many functions and at least three audiences—fellow developers, web standards organizations, and PWDs. Relegating PWDs to the level of tertiary audience explains, in part, the content and ineffectiveness of the WACs.

Because consubstantiality can only occur if rhetors keep the audience in mind and if they can speak the audience's "language by speech, gesture, tonality, order, attitude, idea, thereby identifying [the audience's] ways" with their own, it seems clear that the majority of the corporate WACs examined fail (Burke, 1969, p. 55). An examination of the navigation and content further clarifies this failure to achieve consubstantiality with the PWDs as audience.

2. Navigation Design

For Garrett (2003), navigation design provides "users with the ability to go places" (p. 115) on a website with the goal of finding usable information— what public relation's theorist Springston (2001) calls "high-value information" (p. 614). One of the first steps to establishing consubstantiality is through the website's navigation. "Clear, well-thought-out navigation is one of the best opportunities a site has to create a good impression" (Krug, 2006, p. 60), and by creating a good first impression, users of the site will be more likely to form a favorable opinion of the website and, by extension, the corporation. In terms of effective website navigation, Burke's (1950/1969) theory is useful here: namely that navigation per se is part of the language of identification between the user and the company because both parties have the shared goal of ensuring that the audience finds the web content they need. In this case, locating a WAC results in the acquisition of "equipment for living" for PWDs (Burke, 1941/1973, p. 293). In effect, web navigation becomes a tool of persuasion, thereby enabling consubstantiality (Burke, 1950/1969, p. 55).

Obviously, the homepage is the key to effecting a connection between the user and the corporation (rhetor). It presents the first opportunity for an organization with a web presence to establish its ethos by creating rapport with site users, an affinity achieved partially through the use of good navigational tools that allow users to navigate quickly and easily through the site while looking for relevant materials. The current literature on web navigation, accessibility, and usability underscores the homepage connection—its ability to enable the PWD to easily locate the necessary WAC information. Understandably, accessibility experts recommend—at the very least—placing a clearly visible link from the homepage to the WAC (Clark 2002; Garrett, 2003; Kalbach 2007; Krug, 2006; Pilgrim 2002; Thatcher, Waddell, Henry, Swierenga, Urban, Burks, et. al., 2003). Even so, while WACs may be ubiquitous, navigating to them can be surprisingly difficult. These difficulties seem to be related to the poor positioning of visible links to WACs. People visit websites for information. For that reason, it is highly desirable to find that information "above the fold" on a homepage because that area can be read without scrolling down (Krug, 2006, p. 97). Hence, it would seem reasonable to expect to encounter a WAC in the primary navigation of a page—that is, in the links to the main sections of the website or in the top level of the site's hierarchical structure.

However, in the case of the websites in Table 1, WACs could not be found in the primary navigation area. Instead, when they could be located, they were often in the "utilities" or footer section of the page, where links that assist with using the site are usually found (Krug, 2006, p. 65).

The placement of the WAC in a link in the "utilities" section does nothing to enhance the credibility of the site and build consubstantiality. In fact, such placement is likely to only frustrate a PWD. For example, it may take a screen reader an inconvenient amount of time to get to the bottom of the page. Moreover, persons unable to use a mouse to scroll to the bottom of the page are at an even greater time disadvantage. In both cases, the rhetor fails to appreciate the audience, with the result that the PWD feels disconnected and disadvantaged. This disconnect is only compounded by placing the WAC link beside the site's legal disclaimers in a font size of 8 or 8.5 points. Half of the "high street" companies' WAC links examined by Parkinson (2007) had "a smaller text size than the rest of the text on the page, 50% had poor color contrast, and placement of the link was at the bottom of the page" most often (p. 33). And these findings do not even take into consideration vision-impaired users who do not have screen readers or who do not know how to increase font sizes on their own— because, ironically, such instruction is often located in the very WAC they are struggling to access in the first place. Evidently, for organizations using such navigational practices, the WAC is not a priority. This is illustrated by General Electric's homepage (Figure 3).

Failures such as these undermine both the "reservoir of good will" that users bring to a website and the organizations' credibility with those users (Krug, 2006, pp. 162–163). More savvy PWDs who attempt to locate the WAC through the site's internal search engine generally fare no better. Research for this study found such efforts typically laborious and futile. Often, it was necessary to use an external search engine, such as Google, to locate the WAC. Ironically, even Google's own accessibility site's URL address reveals the lack of straightforward access (http://labs.google.com/accessible).

While Apple has a very thorough and well-documented WAC, repeated efforts to access the WAC from the homepage resulted in no visible link. Finding Apple's WAC begins at the site map and then requires scrolling to access, yet the URL implies effortless accessibility (http://www.apple.com/accessibility/resources/). Of the 20 companies originally examined in Table 1, only 10% had links to the WAC on the homepage. Of the 11 companies with WACs that were accessible through either a Google search or a search of the company's website, not one posted the link to the accessibility statement at the top of the homepage. The footer was the most popular place for the link.

In reality, website visitors usually "glance at each new page, scan some text, and click on the first link that catches their interest or vaguely resembles the thing they're looking for" (Krug, 2006, p. 21). Locating WACs on the sites investigated in Table 1 often required several mouse clicks and much valuable time. And the problem is not limited to the websites represented in this chapter's study. Research by Petrie et al. (2005) on 500 e-commerce and financial websites'

Figure 3. General Electric's Homepage, 2011.
http://www.ge.com/

accessibility statements indicates that the sites made exaggerated claims about the level of accessibility achieved and that more than a quarter incorrectly stated the degree of their compliance with Web Content Accessibility Guidelines (WCAG). This was not interpreted as a symptom of malice on the part of the authors of the WACs but, rather, the result of incomplete or poor testing of accessibility features including navigation design. Nonetheless, the end result is dissociation between the PWDs as potential customers and the organizations. Because ease of use, and by extension accessibility, is understandably the main criterion visitors use to decide whether to revisit a website, this dissociation results in loss of business.

3. Relevance of Content

Establishing consubstantiality depends largely on the relevance of content to the audience. Relevance, in turn, depends upon the ability of the language—that selection of words by rhetors—to convey meaning in a WAC (Burke, 1950/1969, p. 41). Much has been written about WACs since their first appearance around 2000, including what they should contain, as has already been seen. A distinction needs to be made between the content of a WAC and the methodology for writing an effective piece of either technical or professional communication that can be rhetorically persuasive and which has the ability to build consubstantiality. However, the consensus regarding the contents of the WAC seems to be that it should perform multiple tasks, including presenting the following:

- The company's accessibility policy
- Details about the functions of accessibility built into a website
- The methods for reporting failures
- The validation or verification tools used
- Information on browser options
- Links to additional information

General Electric's WAC in Figure 4 is typical of those attempting unsuccessfully to perform these multiple tasks. This is not surprising, given that such an extensive list of tasks seems Herculean for one document that is constrained, at the very least, by the dictates of brevity.

Of the 11 WACs constructed by the Fortune 50 companies in Table 1, the majority began with a single declarative sentence, usually one containing a vision of accessibility for all people before following it with another declarative statement asserting compliance with accessibility standards. Sometimes that sentence is prefaced by a short one- or two-sentence history of the company's journey toward accessibility. A striking feature of the majority of WACs is their lack of user focus and their extremely short (if any) instructions for using assistive technologies (see Figures 4 and 5).

Frequently omitted, too, is helpful troubleshooting advice. Optimally a logical structure for instructions should be expected. In the case of the Coca-Cola Great Britain WAC, for example, it would be reasonable to expect the "Links" information to appear right after "Navigation Shortcuts." Moreover, to underscore the role of the audience or website user, effective instructions are usually written in the active voice, using direct address and the imperative mood (Lannon, 2003). Constrained in part by the demands of brevity, the WACs examined do not provide effective instructions.

WACs are also remarkable for the highly technical and legalistic language that they use. They tend to be jargon-laden and marked by the specialized language of the web developer or designer. General Electric's WAC takes the space to share its pride in having incorporated JavaScript into its website for greater functionality, although this may not be a piece of information high on the audience's "need to know" list of priorities. It may be hard to know, at a glance,

GE Accessibility Statement

GE strives to make its products and services accessible for all users, including people with disabilities. Since 2002, GE has been working to make its Web content accessible to as broad a user base as possible. Our corporate Web site, www.ge.com, complies with best practices and standards as defined by Section 508 of the U.S. Rehabilitation Act and the Web Content Accessibility Guidelines (WCAG) of the World Wide Web Consortium Web Accessibility Initiative (W3C WAI). We have also earned Non-Visual Accessibility (NVA) certification from The National Federation of the Blind (NFB), the largest consumer organization of the visually impaired in the United States.

GE.com is monitored and tested regularly by internal and third party accessibility consultants to identify any usability issues as well as discover new solutions to further improve the accessibility of our site. Our current accessibility features include:

- Alternative text detail for appropriate images and other non-text elements.
- Title attributes for additional information about links and indication of new browser windows.
- Structural markup to indicate headings and lists to aid in page comprehension.
- Association of forms with labels.
- Association of all data cells in a data table with their headers.
- JavaScript and style sheets to enhance the appearance and functionality of the site. If these technologies are not available, alternative content is provided where necessary to ensure graceful degradation.
- Embedded documents and multimedia accessibility efforts are under way. GE will provide reasonable alternative formats upon request until this effort is completed.

As we continue to improve our Web site, we will reflect any changes here within our accessibility statement, so you will know the progress we are making.

We value your opinions. If you have comments or questions, you can send them directly to us via our feedback form.

Figure 4. General Electric's WAC, 2011.
http://www.ge.com/accessibility.html

Navigation shortcuts

There is a short menu at the start of every page that allows screen reader users to jump directly to the most important parts of the page, including main content and navigation.

Changing text-size

Most browsers feature the ability to resize text on screen to a level you feel comfortable with.

This tool is available in the menu of various browsers as follows:

Browser	Instructions
Internet Explorer 7 (PC)	Page > Zoom
Internet Explorer 5, 5.5, 6 (PC)	View > Text Size
Firefox, Netscape 8	View > Text Size
Opera	View > Zoom
Netscape 6, 7, Mozilla	View > Text Zoom
Safari (Mac)	View > Make Text Bigger

Alternatively, if you are using a modern browser and have a mouse with a wheel you can also alter the size of the text size by holding down ctrl (PC) or command (Mac) on your keyboard while scrolling up and down with the mouse wheel.

Contrast

We have made every effort to ensure that we have used sufficient contrast on the Let's Get Together website but if you notice any colour combinations that cause you problems, please contact us.

Links

If a link opens in a new window, this will be indicated by a pop-up title text.

Every effort has been made to ensure that link names are distinct and not repeated on pages.

Figure 5. Excerpt from Coca'Cola Great Britain WAC.
http://www.coca-cola.co.uk/accessibility.html

what Coca-Cola means by a phrase such as "modern browser" or what IBM implies with the term "broadly accessible."

The *Plain Language* initiative seems to be in abeyance in too many WACs. Phrases such as "graceful degradation" and "appropriate structural mark-up language" or parenthetical statements such as ("Section, Access key") say little to a person seeking greater accessibility to a website but who does not have the specialized knowledge of a web developer or extensive computer user (General Electric WAC, n.d., para. 8; Procter & Gamble Careers WAC, n.d., para. 3-4). Cisco Systems's WAC includes a policy statement that contains imprecise and vague language that leaves the reader wondering what actions may ensue from the claim that Cisco intends to report the ways in which its accessibility guidelines "are implemented when competitively, technically, and economically feasible" (n.d., para. 2).[2] While offering a helpful "Accessibility Tips, Tricks, and FAQs" section in its WAC and helpful links designed not to overburden the reader with too much information at one time, Marriott also offers an "assurance" that the company "will enable consumers with disabilities to report website accessibility problems [and] make reasonable efforts to respond to and/or remediate any such problems identified in a timely manner"—which is further underscored by the use of the passive voice (n.d., para. 2). The only way for PWDs to reach Marriott is by email, which in this instance carries no guarantee of immediate response. Indeed, no indications of the length of time for a response are included in any of the initial WACs examined, and email is the only opportunity for interaction with the companies when it comes to performance or accessibility issues relating to a particular WAC. This persistent tendency by corporations toward vagueness in language not only allows for multiple interpretations in meaning but does nothing to further confidence in the ability to verify the accessibility claims made in the content of the WAC.

The abundance of legalistic language points to the compliance statements inherent in the WACs. While Edwards (2006) sees forensic or legal rhetoric at work in corporate annual reports, this type of rhetorical content does not fit logically into the WACs of the Fortune 50 companies, although it abounds. When reading a WAC, PWDs are usually not looking to assess the financial performance of a company from the perspective of shareholders who have invested in the company. Instead, they are looking for ways to easily navigate through and find usable information on a website that they may not have any particular financial investment in.

The WACs build a convincing prima facie case for compliance with laws and regulations and thus stave off any accusation of flagrant disregard for equal access. General Electric's WAC notes that its "corporate Website, www.ge.com,

---

[2] None of the WACS discussed in this study carried publication dates. All were retrieved from the websites in 2010 and 2011.

complies with best practices and standards as defined by Section 508 of the U.S. Rehabilitation Act and the Web Content Accessibility Guidelines (WCAG) of the World Wide Web Consortium Web Accessibility Initiative" (n.d., para.1). This is typical of a majority of the WACs examined. Additionally, compliance is presented in the form of the accessibility features that have been put into operation on the websites. It appears that many of the WACs are nothing more than the closing argument that would be presented at a trial—a listing of all of the laws to which they comply, an argument that PWDs would have no practical interest in or need for. The relevance and usability of this information in the context of a WAC seems questionable.

TOWARD A MODEL WAC:
GLIMPSES OF CSR AND CONSUBSTANTIALITY

A cluster analysis of the WACs studied in Table 2, in particular, reveals several WACs seeking to provide "equipment for living." Burke (1941/1973) suggests that "the words of every writer contains a set of implicit equations" (p. 20). These equations or clusters of subjects (images, ideas, and key terms) clarify the attitudes and focus of the writer/rhetor/organization in the documents and help to access their rhetorical effectiveness (Burke, 1941/1973, p. 20). The earlier examination of the companies in Table 1 revealed a heavy reliance on technical terms, legal references, and claims of compliance, except for IBM. Taking all of these elements together with the predominant use of plural pronouns and corporate names indicates the poor performance of the WACs in Table 1 in terms of achieving consubstantiality with PWDs.

On the other hand, a reading of the WAC statements of the Table 2 group— HelpAge International, Sodexo, Diageo, and Comhlámh, in particular—and IBM (Table 1) reveals a balance between the number of singular and plural pronouns with a clear focus on the person who needs access to the site. For example, Sodexo—rated the top company for PWDs—provides a succinct statement on accessibility when the user first navigates to the link from the Sodexo homepage. The user is greeted by an accessibility homepage. As Figure 6 illustrates, it consists of one declarative sentence that states that the company agrees with W3C's WAI and, by extension, with all standards associated with it.

One easy mouse click away, matters of compliance to laws and standards are dispensed within one sentence, while the benefit of that compliance is user-focused: "As a result [of compliance], this site is accessible to all internet users, including senior citizens or people with disabilities who have functional difficulties" (n.d, para.1) Sodexo continues on in this inclusive vein to note that "a site complying with accessibility standards is of benefit to all internet users" (para. 2) Thus, there is an important recognition that accessibility has universal ramifications. However, it is still worth noting that, although Sodexo's WAC does

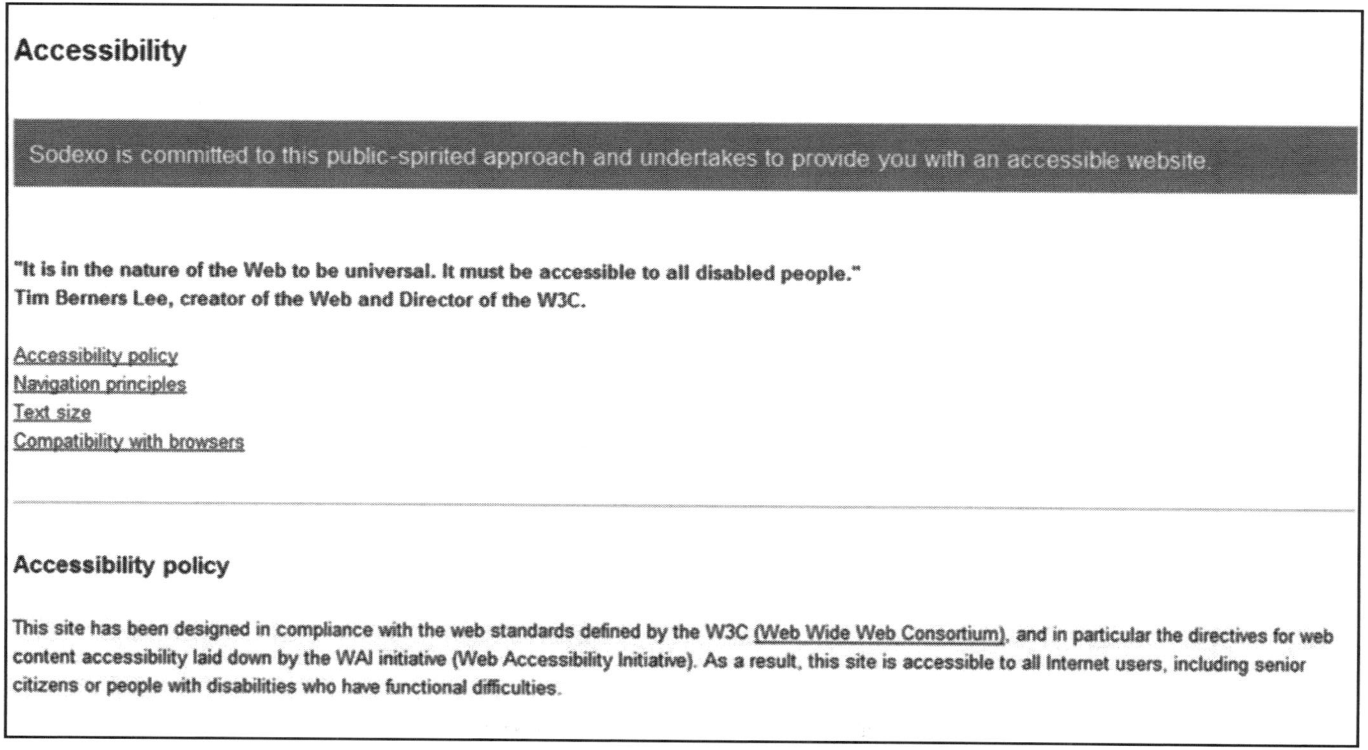

Accessibility

Sodexo is committed to this public-spirited approach and undertakes to provide you with an accessible website.

"It is in the nature of the Web to be universal. It must be accessible to all disabled people."
Tim Berners Lee, creator of the Web and Director of the W3C.

Accessibility policy
Navigation principles
Text size
Compatibility with browsers

Accessibility policy

This site has been designed in compliance with the web standards defined by the W3C (Web Wide Web Consortium), and in particular the directives for web content accessibility laid down by the WAI initiative (Web Accessibility Initiative). As a result, this site is accessible to all Internet users, including senior citizens or people with disabilities who have functional difficulties.

Figure 6. Sodexo's WAC, 2011. http://www.sodexousa.com/usen/accessibility.asp

incorporate the rhetorical elements envisioned for CSR-inspired WACs, it does not mention the WAC in its "Corporate Citizenship" statement.

Starbucks's WAC statement has a predominant focus on the achievements of the company in terms of accessibility, as opposed to the site users, and thus requires further accessibility features, as is so often the case with the Fortune 50 companies examined for this study. Despite this drawback and the familiar listing of features and functions similar to that seen in General Electric's WAC, Starbucks's statement declares that accessibility is part of its mission. The CSR aspect of the WAC is clear in the italicized statement that serves as the introduction in the document: "Starbucks is committed to diversity, inclusion and accessibility in everything we do. These core values are fundamental to the way we do business and come through in the experiences we design for people—both in our coffeehouses and on the Web" (Starbucks, n.d., para.1).

Although IBM is in the business of selling assistive technologies, it still manages to frame these products with the focus clearly on the user, not the company's achievements. IBM has moved beyond feature and function statements to inclusive benefits in describing accessibility browsing software it provides on its website. Surprisingly, this statement is not part of its full WAC even though it is located on a page entitled "Accessibility":

> Easy Web Browsing is an easy-to-install software package that can help you access IBM Web content more conveniently by allowing you to personalize your Web experience. It's ideal if you have limited vision, are experiencing age-related sight loss, if English is a second language for you, or if you simply want to customize how you experience IBM Web pages. (IBM, n.d., para. 2)

While IBM is more adept at creating personal identification through the repetition of personal pronouns with regard to its "Easy Web Browsing" software, it does not follow this same audience focus in its WAC.

In what is the longest WAC studied, Comhlámh insists on equality of access for all. Later in its statement, Comhlámh (n.d.) provides a rationale for the embracing of web accessibility by everyone, and that rationale is corporate social responsibility:

> The Internet offers an unprecedented amount of information for us all, and we must include all members of society when developing websites. We must do all we can to remove barriers . . . as it is our corporate social responsibility to treat all users equally. (para.14)

The word clustering around web accessibility in this instance is *all*, and the equation that can be written to summarize Comhlámh's attitude to accessibility is: CSR + Access to All = Web Accessibility.

As evidenced in Figure 7, Diageo, the maker of Guinness and a strong supporter of CSR initiatives, has one of the shortest WACs examined for this chapter's study. This short statement has the distinction of being free from all compliance references. It is descriptive, instructive, inclusive, and relatively brief. Despite some additional work needed to make the instructions more readable and to provide additional links to compliance issues and contact information, Diageo's WAC statement is highly effective. It does not require scrolling and can be easily accessed from the footer of Diageo's homepage. The terms *disabled*

Accessibility

We have designed Diageo.com to be as accessible as possible for all users. You may wish to alter the way the website looks to help you access information. Step-by-step instructions are below.

Features

HTML Headings

This site uses HTML headings to organise page content. Some assistive technologies will allow you to navigate from heading to heading using a keyboard shortcut.

Text size

You may want to change the text size in this website so the fonts display at a larger size.

To change the font using the browser menu, follow these instructions:

In Internet Explorer, select Text Size from the View menu item. Then choose the preferred size. In Netscape Navigator, select Text Zoom from the View menu item. Then choose the preferred size. The text of the site will change to reflect your choice.

Navigating this website

This site has been designed for ease of use. The main navigation includes all the main sections of the website and runs across the top of each page. Clicking on any of these items will take you to a specific section of the website, where the navigation is displayed down the left. Choosing a section will also reveal any further content pages within a section. This style of navigation is consistent throughout the site.

Images and alt tags

All images used on the site include 'Alt' tags descriptive text alternatives. This allows users to see what the image is meant to convey even if it doesn't load, or if images have been switched off or if using a screen reader to read the web page rather than view.

Figure 7. Diageo's WAC, 2011.
http://www.diageo.com/en-row/Pages/accessibility.aspx

and *disability* do not appear once in the statement, which clusters around inclusive terms such as *all*, *allow*, and *you*. Diageo makes it clear that it intends for its site's visitors to be able to navigate to information and products with ease. Thus, this WAC is all about providing Burke's (1941/1973) "equipment for living." It avoids any phrases that in Burkean terms could result in alienation or dissociation.

The London 2012 Olympic and Paralympics Games (n.d.) WAC again broadens the scope of web accessibility to include everyone, including people "from different cultural and socio-economic backgrounds" and "people from different generations" (para. 4). The key word for the organizers of the 2012 Olympics is *people*—and that includes those with diverse interests and needs: all persons without exclusion.

CONSTRUCTING A BETTER WAC: PROFESSIONAL WRITING AND CSR

If the consensus even among web developers is that WACs are important, then the question remains, how can a WAC meet the needs of its primary audience, which is in fact PWDs? While it might be tempting to blame the web developers for overly technical and impersonal writing styles in the majority of corporate and local government WACs, the demands placed on these statements is really global in nature. They, thus, fall logically under the purview of public relations because PR is largely concerned with communication relationships (Edwards, 2006). In particular, WACs should come under the purview of corporate social responsibility since CSR is primarily tasked with communicating the ways in which a corporation demonstrates its "socially responsible attitude in its interactions with consumers" so that it can "maintain its social capital" and be responsive to all stakeholders, beyond the "traditional confines of shareholders and employees" (Burchell & Cook, 2006, pp. 121–122). Moreover, the use of rhetoric is an extremely effective tool for enabling PR and CSR practitioners to better understand their public (or audience) and thus achieve a heightened awareness of the "interaction among the speaker, the audience, and the societal values that form the basis for shared meaning" (Edwards, 2006, p. 857).

It is now widely accepted that one of those societal values is accessibility and that the achievement of "shared meaning" is the achievement of Burke's (1950/ 1969) consubstantiality. No one would argue that accessibility is not of strategic importance to any Fortune 50 company doing business globally and is not extremely important to its competitive advantage. It is in CSR that we can hope to see the fullest potential for the application of rhetoric as an organization strives to distinguish itself as a good citizen by concerning itself with the greater good of society (Jonker & Marberg, 2007; Sotorrío & Sánchez, 2008). Accessibility consultant Babinszki (n.d.) draws an interesting analogy between the WAC and the "about us" and the "mission statement" pages of a website. Visitors to websites do not necessarily read these pages, but Babinszki (n.d.) argues that such pages are helpful if anyone wants to understand more about the organization, its guiding philosophy and/or its assistive technologies. Hence, the WAC needs to be considered as a document of strategic importance, rather than one of simple compliance to enhance usability, are relevance and accessibility for everyone—not just PWDs. Thus, the difference in message achieved by HelpAge International's placement of its WAC at the top of the homepage is striking, as seen in Figure 8.

As good corporate citizens, organizations need to be aware that at certain stages of life everyone may experience some level of disability; thus, accessibility is global in its reach. In light of the social model of disability,[3] then, situations can arise that can interfere with accessibility: "Among these situations are temporary disabilities that result from accidents, the use of slower internet connections and older browsers, changing abilities due to the aging process (visual, auditory, and manual dexterity), literary levels which can change over the course of time, and even language fluency" (De Andrés et al., 2009, p. 1170). The tale "The Surfer and the Accessibility Statement" (Griffiths, 2005) in the epigraph offers a pertinent lesson. As web surfers grow more confident in their experience with WACs across the web, they share their enthusiasm with friends. Griffiths (2005) captures this interaction: "'Wow' said [The Surfer's] able-bodied web surfer friend 'If only every web site had *general* instructions explaining in detail how to use them. That would be so bloody useful'" (para. 10).

Useful, indeed, but in the world beyond that of Griffith's surfer, to ask a designer or developer to construct a WAC that will meet the requirements of all the people who need accessibility help is unrealistic because of the incredible diversity of the intended audience, the differing rhetorical situations in which users find themselves, and the corporation's branding strategy and levels of web accessibility.

The question of full access captured in WACs is ultimately a matter of being able to create single, concise, rhetorically appropriate, and accessible documents that still provide sufficient information to function as instructional guides and

---

[3] Despite the limitations argued by Shakespeare (2010) with regard to the British social model of disability, it is useful here to underscore that disability is a universal experience. I am one of those who, while surfing the web, am challenged at times by a piece of metal that permanently resides in my right hand, and so I am grateful when sites provide me with fewer clicks and more efficient navigation. My consciousness of the difficulties of reading and retaining information when presented with seemingly endless scrolling through web pages arises from the frequency of dyslexia and vision problems in my extended family. For an argument in favor of the social model, see Playforth (2003).

The social model's nomenclature for a PWD is "DP." There is a certain aptness to the acronym in the context of this article because of its widespread use at the end of WWII to identify the vast numbers of people who lost home and homeland and were thus "displaced persons." Unsuccessful efforts to find access to websites can leave one feeling very much displaced in the virtual world.

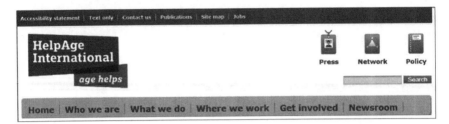

Figure 8. HelpAge's Homepage, 2011. http://www.helpage.org/

vehicles of consubstantiality. By involving professional writers, the likelihood increases that these documents will be more effective because professional writers have the skills, ability, and knowledge to analyze audiences, complex rhetorical situations, and knotty communication problems. Only then can an effective CSR document that is relevant, usable, and accessible be constructed. To ask web designers or developers to step back from their design tasks and write such a document is not feasible and, when done, results in documents that do not generally create consubstantiality.

Consequently, the question becomes, can one document meet all the needs of a diverse set of users and still provide enough information for it to be both a rhetorically suitable, instructional document, and a vehicle for achieving Burke's (1950/1969) consubstantiality/identification between an organization and its disabled clientele or audience? For Burke (1950/1969) the opposite of consubstantiality is alienation or dissociation, and this is what happens when an organization acting in the role of rhetor or persuader fails to identify with its audience. The accessibility statement can produce identification between the PWD and the organization—but only if it is reconsidered as a statement of identification and persuasion rather than as a statement of compliance and defense and if it is disengaged from practicing forensic rhetoric. The WAC cannot achieve all of the goals that are currently envisioned, but those goals are not all necessary if the primary function of the WAC becomes one of consubstantiality rather than compliance.

When WACs are focused on the user and on inclusiveness, and thus on establishing consubstantiality, then the document has persuasive power and is, in fact rather than in theory, usable, relevant, and accessible to its audience. When it is not, it appears to engage in an anticipatory forensic rhetoric in which compliance is the predominant motif, and as a result the goodwill of the audience sinks to the point where, to engage from a different perspective the surfing metaphor used by Griffiths (2005), the surfer no longer has enough water on which to surf. The reservoir is dry and Burke's (1941/1973) "equipment for living," or in this case "equipment for surfing," is lost, and so the web surfer must depart without goodwill toward the organization and without accessibility. Corporations, in particular, need to realize that PWDs will overcome these web access barriers by finding other waters on which to do their surfing. They will seek a far more desirable "waterfront property" for surfing in the pages of competing websites (Krug, 2006, p. 20). And, because of this, WACs are a matter of good business since PWDs are consumers too. Well-written accessibility statements provide "operational benefits" for companies and are directly related to CSR activities, even though they are not currently referenced on the CSR page (De Andrés et al., 2009, p. 1778).

Organizations have a long way to go in terms of creating accessible, usable, and relevant web accessibility statements. However, by utilizing hyperlinks, plain English, practical instructions with examples, and by declaring an inclusive commitment to accessibility, there is reason to believe these documents—created by more rhetorically aware and perhaps empathetic writers in the CSR division— will be as effective and persuasive as the rest of the website. The public relations arm of any corporation has a firm eye on its multiple audiences (or publics), and any communication that is audience-centered is much more likely to be persuasive and build consubstantiality because it is inherently not a postscript.

Clearly the scope of the document should be the establishment of common ground between the organization and PWDs. It should take the form of a descriptive statement, deliberative in nature, which serves as a reassuring guidepost for PWDs. For example, by continuing the practice of including hyperlinks from a basic statement of accessibility (e.g., the WACs adopted by IBM and Marriott), any organization can provide a flexible approach for meeting the particular needs of any PWD visiting its website and achieving an identification with the PWD. That identification can lead to a continuing relationship between the customer or user and the organization or service provider.

An effective WAC can, therefore, be considered a descriptive statement that does the following:

- Acknowledges the need for accessibility for everyone visiting the website
- Assures the user that accessibility help is easily available on the website
- Indicates that accessibility is an integral part of the company's mission
- Provides a clear definition of what the website considers accessibility to be
- Includes an explanation of the ways in which the organization has committed itself to forming a partnership with the PWD to ensure compliance by embracing the best practices in accessibility
- Provides contact information that specifies how the organization can be contacted about problems encountered on the site and gives a time frame for response
- Gives directions to "help" pages dedicated to accessibility

The language of accessibility that the PWD wants to hear in WACs has been achieved in part by several organizations that, although falling short in some of the descriptive content discussed above, nonetheless are striving for consubstantiality (Table 2). Burke (1941/1973) suggests that the rhetor, in this case the organization, helps create identification by defining or naming situations for audiences—accessibility in this case. The WAC is seen, then, as a "strategy for encompassing a situation"—the need for reassurance and assistance in navigating a website to obtain information that allows the users to meet their needs (Burke, 1941/1973, p. 109). Because Burke (1950/1969) views rhetoric as the rhetor's (or corporation's) solution to problems, rhetoric and the artifacts that it produces (in this case the WAC) can indeed provide "equipment for living." Hence, the WAC, the mission statement and the "about us" section of a website are all documents that the audience or user can consult in trying to decide on a particular course of action with regard to the organization's website offerings, whether those be services or products. The WAC can be described as the person with disabilities's "equipment for living" on an organization's website.

REFERENCES

Abrahams, P. (2007, July 23). Accessibility statement—What it should include? Retrieved from http://www.it-director.com/blogs/Abrahams_Accessibility/2007/7/Accessibility_Statement_-_What_it_should_include.html

Aristotle. (2006). *Poetics and rhetoric.* (S. H. Butcher & W. Rhys Roberts, Trans.). New York, NY: Barnes and Noble Classics.

Babinszki, T. (n.d.). Accessibility statement: What is it, and who uses it? Even Grounds. Retrieved from http://www.evengrounds.com/articles/accessibility-statement

British Standards Institution (BSI). (2006). *PAS 78: Guide to good practice in commissioning accessible websites.* Retrieved from http://www.equalityhumanrights.com/uploaded_files/pas78.pdf

Burchell, J., & Cook, J. (2006). Confronting the "corporate citizen": Shaping the discourse of corporate social responsibility. *International Journal of Sociology and Social Policy, 26*(¾), 121–137.

Burke, K. (1969). *A rhetoric of motives.* Berkeley, CA: University of California Press. (Original work published 1950.)

Burke, K. (1973). *The philosophy of literary form: Studies in symbolic action.* Berkeley, CA: University of California Press. (Original work published 1941.)

Caldwell, B., Cooper, M., Reid, L. G., & Vanderheiden, G. (2008). Web content accessibility guidelines (WCAG) 2.0. W3C. Retrieved from http://www.w3.org/TR/WCAG20/

Cheney, G. (1992). The corporate person (re)presents itself. In E. Toth & R. Heath (Eds.), *Rhetorical and critical approaches to public relations* (pp. 165–186). Mahwah, NJ: Lawrence Erlbaum Associates.

Cisco Systems. (n.d.) Accessibility policy. Retrieved from http://www.cisco.com/web/about/responsibility/accessibility/accessibility_policy/index.html

Clark, J. (2002). *Building accessible websites*. Indianapolis, IN: New Riders.

Coca-Cola Great Britain. (n.d.). Accessibility statement. Retrieved from http://www.coca-cola.co.uk/accessibility.html

Comhlámh. (n.d.) Accessibility statement. Retrieved from http://www.comhlamn.org/accessibility-statement.html

Coster, D. (2010, March 22). The world's most ethical companies. *Forbes*. Retrieved from http://www.forbes.com/2010/03/22/ethisphere-ethical-companies-leadership-citizenship-100.html

Coupland, C. (2005). Corporate social responsibility as argument on the web. *Journal of Business Ethics, 62*(4), 355–366.

De Andrés, J., Lorca, P., & Martinez, A. B. (2009). Economic and financial factors for the adoption and visibility of web accessibility: The case of European banks. *Journal of the American Society for Information Science and Technology, 60*(9), 1769–1780.

Diageo. (n.p.). Accessibility statement. Retrieved from http://www.diageo.com/en-row/Pages/accessibility.aspx

Diversity Inc. (2010). The 2010 Diversity Inc. Top 50 List. Retrieved from http://www.diversityinc.com/generaldiversityinformation/the-2010-diversityinc-top-50-list/

Edwards, H. (2006). A rhetorical typology for studying the audience role in public relations communication: The Avon 3-day disruption as exemplar. *Journal of Communication, 56*(4), 836–860.

Fortune. (2010, March 22). World's most admired companies: Industry champions. Retrieved from http://money.cnn.com/magazines/fortune/mostadmired/2010/champions/

Garrett, J. J. (2003). *The elements of user experience: User-centered design for the web*. Berkeley, CA: New Riders.

General Electric. (2011). Homepage. Retrieved from http://www.ge.com/

General Electric. (n.d.). Accessibility statement. Retrieved from http://www.ge.com/accessibility.html

Griffiths, P. (2005, April 11). The surfer and the accessibility statement. Retrieved from http://www.htmldog.com/ptg/archives/000100.php

HelpAge. (2011) Homepage. Retrieved from http://www.helpage.org/

Howell, J. (2006). British standard PAS 78:2006. *Access by Design, 107*, 20–22.

IBM. (n.d.). Accessibility statement. Retrieved from http://www-03.ibm.com/able/access_ibm/accessibility_statement.html

IBM. (n.d.). Browse ibm.com more comfortably with no-charge software. Retrieved from http://www.ibm.com/accessibility/us/en/

Jonker, J., & Marberg, A. (2007). Corporate social responsibility *quo vadis*? A critical inquiry into a discursive struggle. *Journal of Corporate Citizenship, 27*, 107–118.

Kalbach, J. (2007). *Designing for web navigation*. Sebastopol, CA: O'Reilly Media.

Krantz, P. (2006, October 22). Don't provide an accessibility statement. Standards schmandards: A problematic approach to web accessibility. Retrieved from http://www.standards-schmandards.com/2006/just-say-no/

Krug, S. (2006). *Don't make me think: A common sense approach to web usability* (2nd ed.). Berkeley, CA: New Riders.

Lannon, J. (2003). *Technical communication* (9th ed.). New York, NY: Longman.

McAdon, B. (2002). Rhetoric is a counterpart to dialectic. *Philosophy and Rhetoric, 34*, 113–150.

Marriott. (n.d.). Accessibility statement. Retrieved from http://aap.afbconsulting.org/domainpolicy.aspx?ServiceKey=61eb9376-6489-4eb0-9cec-70ef1dfd203e

Parkinson, C. M. (2007). Website accessibility statements: A comparative investigation of local government and high street sectors. *Library and Information Research, 31*(98), 29–42.

Petrie, H., Badani, A., & Bhalla, A. (2005). Sex, lies, and web accessibility: The use of accessibility logos and statements on e-commerce and financial websites. Accessible Design in the Digital World Conference. Dundee, Scotland, August 23–25, 2005. Retrieved from http://www.bcs.org/upload/pdf/ewic_ad05_s5paper2.pdf

Pilgrim, M. (2002). *Dive into accessibility: 30 days to a more accessible website.* Retrieved from http://diveintoaccessibility.info/

Playforth, S. (2003). *Meeting disabled people.* London, UK: Museums, Libraries, and Archives Council.

Playforth, S. (2004). Inclusive library services for deaf people: An overview from the social model perspective. *Health Information & Libraries Journal, 21*(Suppl. 2), 54–57.

Procter & Gamble. (n.d.). Accessibility statement. Retrieved from http://www.pgcareers.com/aboutpg/accessibility/page/242/default.htm)

Quinn, P. (2008, July 29). Accessibility statements. University of Oxford. Retrieved from http://www.ox.ac.uk/web/guides/accessibility.html

Shakespeare, T. (2010). The social model of disability. In L. J. Davis (Ed.), *The disabilities studies reader* (3rd ed., pp. 266–293). New York, NY: Routledge.

Sodexo. (n.d.). Accessibility Statement. Retrieved from http://uk.sodexo.com/uken/accessibility.asp

Sotorrío, L., & Sánchez, J. (2008). Corporate social responsibility of the most highly reputed European and North American Firms. *Journal of Business Ethics, 82*(2), 379–390.

Springston, J. K. (2001). Public relations and new media technology: The impact of the Internet. In R. L. Heath (Ed.), *Handbook of public relations* (pp. 603–614). Thousand Oaks, CA: Sage.

Starbucks. (n.d.). Accessibility statement. Retrieved from http://www.starbucks.com/about-us/company-information/online-policies/web-accessibility

Thatcher, J., Waddell, S., Henry, S., Swierenga, S., Urban, M., Burks, M., et al. (2003). *Constructing accessible websites.* Birmingham, UK: Glasshaus.

Tomlinson, L. (2008, September 16). Understanding disabilities when designing a website. *Digital Web Magazine.* Retrieved from http://www.digital-web.com/articles/understanding_disabilities_when_designing_a_website/

United Nations. (2007). Convention on the rights of persons with disabilities. Retrieved from http://www.un.org/disabilities/convention/conventionfull.shtml

U.S. Department of Justice. (2009). Americans with disabilities act of 1990, as amended. Retrieved from http://www.ada.gov/pubs/ada.htm

U.S. Government. (1973, 1998). The rehabilitation act amendments (Section 508). Retrieved from http://www.access-board.gov/sec508/guide/act.htm

Wriston, W. (1992). *The twilight of sovereignty.* New York, NY: Charles Scribners.

CHAPTER 10

Accessibility as Context: The Legal, Fiscal, and Social Imperative to Deliver Inclusive e-Content

Lisa Pappas

In recent decades, as computer access has become ubiquitous, great attention has focused on the accessibility of computer and information technologies. With the casting of the World Wide Web, the Internet—previously a character-driven, command-line interface—became a barrier-ridden sea for people with disabilities using computers. Ironically, technological advances and proliferation of web content resulted in regressions in connectedness for tech-savvy users with disabilities.

Accessibility refers to inclusiveness for people of all functional abilities, whether as an architectural attribute or functionality in information and computer technology (ICT). The term first became concrete in popular culture with the passage of the Americans with Disabilities Act (ADA) in 1990. This landmark legislation dictated that public facilities be navigable and usable by people with disabilities. Common hallmarks included curb cuts on sidewalks, designated parking spots with ramps, and wide restroom stalls to accommodate a wheelchair. Beyond the most visible architectural aspects, the ADA protects the civil rights of people with disabilities to access telecommunications services, public transportation, voter registration and voting facilities, as well as public education (U.S. Dept. of Justice, 2005).

Recognizing the resultant accessibility gap and its impact on employment and education opportunities for citizens with disabilities, the U.S. Congress in 1998 amended the Rehabilitation Act of 1973, adding Sections 508 and 504.

203

Section 508 mandated that most electronic information and technology (EIT) purchased by the U.S. federal government must provide to federal government employees who have disabilities information and data access that is comparable to the access that is provided to federal government employees who do not have disabilities. In addition, for information that it disseminates to the public, the U.S. federal government must provide to members of the public who have disabilities data access comparable to the data access provided to members of the public who do not have disabilities. The regulations developed by the U.S. federal government to implement Section 508 generally require that U.S. government agencies purchase software solutions that are most compliant with Section 508 requirements.

In the two decades since Section 508 has been in force, U.S. federal procurers, state and municipal governments, and international entities increasingly require compliance with accessibility standards when making procurement decisions. Concurrently, individuals' and advocates' demands for accessible EIT have increased, as has their use of social and other media to promote their cause. These two trends converge in the technical communication arena. To meet the information needs of users, including those with disabilities, technical communicators must deliver their information products in a format that meets the aforementioned accessibility standards and can be used by people with disabilities using special hardware and software. Moreover, their content must describe accessibility features or deficiencies present in the software, products, websites, or other EIT about which they are communicating.

In this chapter, I explore the legal and policy drivers for accessible e-Content, not only addressing the need to document accessibility in EIT, but also introducing the standards against which compliance is measured. Next, moving to information design and learning, I survey legal obligations for public education and people with disabilities, covering primary through continuing education. Through e-government initiatives, agencies increasingly deliver services to citizens via the web. I next consider the accessibility of government services, the cost of providing alternatives, and the broader benefits of accessibility included in design. Beyond the public sector, accessibility compliance affects businesses, both from employee access and from the recruiting pool. With this broad understanding of accessible EIT in society, I focus on implications for technical communicators, their responsibility to end-users with disabilities as well as to the firms for whom they develop content. I conclude with a look forward and identify additional research to inform technical communication accessibility.

LEGAL AND POLICY DRIVERS FOR ACCESSIBLE INFORMATION PRODUCTS

Effective technical communicators exhibit a clear understanding of context, the framework within which their information products will be consumed. Regarding accessibility, technical communicators have a responsibility to their employers and an obligation to end users to know the legal and policy requirements on their information products. One challenge for global corporations is that countries and regions have adopted their own accessibility standards, and demonstrating conformance to each can prove onerous.

As previously mentioned, the U.S. Congress passed Section 508 law, making EIT accessibility a consideration in procurement decisions. With civil rights as a clear motivator, it is useful to understand the underlying fiscal drivers for accessibility legislation. According to the U.S. Bureau of Labor Statistics, among working age adults (people 16 years of age and over), more than 10% have a disability (U.S. Department of Labor, 2010).[1] In 2009, the unemployment rate of working age adults with disabilities was 14.5%, compared to 9% among adults without a disability (U.S. Department of Labor, 2010). Working citizens paying into a system are far less costly per capita than non-working citizens, so governments have financial incentive to improve the employment status of people with disabilities. In addition, the U.S. government is the nation's largest employer of people with disabilities. Accessible EIT can also help to retain workers who possess accumulated years of domain knowledge but who may develop a disability over time. Companies can protect their investment in employees by providing tools to help these employees maintain their competitive edge in the workplace despite age-related impairments such as diminished visual and audio acuity and decreased manual dexterity.

With the tremendous purchasing power of the federal government and as enforcement increased, accessibility conformance became a marketing asset for firms selling EIT in the public sector.

The Section 508 standards apply to a range of EIT:

- 1194.21 Software applications and operating systems
- 1194.22 Web-based intranet and Internet information and applications
- 1194.24 Video and multimedia products
- 1194.31 Functional performance criteria (U.S. Access Board, 2000)

Recognizing the potential of Section 508, the European Union adopted the EU 376 Mandate for Accessible ICT Procurement, n.d.). The European Union has witnessed demographic trends putting pressure on the public sector to provide services to a growing, older population. As the average life expectancy has risen,

---

[1] The U.S. Bureau of Labor Statistics defines a person with a disability as having one or more of the following conditions: "is deaf or has serious difficulty hearing; is blind or has serious difficulty seeing even when wearing glasses; has serious difficulty concentrating, remembering, or making decisions because of a physical, mental, or emotional condition; has serious difficulty walking or climbing stairs; has difficulty dressing or bathing; or has difficulty doing errands alone such as visiting a doctor's office or shopping because of a physical, mental, or emotional condition" (U.S. Department of Labor, 2010).

people are staying in the workforce longer. A global survey of economically active populations in developed countries, conducted by the International Labor Organization, shows the number of workers 55 or older on pace to nearly double from 2000 to 2020 (2010). Combined with the declining trend in birth rates in industrialized nations, corporations face a dwindling supply of trained, experienced workers and a rising battle for talent. "As the pool of younger workers contracts, recruiting and retaining mature, experienced workers becomes increasingly critical for employers who seek to maintain a competitive edge in today's marketplace" (Barrington, 2004).

As in the United States, the European Union's EIT budget proved a sufficient attraction to motivate technology producers to make accessibility accommodations. While this may have improved work tools for some government employees, the greater body of material—and that often developed by technical communicators—comprises the plethora of e-government websites.

In response to human rights advocacy, many countries and regions enacted laws requiring public-facing websites to meet the needs of people with disabilities:

- Canadian Common Look and Feel for the Internet (Treasury Board of Canada Secretariat, 2011)
- Italy's Stanca Law (Government of Italy, 2004)
- Germany's Barrier-Free Information Technology (German Federal Ministry of the Interior, 2002)
- British Standard BS8878:2010—Web Accessibility Code of Practice (British Standards Institute, 2010)

Of interest in these laws is that they cite the World Wide Web Consortium (W3C) Web Content Accessibility Guidelines (WCAG) guidelines as authoritative. Version 1 of these guidelines (W3C, 1999) pre-dated Section 508 and became technologically obsolete. In 2008, the W3C issued version 2 (W3C, 2008), which is technology agnostic, focusing on the functional result for end users.

As governments increasingly rely on the Internet to deliver content and services, the need of citizens with disabilities for accessible content also escalates. However, investigation reveals that many government websites fail to meet the needs of citizens with disabilities:

- In the UK, a survey from Southampton University found that the majority of UK government websites failed to comply with the Web Content Accessibility Guide (Goldie, 2006).
- In India, the Centre for Internet and Society (CIS) found that 23 government agencies failed to make even their homepages accessible (Miuli, 2008).

- In the United States, the National Foundation for the Blind (NFB) filed administrative complaints against three federal entities, citing violations of Section 508 resulting in disenfranchisement of blind people who use text-to-speech screen access technology or Braille displays to access information:
  - On the Small Business Administration site, blind people cannot fill out forms on the site or take online courses offered by the SBA.
  - On the Social Security Administration site, blind people cannot fill out forms and questionnaires or access information about their benefits.
  - On the Department of Education's U.S.A. Learns site, blind people cannot access or navigate through the content of the English vocabulary, spelling, and pronunciation lessons offered. (SSB Bart Group)

As awareness of accessibility—and successful litigation—has increased, so too has the burden on private corporations to deliver accessible EIT, including its information products.

With an understanding of the legal and policy drivers for accessible EIT and their supporting information products, I next consider accessibility in the educational arena. As many technical communicators design learning products—textbooks, online learning products, and educational websites—they must understand the obligations of educational entities to their students with disabilities. This discussion will focus primarily on the United States; however, similar legislation exists in many developed nations.

ACCESSIBLE PUBLIC EDUCATION
AND e-LEARNING

All U.S. schools that receive any federal financial assistance must comply with Section 504 of the Rehabilitation Act of 1973, and each must have a designated 504 coordinator. Under Section 504 provisions, students with disabilities, as defined by the ADA,[2] cannot be denied the opportunity to participate in activities available to students without disabilities. In practice, this can mean accommodations such as:

- Electronic versions of textbooks with software that can read aloud to students with vision deficiencies or learning disabilities
- School websites that can be navigated via keyboard, voice, or touch screen by students with dexterity impairments preventing their use of a mouse device
- Online courses with captioned video and text descriptions of graphics for students who are blind or who have attention deficits

---

[2] The Americans with Disabilities Act (ADA) states that an individual has a disability if they possess a "physical or mental impairment that substantially limits one or more major life activities" (U.S. Department of Justice, 2005).

To meet the civil rights of students with disabilities, the curriculum materials—whether hard copy or electronic—must meet myriad functional requirements. From a technical communicator's perspective, this has significant implications for, among many other aspects:

- Information architectures—flexible and intuitive navigation structures not reliant on visuals
- Electronic format—delivering books in files readable by assistive technologies such as screen readers that read electronic files aloud to blind or vision-impaired people
- User-Task analysis—procedures written in terms not dependent on a specific device, such as a mouse (e.g., Press Alt+F to open the File menu, then choose Open.)
- Interface design—providing keyboard shortcuts and documenting them for efficient navigation to most-used functions (e.g., think of the common Ctrl+P for printing).

As awareness and advocacy for students with disabilities have expanded, so too has successful litigation against educational entities failing to protect students' civil rights under Section 504 and related legislation.

- In 2002, in a landmark settlement costing over $1 million, the University of California at Berkeley and UC Davis, without admitting wrongdoing, agreed to "provide additional listening devices" for students' use and make sure all videos, films, and DVDs used in classes with a deaf or hearing-impaired student have captions," among other accommodations (Scully, 2002).
- In 2009, with support from the National Federation for the Blind (NFB), a blind applicant filed a discrimination suit against The Law School Admissions Council (LSAC), which administers the national law school admissions test. According to the suit, the LSAC "Web site and Law School Admission Test (LSAT) preparation materials are inaccessible to the blind" (Qualters, 2009).

Pressure on educational entities to comply with accessibility laws will only increase as institutions increasingly deliver materials and courses virtually. Moreover, computer savvy adult learners who have acquired disabilities are a growing segment of those seeking continuing education opportunities. Their expectations for accommodations means institutions are now expected to meet the needs of diverse learners. As developers of learning material, technical communicators must understand what is needed to deliver their information products in ways that accommodate the needs of students with disabilities.

THE ROLE OF TECHNICAL COMMUNICATORS
IN e-CONTENT DELIVERY

An understanding of accessibility—implications for deliverables, needs of end users, and obligations of vendors—is highly complementary to core competencies of technical communication. In this section, I explore aspects of this partnership and identify how accessibility expertise can aide professional development.

Audience Analysis and Awareness of
Disability Statistics

From the onset of their careers and in whatever medium they publish, technical communicators must consider for whom they are writing. Are they novices or experts in the subject matter? In what context will they encounter the information: frequently or seldom? Is the information critical? What is the demographic make-up of the elusive "primary persona"? How varied is the audience? The answers to these questions inform the design and information architecture of the communication. "For most technical writers," claims textbook author McMurray, audience analysis "is *the most important* consideration in planning, writing, and reviewing a document. You 'adapt' your writing to meet the needs, interests, and background of the readers who will be reading your writing" (McMurray, 2001).

With audience analysis as your tool, calibrate it to factor in users with disabilities. As noted earlier in this chapter, more than 10% of working age adults self-report some disability. But what if your audience includes people who may not be in the workforce currently? According to the U.S. Census Bureau's (1994) Survey of Income and Program Participation (SIPP), a full 20% of U.S. citizens have a disability, with the incidence rising to 29% among those aged 45 to 64. To understand the potential impact of these statistics to web content design and delivery, consider the work of Fidelity Investments.

Fidelity Investments was an early adopter of online banking and investment management. Their market strategy was to empower their customers to research investments, conduct transactions, and manage their financial portfolios from their Internet browser. Fidelity recognized that their user distribution would likely be skewed to older individuals, those more likely to have a disability.

For example, out of Fidelity's 22 million customers, statistics would suggest that roughly 1 million have significant vision impairment, while about 100,000 are likely to be legally blind. For Fidelity, accessibility is not an abstract concept but an important business driver for its customer (McNally, 2008).

Fidelity's web technology team also recognized that those same tech savvy users (themselves early adopters of online investing) would expect user interfaces and information to accommodate their functionality needs. Their proactive adoption of accessibility earned them great customer loyalty.

Technical Editing for Standards Compliance

In many organizations, technical editors are the arbiters of standards and, with a view spanning information products, are well positioned to introduce accessibility into a technical communication library. To fulfill that role, however, technical editors first need to understand which standards or guidelines apply to the information based on its type (electronic book, e-learning with audio and video, webpage, etc.) and based on the geography of the company producing and of the community receiving the communication. The following are two sources for that information:

- "International Standards for Accessibility in Web Design and the Technical Challenges in Meeting Them" in the *Handbook of Human Factors Web Design* (Pappas, Roberts, & Hodgkinson, 2011)
- "Policies Relating to Web Accessibility" on the W3C Web Accessibility Initiative (WAI) website (W3C, 2006)

Raising awareness of accessibility obligations among communication producers and project managers, all the way up to management, the technical editor can help to mitigate the company's risk of litigation or bad public opinion by promoting compliance. No treatment of accessibility standards is complete without acknowledgment of ISO 9241-171:2008 ("Ergonomics of human-system interaction—Part 171: Guidance on software accessibility) (International Organization for Standardization, n.d.). As an international standard, ISO 9241-171 has the broadest application and by far the greatest specificity. However, as of this writing, it is not widely adopted as authoritative but rather as highly informative.

Another aspect of accessibility to which technical editors can contribute is through careful review of supporting materials. For example, any substantive graphic requires alternative text so that a non-sighted individual, who may be using screen reading software, can discern its meaning. Well-written alternative text is not a repeat of a caption, if present, or, even worse, the dreaded description of only the text, "Graphic."

Consider this example from the U.S. Library of Congress (n.d.). The Library of Congress is a treasure trove of artifacts in many formats, including old audio recordings, photographs, and much more. As a free resource for the public, it is subject to Section 508 law and must ensure that all citizens with disabilities can access the information available.

Browsing the Culture and Folklife section, the user finds a black-and-white photo with little context. For someone who has low vision or cannot read, more information is needed. Note the text link "About this image" (see Figure 1).

Fiddle Tunes of the Old Frontier

The Henry Reed Collection

Josh and Henry Reed, ca. 1903.
About this image

Overview

Fiddle Tunes of the Old Frontier: The Henry Reed Collection is a multi-format **ethnographic field collection** of traditional fiddle tunes performed by Henry Reed of Glen Lyn, Virginia. Recorded by folklorist **Alan Jabbour** in 1966-67, when Reed was over eighty years old, the tunes represent the music and evoke the history and spirit of Virginia's Appalachian frontier. Many of the tunes have passed back into circulation during the fiddling revival of the later twentieth century. This online collection incorporates 184 original **sound recordings**, 19 pages of **fieldnotes**, and 69 **musical transcriptions** with descriptive notes on tune histories and musical features; an illustrated **essay** about Reed's life, art, and influence; a **list** of related publications; and a **glossary** of musical terms.

Figure 1. Initial photo in Library of Congress example.
Source: U.S. Library of Congress.

A blind user of screen reading technology could navigate to the link and press "Enter"; a new window, with a much larger photo and descriptive text, would display (see Figure 2).

This approach benefits not only a user with a disability such as blindness or low vision but also provides enhanced experience for all users, who can choose to expand or collapse details as needed.

User Experience and Adaptive Design

Research shows that techniques used to deliver accessible content generally raise its overall usability and flexibility. In a presentation to the U.S. Access Board advisory committee, Clayton Lewis "pointed out that many features that make Web sites accessible to people with cognitive disabilities also improve the general usability of sites, because such disabilities can amplify mild annoyances into absolute barriers" (as cited in Quesenberry, 2009). As noted in the Library of Congress example above, flexibility for accessibility purposes can yield general usability improvements.

User experience designers are often tasked with developing flexible designs, ones that enable users to personalize their interface or that adapt to alternative devices. This requirement has gained momentum as people use mobile devices

Figure 2. Information displayed from "About this image" link in Figure 1.
Source: U.S. Library of Congress.

such as smartphones and tablets to access web content, applications, and business networks. Many principles of web accessibility apply readily to mobile best practices.

Most mobile web specialists don't know about design issues for people with disabilities. Likewise, most web accessibility specialists don't know mobile web design best practices. Websites can more efficiently meet both goals when developers understand the significant overlap between making a website accessible for a mobile device and for people with disabilities. The similarities are introduced below along with benefits of addressing both and resources with technical details of the overlap (W3C, 2008).

People with low vision or cognitive disabilities may require enlarged views and the ability to close or move extraneous panels in an interface. Traditional users of a mobile device may have the same challenges, and providing a linearized view (versus horizontal) may aide usability (think flick to scroll). As noted earlier, for accessibility, visuals require text equivalents. On a mobile device, due to bandwidth issues, a user may disable graphics to boost speed performance. Providing alternative text in graphic placeholders can tell the sighted user what he or she is missing, prompting the user to selectively enable graphics on mobile sites.

IMPLICATIONS FOR
TECHNICAL COMMUNICATION RESEARCH

Significant research from the W3C WAI and other entities has proven that accessibility promotes overall usability. As technical communicators, we want our work products to be used, to have value, and, ultimately, to help someone. With the rapid shift from traditional media to online, from printed to e-books, from desktop tutorials to web-based e-learning, people with disabilities continue to face significant challenges accessing those assets, and lack of access contributes to professional development challenges and, ultimately, employment challenges.

As the body of laws and regulations governing the work technical communicators produce has grown—and the penalties for deviation have increased—as communication professionals, we are obliged to educate our communities of practice about accessibility to enable them to educate their employers, reducing risk of litigation. But we must go beyond the legality and risk. We must consider the ethical ramifications of these laws and regulations on the work we do.

> By *ethics* we mean a critical-rational reflection on the customs or habits. . . .
> This reflection is conducted with a distance in order to see whether the
> moral responses that guide behaviour have become obsolete because they
> arose in a highly specific and determined context (a context with given
> values and knowledge), or whether they remain valid and why. . . . The
> ethical question . . . is why we should do it. (Román 2010, "Introduction,"
> para. 2)

Why should we advocate for the ethics of accessibility? This is a question ideally suited for technical communicators to help answer. Technical writing ethics is not simply ensuring that the letter of the law is followed. Rather, the role of the technical communicator is one of interpretation, humanistic perspective, and ensuring that communication decisions best serve the users' interests. In other words, the question of ethics—why we should do it—moves the focus from simply ends to the means. Aristotle's (1980) philosophy and ethics claim that people do not deliberate about ends; they deliberate about means. Aristotle (1980) gives the example of a doctor not deliberating about the end of wanting to heal or make better; rather, the doctor deliberates on how and by what means the end should be attained (pp. 55–56).

Now move this example to the realm of technical communication, specifically to issues of disability and accessibility. Technical communicators understand the end goal of ensuring that a website or product meets minimum measures of legal compliance. But we should be spending time considering the means. We cannot know what people with disabilities need better than they themselves do, which is an inherent assumption in many of the laws and regulations. Since laws and regulations stipulate "minimum compliance," there is an implicit acknowledgement that people with disabilities need only this minimum. Technical communicators know that most users need more than the minimum. Thus, one way to ensure ethical action is to consider what the user needs to achieve the action, which means thinking about the means rather than the end. For people with disabilities, the necessary technological means differs from those of people without disabilities; thus, ethical considerations are paramount in ensuring universal design.

In this deliberation about means, however, technical communicators often report feeling that they have little power to drive change.

> Employees are paid to render a service to employers and to further their goals. . . . Institutional readers "need" a document that does a certain job, and they won't accept one that does not do it to their satisfaction, no matter how lofty the social sentiments of the writer." (Ornatowski, 1992, p. 100)

But technical communicators should question their organizations' practices, especially if those practices could be improved to better serve diverse and inclusive audiences. By questioning internal processes, technical communicators improve their chances to identify opportunities to influence the means. Ensuring the inclusion of minor changes that can have major impacts—such as the simple act of adding ALT tags to websites—is definitely something within the power of many technical communicators. One specific area that could provide an arena for more involvement is in situations where "reasonable accommodation" is invoked as a means to avoid adding accessibility features. And how much can a business reasonably expect to invest in such accommodations? What, exactly, governs "reasonable accommodation"? The ethical consideration of deliberating about means can help with this ethical dilemma. Moreover, technical communicators do have the power to argue for and to be advocates for the user and for more universal design features.

I firmly believe that expanding technical communication research to encompass accessibility considerations is in line with the profession's ethical principles. Consider those put forth by the Society for Technical Communication (1998), the leading professional organization of the field, regarding legality and fairness:

As technical communicators, we observe the following ethical principles in our professional activities.

Legality: We observe the laws and regulations governing our profession. (para. 1)

Fairness: We respect cultural variety and other aspects of diversity in our clients, employers, development teams, and audiences. We serve the business interests of our clients and employers as long as they are consistent with the public good. (para. 5)

The ethical question of why we should do it can also be framed within the issue of fairness. "Resolving such difficult questions on disabilities and accessibility demands a delicate balance of ethics, law, technology, and economics—the fulcrum of which is the principle of fairness" (Voss, 2003, p. 103). The fairness guideline opens up a space for the technical communicator to consider multiple stakeholders. Fairness moves from production to conduct, but it is important to include fair conduct in the deliberations associated with production. Out of respect for the diversity of our information consumers, technical communicators must conduct research to ensure that newer technologies do not create further barriers to information for audiences. For example, rather than including a "skip navigation" option for blind or low vision users, change it to "skip to main content." This small change can have big results not only for blind or low vision users but for all users who opt for keyboard navigation over mouse navigation. Other examples well within the control of technical communicators include writing descriptive tagged headings, putting the most important information first, and writing content in manageable chunks. This latter example helps a wide range of people with disabilities from blind and low vision users to the aging population to low literacy users.

Is this ethic, premised on the process of production (means) and fairness conceivable and realistic for technical communicators? Is this ethic worthwhile to organizations? Is this ethic an effective means to address difficult questions regarding disability and accessibility? It's a specific start that can be implemented with relative ease. Technical communicators should consider taking the lead role in applying the laws and regulations that govern their work to advance the rights of people with disabilities and a growing aging population. The ethical burden cannot be left to laws and regulations, nor can it be made solely the responsibility of people with disabilities to litigate to provoke change. Rather, it should fall within the purview of technical communication to consistently invoke an ethic that considers the best means to meet the end needs of all users.

In this chapter, much time has been devoted to the "stick" of accessibility regulation, but in closing, consider the very rich "carrot" aspect as well.

Many times focusing on standards and guidelines puts the focus on the technical aspects of accessibility, and the human interaction aspect is lost. This problem can be avoided by adopting the broader definition of accessibility as a guiding principle. Instead of focusing only on the technical aspects of accessibility, it is important to recognize that usability is also an important aspect of accessibility. Consciously addressing "usable accessibility" helps clarify the difference between what meets minimum accessibility standards and what is usable by people with disabilities. (Henry as cited in Quesenberry, 2009)

REFERENCES

Aristotle. (1980.) *Nicomachean ethics*. (D. Ross, Trans.). Oxford, UK: Oxford University Press.

Barrington, L. (2004, November 10). Demographic trends and the aging workforce. *Maximizing your workforce: Employees over 50 in today's economy*. Philadelphia, PA: Wharton Impact Conference sponsored by the American Association of Retired Persons' (AARP's) Global Aging Program and the Wharton School's Center for Human Resources, in collaboration with the Boettner Center for Pensions and Retirement Research.

British Standards Institute (BSI). (2010, November 30). *BS 8878: 2010. Web accessibility. code of practice.* Retrieved from http://shop.bsigroup.com/en/ProductDetail/?pid= 000000000030180388

German Federal Ministry of the Interior. (2002, July 17). Federal ordinance on barrier-free information technology. Einfach für Alle. Retrieved from http://www.einfach-fuer-alle.de/artikel/bitv_english/

Goldie, L. (2006, July 3). *Inaccessible government web sites named and shamed*. New Media Age. Retrieved from http://www.nma.co.uk/news/inaccessible-government-sites-named-and-shamed/28363.article

Government of Italy. Information Systems Accessibility Office at CNIPA (National Organism for ICT in the Public Administration). (2004, January 9). *Provisions to support the access to information technologies for the disabled*. Pubblic Accesso. Unofficial Translation to English. Retrieved from http://www.pubbliaccesso.gov.it/ normative/law_20040109_n4.htm

Human Factors (HF); European accessibility requirements for public procurement of products and services in the ICT domain (European Commission Mandate M 376, Phase 1). ETSI TR 102 612 V1.1.1 (2009-03). Retrieved from http://www.mandate 376.eu/tr_102612v010101p.pdf.

International Labour Organization Department of Statistics. Estimates and Projections of the Economically Active Population, 1980-2020 (5th edition, Geneva 2007, Update August 2008, Update December 2009).

International Organization for Standardization (ISO). (n.d.). *Ergonomics of human-system interaction—Part 171: Guidance on software accessibility (ISO 9241-171:2008)*. Retrieved from http://www.iso.org/iso/iso_catalogue/catalogue_ics/catalogue_ detail_ics.htm?csnumber=39080&ICS1=35&ICS2=180

McMurray, D. A. (2001). *Power tools for technical communication*. Boston, MA: Thomson Learning/Heinle Publishers.

McNally, P. (2008, June). *Universal usability of dynamic content: Three case studies in making DHTML, Ajax, and Flash accessible*. Boston-IA Association. Retrieved from http://www.boston-ia.org/news/article_28.html

Miuli, U. (2008, December 8). Government web sites are inaccessible to disabled people. *IT Examiner.* Retrieved from http://www.itexaminer.com/government-websites-are-inaccessible-to-disabled-people.aspx

Ornatowski, C. M. (1992). Between efficiency and politics: Rhetoric and ethics in technical writing. *Technical Communication Quarterly 1*(1), 91–103.

Pappas, L., Roberts, L., & Hodgkinson, R. (2011). International standards for accessibility in web design and the technical challenges in meeting them. In K. Vu & R. Proctor (Eds.), *Handbook of human factors in web design* (2nd ed., pp. 399–411). Long Beach, CA: CRC Press.

Qualters, S. (2009, February 20). *Blind law student sues Law School Admissions Council over accessibility. National Law Journal.* Retrieved from http://www.law.com/jsp/nlj/PubArticleNLJ.jsp?id=1202428419045&slreturn=1&hbxlogin=1

Quesenberry, W. (2009, February 23). *Usable accessibility: Making web sites work well for people with disabilities.* UXmatters. Retrieved from http://www.uxmatters.com/mt/archives/2009/02/usable-accessibility-making-web-sites-work-well-for-people-with-.php

Román, B. (2010). Ethics in caregiving services for people with serious intellectual disabilities. *Ramon Llull Journal of Applied Ethics, 1*(1), 121–142. Retrieved from http://www.rljae.org/text.asp?2010/1/1/121/70660

Scully, J. M. (2002, November 20). Universities settle suit brought by hearing impaired students. *Los Angeles Times.* Retrieved from http://articles.latimes.com/2002/nov/20/local/me-deaf20

Society for Technical Communication. (1998, September). STC's ethical principles for technical communicators. Retrieved from http://www.stc.org/about/ethical-principles-for-technical-communicators.asp

SSB Bart Group. (2010, February 24). Current state of US accessibility standards – Section 508. Retrieved from https://www.ssbbartgroup.com/blog/2010/02/24/current-state-of-us-accessibility-standards-%E2%80%93-section-508/

Treasury Board of Canada Secretariat. Common Look and Feel for the Internet 2.0. (n.d.). Retrieved from http://www.tbs-sct.gc.ca/clf2-nsi2/index-eng.asp

U.S. Access Board. (2000, December 21). Electronic and information technology accessibility standards (Section 508). Retrieved from http://www.access-board.gov/sec508/standards.htm

U.S. Census Bureau. (1994, January). *Americans with Disabilities (94-01).* Survey of Income and Program Participation (SIPP). Retrieved from http://www.census.gov/sipp/stat_briefs.html

U.S. Department of Justice, Civil Rights Division. (2005, September). A guide to disability rights laws. Retrieved from http://www.ada.gov/cguide.htm

U.S. Department of Labor, Bureau of Labor Statistics. (2010, February 5). Table A-6. Employment status of the civilian population by sex, age, and disability status, not seasonally adjusted. Retrieved from http://www.bls.gov/webapps/legacy/ cpsatab6.htm

U.S. Library of Congress. (n.d.). Fiddle tunes of the old frontier: From the Frank Reed collection. Library of Congress, American Memory. Retrieved from http://memory.loc.gov/ammem/collections/reed/

Voss, D. (2003). *The ethics of special needs: It's a matter of fairness.* Proceedings of the 50th International STC Conference. Dallas, TX, May 18–21, 2003.

W3C. (1999, May 5). *Web content accessibility guidelines 1.0.* Retrieved from W3C: http://www.w3.org/TR/WCAG10/

W3C. (2006, August 25). *Policies Relating to Web Accessibility. Retrieved August 13, 2010, from W3C Web Accessibility Initiative (WAI).* Retrieved from http://www.w3.org/WAI/Policy/

W3C. (2008, October 14). *Making a web site accessible both for people with disabilities and for mobile devices.* Retrieved from http://www.w3.org/WAI/mobile/

W3C. (2008, December 11). *Web content accessibility guidelines (WCAG) 2.0.* Retrieved from W3C: http://www.w3.org/TR/WCAG20/

http://dx.doi.org/10.2190/RAAC11

CHAPTER 11

Resources

Allison Maloney

The following includes a series of resources that can help technical communicators and disability studies scholars to become better acquainted with laws, guidelines, tools, and other information about disability and accessibility. These resources are not comprehensive, but they provide a verified and tested place to start.

SECTION 508 WEB-BASED STANDARDS

- www.section508.gov
- www.section508.gov/index.cfm?fuseAction=stdsdoc#Web

Section 1194.22: Web-based intranet and Internet information and applications

(a) A text equivalent for every non-text element shall be provided (e.g., via "alt," "longdesc," or in element content).
(b) Equivalent alternatives for any multimedia presentation shall be synchronized with the presentation.
(c) Web pages shall be designed so that all information conveyed with color is also available without color, for example from context or markup.
(d) Documents shall be organized so they are readable without requiring an associated style sheet.
(e) Redundant text links shall be provided for each active region of a server-side image map.
(f) Client-side image maps shall be provided instead of server-side image maps except where the regions cannot be defined with an available geometric shape.

219

(g) Row and column headers shall be identified for data tables.

(h) Markup shall be used to associate data cells and header cells for data tables that have two or more logical levels of row or column headers.

(i) Frames shall be titled with text that facilitates frame identification and navigation.

(j) Pages shall be designed to avoid causing the screen to flicker with a frequency greater than 2 Hz and lower than 55 Hz.

(k) A text-only page, with equivalent information or functionality, shall be provided to make a web site comply with the provisions of this part, when compliance cannot be accomplished in any other way. The content of the text-only page shall be updated whenever the primary page changes.

(l) When pages utilize scripting languages to display content, or to create interface elements, the information provided by the script shall be identified with functional text that can be read by assistive technology.

(m) When a web page requires that an applet, plug-in or other application be present on the client system to interpret page content, the page must provide a link to a plug-in or applet that complies with §[Section]1194.21(a) through (l).

(n) When electronic forms are designed to be completed on-line, the form shall allow people using assistive technology to access the information, field elements, and functionality required for completion and submission of the form, including all directions and cues.

(o) A method shall be provided that permits users to skip repetitive navigation links.

(p) When a timed response is required, the user shall be alerted and given sufficient time to indicate more time is required.

AMERICANS WITH DISABILITY ACT OF 1990, AS AMENDED

- http://www.ada.gov
- http://www.ada.gov/pubs/adastatute08.htm

Section 12102: Definition of disability

(1) Disability

The term "disability" means, with respect to an individual

(A) a physical or mental impairment that substantially limits one or more major life activities of such individual;

(B) a record of such an impairment; or

(C) being regarded as having such an impairment (as described in paragraph (3)).

(2) Major Life Activities
   (A) In general
      For purposes of paragraph (1), major life activities include, but are not limited to, caring for oneself, performing manual tasks, seeing, hearing, eating, sleeping, walking, standing, lifting, bending, speaking, breathing, learning, reading, concentrating, thinking, communicating, and working.
   (B) Major bodily functions
      For purposes of paragraph (1), a major life activity also includes the operation of a major bodily function, including but not limited to, functions of the immune system, normal cell growth, [and] digestive, bowel, bladder, neurological, brain, respiratory, circulatory, endocrine, and reproductive functions.
(3) Regarded as having such an impairment
   For purposes of paragraph (1)(C):
   (A) An individual meets the requirement of "being regarded as having such an impairment" if the individual establishes that he or she has been subjected to an action prohibited under this chapter because of an actual or perceived physical or mental impairment whether or not the impairment limits or is perceived to limit a major life activity.
   (B) Paragraph (1)(C) shall not apply to impairments that are transitory and minor. A transitory impairment is an impairment with an actual or expected duration of 6 months or less.

INFORMATION RESOURCES ON SECTION 508

U.S. Access Board
(http://access-board.gov/sec508/guide/1194.22.htm)

The U.S. Access Board operates as an independent federal agency that is committed to providing information on accessible design; their core mission is to inform people about accessibility for individuals with disabilities. The U.S. Access Board's guide to Section 508, "Web-based Intranet and Internet Information and Applications (1194.22)," clearly explains the regulations and provides actionable information on how to implement them.

The guide splits the information into 15 sections, with each section dedicated to one or two Section 508 standards. The sections explain what the respective standard or standards mean and why they are important. It also provides instructions on implementing the standards and offers examples depicting compliance.

WebAIM
(http://webaim.org/standards/508/checklist)

The WebAIM (Web Accessibility in Mind) organization is part of the Center for Persons with Disabilities at Utah State University. Its focus is to make the web more accessible for people with disabilities. As a part of the initiative, WebAIM provides a detailed checklist of Section 508 standards that is intended to help web developers determine if their website passes or fails the standard.

JimThatcher.com
(http://jimthatcher.com/webcourse1.htm)

Jim Thatcher is an independent consultant on accessibility. Prior to consulting, he spent 37 years working for IBM, where he helped develop the first screen reader for DOS. He also served on the committee that was commissioned by the U.S. Access Board to recommend standards for Section 508.

Jim Thatcher's website offers a web-based course on the standards of Section 508. Each module explains a few of the standards and then offers several examples of how they can be implemented. The modules are organized by theme, and each one covers several standards. Given the thematic organization of the course, this resource will be most useful for people who are already familiar with the regulations and are just seeking more information about how to implement them. The site also provides links to many other online resources for accessibility.

Section 508 Universe Training
(http://www.section508.gov/index.cfm?fuseAction=Training)

Section508.gov offers a tutorial, "Designing Accessible Web Sites," on how to interpret and implement the Section 508 accessibility regulations. Divided into eight modules, the lessons explain why a particular accessibility element is needed, provides examples of how disabled users would experience an improper site, provides information on how to create the site correctly, and then sometimes offers design suggestions. The modules can be viewed either as a slideshow on the website or in a format that can be printed and saved for reference.

To access the tutorial, navigate to the link provided above, register as a new user, log in using your new registry information, click the left panel link that says "508 Training Course," and then choose the link that says "Designing Accessible Web Sites."

Usability.gov
(http://www.usability.gov/guidelines/index.html)

Usability.gov provides a quick overview of Section 508 regulations. The "accessibility" guidelines are a useful snapshot of what each regulation means in terms of elements on a webpage.

Accessibility Forum 2.0
(http://buyaccessible.net/blog/)

The objective for this blog is to become the central point of dialogue for all varieties of Section 508 stakeholders and to be the solution-space for any Section 508-related issue, including acquisition, development, and implementation of new accessibility enhancing technologies. The site authors intend to open discussion on a host of issues: web accessibility, agency good practices, shared experiences, new technologies, acquisition insights, Section 508 events, and more.

ADDITIONAL RESOURCES FOR WEB ACCESSIBILITY

National Center for Accessible Media
(http://ncam.wgbh.org/invent_build/web_multimedia/ accessible-digital-media-guide)

The National Center for Accessible Media organization provides a comprehensive guideline for making web content accessible to disabled users. Their section "Accessible Digital Media Guidelines" is geared toward making online media—such as digital publications, websites and educational software—more available to students; however, the proposed standards and techniques for execution are applicable to all web designers. The main topics addressed for accessibility include images, forms, tables, digital publications, interactivity, graphs, math, multimedia, multimedia in e-books, and multimedia in digital talking books (DTBs). Each section begins by describing why the respective adaptation is necessary, and then provides several options for implementing the standard.

British Standard

The British Standards Institution (BSI) created the British standards for developing accessible websites for disabled and elderly people, referred to as "BS 8878: Web accessibility. Code of practice." Officially released on December 7, 2010, the standards build on and replace the previous guidelines published in 2006: "PAS 78: Guide to good practices in commissioning accessible websites."

BS 8878 recognizes that many private and public organizations do not have processes in place to develop accessible websites; therefore, "it is a non-technical standard that explains how organisations [sic] should create policies and production processes to identify and remove barriers that result in websites excluding disabled and elderly people" (Out-Law.com, para. 2). Jonathan Hassell, BBC's Head of Usability and Accessibility and chair of the committee that created the BS 8878 standards, commented that "Site owners urgently need an end-to-end guide to help them to ensure their products consider the needs of disabled and elderly people at all stages of the web production process, from initial requirements gathering, through selection of technologies and platforms, testing, launch and maintenance. . . . BS8878 is that guide" (as cited in Out-Law.com, 2010, para. 17).

Hassell (2010) notes that the BS 8878 looks to the future of where web production is heading, and addresses topics such as inclusive design and personalization, accessibility across devices (e.g., mobile apps and Internet TV), accessibility under new legislation, and accessibility in web product procurement. In regard to new legislation, the Equality Act 2010 was recently passed and dictates website accessibility requirements; BS 8878 reviews the legal obligations of the Equality Act 2010 and outlines what needs to be done to be in compliance with the law.

The standards do not address technical specifications of the websites; rather it "states that the ideal situation for assuring accessible experiences is that organizations produce web products that confirm [*sic*] to W3C's Web Content Accessibility Guidelines (WCAG) and associated standards" (Akirkpat, 2010, para. 3).

The BS 8878 web accessibility code of practice can be purchased on BSI's website at http://shop.bsigroup.com/en; search for "BS 8878" to find the standards. The purchase page provides an in-depth overview of the purpose of the standards and provides a table of contents for the document.

BSI was founded in 1901 to create engineering standards; since its inception, it has expanded to become a business services company that is active in over 140 countries. BSI focuses on developing standards that promote best practices and provide solutions.

World Wide Web Consortium (W3C)
Web Accessibility Initiative (WAI)

- http://www.w3.org/WAI/impl/Overview.html: An implementation plan that can help an organization make its website accessible.
- http://www.w3.org/WAI/impl.software.html: Selecting and using authoring tools for web accessibility.

The WAI is one of four domains of the W3C and operates with the mission of making the web more accessible for people with disabilities. To pursue this commitment, the WAI's website serves as a comprehensive resource on web accessibility. The information it provides includes explaining why accessible websites are necessary, listing and describing the WAI 2.0 standards for creating accessible sites, and offering instructions on how to plan for, manage, evaluate, and test the accessibility of websites.

While the WAI's content is comprehensive and covers every angle of creating an accessible website, finding the right information can be cumbersome for someone new to accessibility. The sheer amount of material on the site makes it difficult to find actionable information. The best place to start is in the "Guidelines & Techniques" section, which can be found on the left panel of the WAI homepage. The second link on the "Guidelines & Techniques" page, "How to Meet WCAG 2.0" (http://www.w3.org/WAI/WCAG20/quickref), navigates you to a document that provides an overview of the WAI's suggested accessibility standards. Each standard is accompanied with several techniques for implementation, as well as methods to use to determine if a standard is not met within a webpage. Furthermore, if a technique catches your attention and you would like to learn more information about it, you can simply click a link and get a document explaining it in more detail.

Another useful portion of the site can be found by clicking the "Evaluating Accessibility" section on the left panel. The section expands to reveal subsections, including a "Tools Search" (http://www.w3.org/WAI/ER/tools/Overview.html) that allows you to search for automated tools that will help you check the accessibility of a website. Overall, the WAI is a great resource for people who are interested in website accessibility.

WEB ACCESSIBILITY TOOLS

There are several free tools available for web designers to test their sites for accessibility. While many of the tools test for compliance with Section 508 or WAI standards, one tool cannot check every aspect of a website's accessibility. Therefore, to get a complete picture of how a website measures up to accessibility standards, you must also perform a manual check.

There are tools available to aid your manual check. W3C's Markup Validation Service (http://validator.w3.org) is a good place to start.

WebAnywhere (http://webanywhere.cs.washington.edu/wa.php) is a tool that functions as an actual screen reader. It was created to allow visually impaired people to use the Internet at any location without having to bring a reader with them. By entering the URL into the tool, the system will read the website to you. If you have the time and patience, hearing the website as a disabled person may help you pinpoint problematic areas.

Alternatively, Firefox's add-on Fangs (https://addons.mozilla.org/en-US/firefox/addon/402) provides an output of a website in all text, displaying it how a screen reader would read it.

In addition to the text output, there are a few program extensions you can add to a Firefox or Chrome browser that expands your reviewing capabilities. The Web Developer Extension (http://chrispederick.com/work/web-developer) places an accessibility toolbar on the browser that you can use while viewing any website. Selecting an option on the toolbar menu changes the webpage or displays pertinent information. Options include disabling java, background page colors, and images; displaying form details and alt text; and validating CSS, links, HTML, and Section 508 and WAI standards.

If you choose to validate the Section 508 or WAI standards, the option redirects you to an automated tool, Cynthia Says (http://www.cynthiasays.com), and automatically provides you with a report on the respective webpage. The Cynthia Says tool allows you to check your webpage against Section 508 standards or Web Content Accessibility Guidelines (WCAG). Simply enter the site's URL into the tool, and it will quickly produce a detailed report. The report lists each guideline and indicates whether that guideline is failed anywhere on the site. If a failure exists, the line and column number are provided.

There are two other great tools for automated accessibility reporting. WebAIM.org offers a tool called WAVE (http://wave.webaim.org) that displays the accessibility report overlaid on top of the actual website; icons appear on the website where accessibility problems may exist. The Fujitsu Web Accessibility Inspector 5.1 (http://www.fujitsu.com/global/accessibility/assistance/wi) is also an extremely useful tool that checks for accessibility based on WCAG 1.0. You must download the program onto your computer, but it produces a comprehensive report. The report provides a list that describes the accessibility problems found, displays the line the problem is on, and shows the beginning of the source code behind the problematic area. It also offers an option to view where the problem occurs on the website; by clicking the "View" option, it will pull up the actual webpage and indicate where the issue is occurring. At the bottom of the report, a Source list displays the entire HTML coding behind the webpage. Line numbers are provided for the coding, making it easy to locate the problems previously listed on the report. Web designers can use this tool to check both websites and files.

Lastly, most automated tools are unable to check the contrast of the website to ensure it is viewable for a visually impaired person; therefore, using a color checker is useful. The Juicy Studio Accessibility Toolbar (https://addons.mozilla.org/en-US/firefox/addon/9108) is an add-on for Firefox that will check the contrast on the webpage and identify areas that may need adjusting.

MISCELLANEOUS RESOURCES

The resources listed here are united by a focus on the ideas and concepts discussed throughout this volume.

- http://www.thinkbeyondthelabel.com: Information for businesses and job seekers to create a more inclusive workforce
- http://www.usabilityprofessionals.org/civiclife/access:
  Usability Professional's Association Accessibility Information

- http://www.icdri.org/section508/: International Center for Disability Resources on the Internet
- http://www.stc-access.org: Society for Technical Communication, Special Interest Group (also see Twitter hashtag #stcaccess)
- ISO related to disability/accessibility:
  - ISO 9241 series, which has had the most impact and includes ISO 9241:11: Guidance on Usability, which provides a definition of *usability*
  - ISO/IEC 9126: Software engineering—product quality, which defines usability in terms of understandability, learnability, operability, and attractiveness
  - ISO 20282: Ease of Operation of Everyday Products, which specifies the usability of the user interface of everyday products
  - ISO 9241: Ergonomic requirements for office work with visual display terminals
  - ISO 14915: Software ergonomics for multimedia user interfaces
  - IEC TR 61997: Guidelines for the user interfaces in multimedia equipment for general purpose use
  - ISO CD 9241-151: Software ergonomics for World Wide Web user interfaces
  - ISO 13406: Ergonomic requirements for work with visual displays based on flat panels
  - ISO 13407: Specifications for the activities required and internationally accepted good practice in user-centered design
  - ISO 16982: An outline of the types of methods that can be used in user-centered design
  - ISO WD 20282: A multi-part standard that is being developed to specify the usability information required about a consumer product to enable purchasers to determine whether they will be able to use it easily. This includes the characteristics of a "normal" user and how to specify characteristics of users with "special needs."
- Organizations with an emphasis or concern with disability:
  - Action on Disability and Development (ADD): http://www.add.org.uk/
  - Disability Awareness in Action (DAA): http://www.daa.org.uk/
  - Disabled Peoples' International (DPI): http://www.dpi.org/
  - Handicap International: http://www.handicap-international.org.uk/
  - Include Everybody.org: http://www.includeeverybody.org/index.php
  - Inclusion International: http://www.inclusion-international.org/
  - Independent Living Institute: http://www.independentliving.org/
  - Institute of Development Studies: http://www.ids.ac.uk/
  - International Disability Alliance: http://www.internationaldisabilityalliance.org/
  - International Disability and Development Consortium: http://iddc.org.uk/
  - Rehabilitation International: http://www.riglobal.org/
  - United Nations Enable: http://www.un.org/disabilities/

DISABILITY STUDIES

To learn more about the academic field of disability studies, the following websites are recommended places to start:

- http://www.disabilitystudies.net/: UK center with links to centers in the UK
- http://thechp.syr.edu/Disability_Studies_2003_current.html:
  Comprehensive listing of resources (including an annotated list of books, book chapters, and articles) for those wanting to learn more about the field of disability studies
- http://disabilitystudies.syr.edu/what/whatis.aspx: Defines disability studies
- http://www.disabilityrhetoric.com/: Online space for scholars who work in rhetoric and disability studies
- http://www.bbc.co.uk/blogs/ouch/: Blog featuring entries about all things disability
- http://disstudies.org/: Society for Disability Studies website
- http://www.dsq-sds.org/: The leading journal in disability studies—Disability Studies Quarterly

REFERENCES

Akirkpat. (2010, December 6). New British standard: Web accessibility code of practice, BS 8878:2010. Adobe.com blog. Retrieved from http://blogs.adobe.com/accessibility/2010/12/new-british-standard-web-accessibility-code-of-practice-bs-88782010.html

Hassell, J. (2010, December 3). UN International Day of Persons with Disabilities: A preview of why the new BS8878 British standard for web accessibility matters. BBC Internet Blog. Retrieved from http://www.bbc.co.uk/blogs/bbcinternet/2010/12/on_un_international_day_of_per.html

Out-Law.com, Pisent Masons. (2010, June 3). iPad apps may need to be disabled-accessible, possible legal duty, says BSI. The Register. Retrieved from http://www.theregister.co.uk/2010/06/03/ipad_accessible/

Contributors

Lora Arduser is a faculty member in the Rhetoric and Professional Writing track of the University of Cincinnati's English & Comparative Literature department, where she teaches technical and professional writing courses. Her research focuses on issues of rhetorical agency in collaborative and online spaces in chronic care.

Kimberly Elmore is a technical communication instructor at Louisiana State University at Alexandria and a PhD student in the Technical Communication and Rhetoric program at Texas Tech University. She is researching the online rhetoric of organizational stakeholders in autism research to find out how diverse constructions of autism affect research funding, questions, and applications.

Margaret Gutsell is the principal and owner of Inclusive Quality in Cincinnati, Ohio. She assists businesses and organizations in discovering and implementing inclusive practice through conducting quality reviews to explore spaces, strategies, and features; providing consultation on best and emerging practices; and designing and facilitating related training.

Beth L. Hewett is a consultant in online communication in educational settings. She is an adjunct associate professor with the University of Maryland University College. She is the author of *The Online Writing Conference: A Guide for Teachers and Tutors*, co-author of *Preparing Educator's for Online Writing Instruction: Principles and Processes*, and author of various journal articles about writing, technology, and rhetoric.

Kathleen M. Hulgin is an associate professor of education at the College of Mount St. Joseph in Cincinnati, Ohio. Her areas of interest include disability studies pedagogy, contextual considerations for building inclusion, and collaborative learning.

Caroline Jarrett was working with the UK tax authorities on processing forms when she became fascinated with the problem of how to design forms so that people found them easy to use—a fascination that shows no sign of wearing off more than 15 years later. She is the co-author of *Forms That Work: Designing Web Forms for Usability* and co-founder of the Design to Read project.

Antoinette Larkin is an associate professor of professional writing at the University of Cincinnati, where she teaches graduate and undergraduate courses. Her research examines corporate publications from both professional writing and public relations perspectives. She has a strong interest in the theory and practice of visual rhetoric as well as in print and digital publishing.

Sarah Lewthwaite is a post doctoral research associate at the King's Learning Institute, Kings College London. Her research interests integrate disability studies, social media, accessibility, and human computer interaction, and her PhD examines the socio-technical dimensions of disability in social networks and higher education. Her growing publication record reflects this as well as her wider ambition to engage technical disciplines with an account of disability that is driven by social theory and research.

Allison Maloney works for a leading global information and measurement company. She works on research and data interpretation about the use and deployment of social media and other Internet technologies.

Lisa Meloncon is an assistant professor of professional and technical writing at the University of Cincinnati, where she teaches graduate and undergraduate courses. Her research interests examine medical rhetoric and the Internet, visual rhetoric, the history of technical communication and health communication, as well as pedagogical practices and programmatic concerns.

Sushil K. Oswal is a faculty member in the Technical Communication department at the University of Washington. Whereas Oswal's earlier research focused on environmental policy, development process, and technical communication, his present work encompasses disability theory, accessibility, and visual impairment.

Lisa Pappas is currently a global product-marketing specialist for SAS, focusing on business intelligence and data visualization. She has authored several papers, articles, and scholarly chapters on accessibility, information architecture, and web usability, and she was a contributing editor on the W3C Web Accessibility Initiative's Accessible Rich Internet Application specification.

Elizabeth Pass is an associate professor in the School of Writing, Rhetoric, and Technical Communication at James Madison University in Harrisonburg, Virginia. She teaches technical communication, focusing on the study and production of online and webbed environments, primarily to prepare students for cutting-edge industries in technical communication.

Janice (Ginny) Redish has helped clients and colleagues communicate clearly to a wide variety of audiences for more than 30 years. Her passion is getting people to understand that good information design and plain language help everyone. In her book *Letting Go of the Words—riting Web Content That Works*, she gives practical guidelines for creating websites that meet an organization's business goals by satisfying site visitors' needs.

Kathryn Summers focuses on making medical information easier for people with lower literacy skills to find, navigate, and read on the web. She teaches user research, usability testing, and interaction design for the University of Baltimore's master's program in Interaction Design and Information Architecture.

Henny Swan has over 10 years of experience working in the UK in accessible web design and universal access, providing consultancy, audits, and training to both large and small organizations. Frustrated at the disparate levels of access to users dependent on country and context, she co-leads the International Liaison Group (ILG), part of the grass roots Web Standards Project (WASP), where she helps promote web standards and accessible web design through a network of volunteers in different countries.

Index